THE
McGRAW-HILL
STYLE MANUAL

THE McGRAW-HILL STYLE MANUAL

A CONCISE GUIDE FOR WRITERS AND EDITORS

EDITED BY

MARIE LONGYEAR

McGRAW-HILL BOOK COMPANY

New York   St. Louis   San Francisco   Auckland   Bogotá   Hamburg
London   Madrid   Mexico   Montreal   New Delhi
Panama   Paris   São Paulo   Singapore   Sydney   Tokyo   Toronto

Library of Congress Cataloging in Publication Data
Main entry under title:
    The McGraw-Hill style manual.
    Bibliography: p.
    Includes index.
    1. Authorship—Style manuals. I. Longyear, Marie
II. McGraw-Hill Book Company.
PN147.M47   1982   808'.02   82-195
ISBN 0-07-038676-5
ISBN 0-07-038684-6 (PBK.)

    67890 DOCDOC 898

ISBN 0-07-038676-5
ISBN 0-07-038684-6 {PBK.}

The editors for this book were William A. Sabin and Rose Arny,
the designer was Nicholas Krenitsky,
and the production supervisor was Teresa F. Leaden.
It was set in Electra by University Graphics, Inc.

Printed and bound by R. R. Donnelley & Sons Company

CONTENTS

PREFACE

This book is addressed to professional editors and to writers who are, or would like to become, professional authors—to anyone who intends to prepare a manuscript for publication and wants to do it with style.

In publishing, *style* refers to the standards governing abbreviation, capitalization, bibliographic form, use of italics and quotation marks, and many other editorial and typographic details that require consistency. Most publishers combine and modify various established standards to create their own "house style."

It might be useful to point out at the start that in book publishing, where products are as different as the authors who write them, standards of style usually take the form of recommendations rather than a set of rigid rules. In magazines and newspapers, on the other hand, articles are edited to conform to a more prescriptive pattern, because these publications have to maintain a recognizable format and a unified tone from issue to issue.

McGraw-Hill Book Company's style standards have evolved over many years of editing and publishing manuscripts on a wide variety of subjects. The recommendations set forth here are especially suited for general nonfiction; for educational texts at the high school, vocational school, business school, college, and postgraduate levels; and for professional texts and reference books in almost every field.

As times change, styles change. Publishing style is no exception. New methods of typesetting are rendering some of the old standards obsolete. (For example, certain styles of mathematical notation were originally devised to avoid time-consuming hand operations, but electronic typesetting has made alternative styles permissible and often preferable.)

Many of the procedures of book production are changing rapidly as well. This manual cannot describe them all, but readers should be able to adapt the recommendations set forth here to whatever new system they are using.

Chapters 1 to 8 are based on McGraw-Hill Book Company's in-house style manual, *Editing and Composition Standards*. To acknowledge everyone who has ever had a hand in the development of these standards would require powers of recall that are beyond me. Even so, the list is long, indicating the debt that this book owes to the many editors whose knowledge and effort have gone into the evolution of McGraw-Hill style over the years: James Amar, Timothy Armstrong, Rose Arny, Virginia Blair, Gretlyn Blau, Frances Bond, James Bradley, Matthew Cahill, Beatrice Carson, Olive Collen, Mark Cowell, David Damstra, Donald Douglas, David Dunham, Madeleine Eichberg, Geraldine Fahey, Carol First, Charles Freedhand, Susan Gamer, Annette Hall, Antonia Halston, Edwin Hanson, Claire Hardiman, Milton Horowitz, Ron Kirchem, Ellen LaBarbera, Michael LaBarbera, Margaret Lamb, Richard Laufer, Marie Longyear, Jack Maisel, Alice Manning, Margaret Merritt, Mary Lou Mosher, Carolyn Nagy, Josephine Neal, Cynthia Newby, Stanley Redka, Lester Strong, Claire Trazenfeld, Anne Vinnicombe, Lee Walters, and Sylvia Warren.

Chapters 9 and 10 were written by Marie Longyear, who also revised *The McGraw-Hill Guide to Manuscript Preparation*, which is incorporated in Chapter 11.

The portions of Chapter 12 that deal with proofreading are based substantially on McGraw-Hill's proofreading procedures as set forth by Earle Resnick. Section 12-6 reflects McGraw-Hill's in-house guidelines for bias-free publishing, quoting especially from material on minority groups developed by Mary Ann Drury, Linda Richmond, Stephen Wagley, Sylvia Warren, and Timothy Yohn. Others who were active in the development of these policies were Martin Hamer (multiethnic guidelines); Robert Davidson, Marie Longyear, Helen Morris, Carole O'Keefe, and John Rothermich (fair representation of disabled people); and Lisa Del Gado, Mary Ann Drury, John J. Fitzpatrick, Susan Gamer, Katharine Glynn, Alma Graham, Maryann Jones, Marie Longyear, Gary Schwartz, and Timothy Yohn (equal treatment of the sexes). Other portions of Chapter 12 are original material.

Chapter 13, "Making the Index," is based on McGraw-Hill standards originally devised by Delight Ansley (winner of the H. W. Wilson award for the best index of 1980). Delight kindly updated the material for inclusion in this book, and Helen Ferguson and Audre Hanneman provided additional insight.

Most of the illustrative material in this manual has been adapted from actual manuscripts and books. In some instances the wording has been freely changed or errors have been added for the purpose of illustrating and discussing stylistic problems and editing procedures. In such illustrations, any "authors" cited are fictitious.

Many excellent editorial suggestions were made throughout the manuscript by Rose Arny, Roy Hughson, Edward Millman, Elizabeth Richardson, and Sylvia Warren, to all of whom I extend my thanks.

Most of all, I wish to acknowledge the influence of Elizabeth Gile, who from the late 1920s to the mid-1960s was the chief arbiter of McGraw-Hill style. The continuing preoccupation of McGraw-Hill editors with standards of quality is due largely to Betty Gile's example and to the influence of her teaching.

In adapting McGraw-Hill's *Editing and Composition Standards* for this book, I may have inadvertently introduced errors or inconsistencies, for which I take sole responsibility. I urge readers to send me their suggestions for future improvements.

Marie Longyear

THE
McGRAW-HILL
STYLE MANUAL

GENERAL
STANDARDS

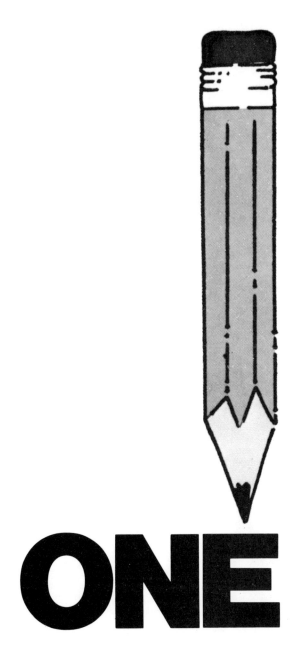

ONE

1

SPELLING, HYPHENATION, ITALICS AND QUOTATION MARKS

1-1

SPELLING

George Bernard Shaw, distressed by the inability of our twenty-six-letter alphabet to represent all the sounds of the English language, left provision in his will for the design of a new alphabet of at least forty letters. A worldwide design competition resulted in the publication of a new alphabet in 1962, twelve years after Shaw's death. It didn't catch on, however, and we are still struggling to express complex English sounds with a woefully inadequate alphabet in which there is often no correlation between orthography and pronunciation. Rules of spelling, when they exist, are not absolute ("*i* before *e* except after *c*" usually works, but not for *freight* and *seize* and *seismograph*).

The diverse linguistic sources of the English language are responsible for this state of affairs, as well as for its richness and variety. Perhaps we should spend as much time enjoying the language as we spend trying to regulate its spelling.

Dictionaries

McGraw-Hill generally uses *Webster's New Collegiate Dictionary* as a standard desk reference, and the latest edition of *Webster's New International Dictionary* (unabridged) for words not listed in the *Collegiate*. When equal weight is given to variant spellings in the dictionary, choose the first, for consistency. Some terms in medicine, electronics, and other specific fields are often spelled in accordance with accepted practice in the literature rather than as given in the dictionary.

Commonly Used Terms

For quick reference, preferred forms for a few commonly used (and sometimes troublesome) terms are given below. An asterisk indicates that the spelling shown in the list is an exception to *Webster's* or not *Webster's* first form.

accommodate
adviser
airspeed
alphanumeric
analog (computers)
analogue (something analogous)
bandpass *
birthrate
blackbody
broadband
busing
bypass
canceling
cancellation
catalog
centerline
checklist
collinear
conveyer (one who conveys)
conveyor (moving belt)
coworker *
death rate
deemphasize *
diagramed
disk (*but* disc harrow)
dos and don'ts
dropout (n.)
end point (completion)
endpoint (of line segment or
   interval)
ensure (to make sure)
firstborn
flip-flop
flowchart
follow-up (n.)
formulas
gauge (*sometimes* gage)
goodwill
groundspeed *

guideline
gyrocompass
half-life
half plane
halfway
henrys
highlight
insofar as
installment
insure (provide insurance)
kilowatthour *
know-how (n.)
labeled
life cycle
lifestyle *
loudspeaker
makeup (n. and adj.)
marijuana
midbrain
midpoint
mold
naive
narrowband
online * (computers)
overall
paperwork
paralleled
passband
payload
payroll
percent
photocell
printout (n.)
print out (v.)
programmed
proved (past part.)
proven (adj.)
résumé
roentgen ray

sawtooth	toward
schoolchild	trademark
schoolwork	trade name
servoamplifier*	tradeoff* (n.)
shortcut	traveled
sideband	vice president*
straightedge	waveform
subclass	waveshape
sulfur	wave train
synonymous	workload*
teenager	worthwhile
timesharing*	x-ray (n.* and v.)

Compound Nouns

To determine whether a compound noun should be one word, two words, or hyphened, consult the dictionary; there is no simple formula that can satisfactorily explain the following discrepancies in compounding:

half-life	childbearing
halftime	flag-waving
half title	problem solving

If the term is not listed in either the abridged or the unabridged dictionary, assume that it is spelled as two words.

Nouns formed of coequal terms are hyphened:

author-critic
owner-manager
programmer-encoder

Hyphens are not necessary in most terms consisting of a letter or symbol and a noun:

I beam
RC circuit
x axis
but x-ray

Simple spelled fractions are hyphened:

one-half
thirteen-sixteenths

Compound Verbs

Compound verbs are either hyphened or closed up. If a compound verb does not appear in *Webster's*, it should be hyphened:

to class-test	to pinpoint
to factor-analyze	to waterproof

The form of a compound noun does not affect the form of the related compound verb:

to dry-clean	*but*	dry cleaning (n.)
to heat-treat	*but*	heat treatment (n.)

Compound Adjectives

See Section 1-2.

Prefixes and Suffixes

Prefixes and suffixes are generally attached to the base word without a hyphen:

afterimage	isoenergetic
antitrust	midcourse
audiovisual	multidimensional
bipolar	nonexempt
branchlike	nonnegative
citywide	overrepresented
coenzyme	posttest
coordinate	pretest
counterrevolutionary	prewar
coworker	reemphasize
earthward	semiannual
electroosmosis	socioeconomic
extrasensory	substrata
foolproof	superimpose
fourfold	unnerving
interrelations	uppermost
intraarterial	

However, a hyphen is used between a prefix and a base word in the following instances:

1   When the letter *i* is repeated:

anti-inflationary

2 To distinguish homonyms or when otherwise needed for sense:

co-op   re-form
pre-position   re-mark
re-collect   un-ionized
re-cover

3 When a prefix is repeated:

re-reflected
sub-subcommittee

4 When the base word is capitalized or is a number:

pre-Euclid
un-American
post-1945

5 When the base word is a hyphened or unhyphened compound (note that a hyphen, not an en dash, is used):

non-interest-bearing account
pre-Civil War era

En dashes are discussed in Sections 1-2 and 10-6.

The following paragraphs offer some rules for a few common word combinations and combining forms.

cross- Usage varies; consult *Webster's*. As examples, note:

crossover
cross-reference
cross section

-elect Link *-elect* to a one-word title with a hyphen; use a space before it with multiple-word titles:

president-elect
attorney general elect
secretary-treasurer elect

ex- Hyphenate ex- unless the term is spelled solid (as one word) in *Webster's* or is a Latin term:

ex-chancellor
excurrent
ex officio

-fold   Spell *-fold* solid except with figures and with hyphened numbers:

> hundredfold
> 15-fold
> twenty-five-fold

great-   Hyphenate all relationship terms beginning with *great-:*

> great-aunt
> great-great-grandchild

-in-law   Hyphenate all relationship terms ending with *-in-law:*

> father-in-law

-like   Attach the suffix *-like* to the base word without a hyphen unless the base word is capitalized, ends with an *l*, or is a hyphened or open compound:

> doglike   gull-like
> featherlike   great-aunt-like
> Alaska-like   civil war-like
> gel-like

The hyphen is often used with multisyllabic technical terms:

> acetylcholine-like

-odd   Hyphenate compounds ending with *-odd:*

> fifty-odd

pseudo-   Permanent compounds (that is, terms given as an entry in the dictionary) are spelled solid. *Pseudo* used as an adjective is not usually linked by a hyphen to the word it modifies, unless it is part of a compound adjective.

> pseudopod   pseudo humanism
> pseudoscience   pseudo-intellectual approach

quasi-   The rules cited above for *pseudo-* apply to *quasi-* as well:

> quasiparticle

a quasi corporation
quasi-scientific literature

self-   When *self-* is used as a combining form, it is hyphened unless *self-* is the base word (exception: *unselfconscious*):

self-defense
self-respect
selfless

When *self* is used as an adjective, omit the hyphen:

self antigen

under-   *Under-* is generally spelled solid:

undereducated

-wide   In the sense of *throughout*, *-wide* is spelled solid:

citywide	nationwide
industrywide	worldwide

Proper Names
For the spelling of proper names the Webster biographical and geographical dictionaries are the usual authorities, although not all the spellings shown in the specialized dictionaries have been generally adopted. Non-Webster spellings are acceptable when used consistently and recognized as standard variants. Verifying the spelling of proper names, including company names, is a responsibility that rests with the author.

British Spellings
Avoid British spellings in textbooks and other forms of nonfiction written for U.S. markets:

analyze (*not* analyse)	toward (*not* towards)
center (*not* centre)	traveled (*not* travelled)
color (*not* colour)	

Possessives
The following rules, based on *Webster's*, have wide acceptance. In most instances, form is dictated by sound.

1   For singular or plural nouns that do not end in a sibilant sound, add 's:

> Jacques's
> kitten's
> men's

2   For singular nouns that end in an s or z sound:

a. When of one syllable, generally add 's:

> Jones's
> Mars's
> Zeus's

Some specific exceptions:

> Bayès' theorem   Gauss' equations
> Boas' reagent   Stokes' law

b. When of two or more syllables with accent on the last, add 's:

> Louise's

c. When of two or more syllables with no accent on the last:
   (1) Add 's if the last syllable is not preceded by an s or z sound:

> Corliss's
> Pythagoras's
> Thomas's

(2) For proper nouns add only the apostrophe if the last syllable is preceded by an s or z sound:

> Croesus'   Jesus'
> Dos Passos'   Xerxes'

3   For classical proper nouns ending in es (pronounced eez), add only the apostrophe if the accent is on the penult. In other cases add 's.

> Achilles'   Aristophanes's
> Ulysses'   Hercules's

4   For abbreviations that are part of titles, firm names, etc., add 's:

> Henry IV's
> McGraw-Hill, Inc.'s

5   For plural nouns ending in s or es, add apostrophe only:

> elves'
> teachers'

6   For plural nouns not ending in *s*, add *'s:*

geese's
women's

When more than one possessor is listed, the number of apostrophe *s*'s depends on whether possession is joint or individual:

Lord and Taylor's display windows
Smith and Braun's findings (joint research)
Smith's and Braun's findings (separate research)

Plurals

The only plurals likely to cause difficulty for writers and editors are the plurals of foreign and assimilated words—especially those which come to us from Latin and classical Greek. The choice between a foreign and an anglicized plural ending is often determined by usage in a given field; sometimes alternative endings convey different meanings. It is therefore difficult to formulate rules. Use the latest edition of *Webster's New International Dictionary* or *New Collegiate Dictionary* as a general guide to problematic plural forms. For plurals used in medicine and the life sciences, see Table 8-5 or consult the latest edition of the *Gould Medical Dictionary*. Some commonly encountered plurals follow.

Singular	*Plural*
alumna	alumnae
alumnus	alumni
antenna	antennae (biology); antennas (radio)
apex	apices
appendix	appendices (biology); appendixes (books)
automaton	automata *or* automatons
axis	axes
basis	bases
cactus	cacti
chargé d'affaires	chargés d'affaires
coup d'état	coups d'état
curriculum	curricula

Singular	Plural
delphinium	delphiniums
diagnosis	diagnoses
focus	foci
formula	formulas
fulcrum	fulcrums
genus	genera
gladiolus	gladioli
grafitto	grafitti
helix	helixes
index	indices (mathematics); indexes (books)
larva	larvae
matrix	matrices
memorandum	memoranda
nucleus	nuclei
octopus	octopuses
ovum	ova
plexus	plexuses
sinus	sinuses
species	species
tempus	tempora
vertebra	vertebrae

1-2

HYPHENATION OF COMPOUND MODIFIERS

The hyphenation of compound modifiers is often a question of judgment. Many compound modifiers are so familiar in particular fields that they need not be hyphened (see "Exceptions" below for a representative list of such terms).

In deciding whether to hyphenate a compound modifier, remember that *clarity* is the goal. A hyphen must always be used, for example, when its absence could lead to misreading:

a slow-moving van (signifying a van that is slow-moving, not a moving van that is slow)

In other situations, use of the hyphen in the attributive position (before the noun) and the predicative position (after the verb) usually depends on the type of combination and the context in which it appears. The following paragraphs offer some general guidelines.

Common Combinations

adjective plus noun   Usage often governs whether hyphens are used. When a hyphen is appropriate, it is generally used in both the attributive position and the predicative position. This rule covers combinations with comparatives and superlatives.

all-city team
short-term loan; the loan was short-term
stainless-steel sink
best-quality fabric

adjective plus adjective   Hyphenate coordinate expressions in both the attributive and the predicative positions. When the first word modifies the second, use a hyphen in the attributive, but not generally in the predicative, position.

blue-green sea; the sea is blue-green
bluish-green dress; is bluish green
dark-green color; is dark green

Do not use a hyphen, even in the attributive position, if an adverb precedes the pair of adjectives:

a very dark green color

adjective plus adjective formed by adding -ed to noun   Use a hyphen in both the attributive and the predicative positions. This rule covers combinations with comparatives and superlatives.

full-bodied wine; the wine is full-bodied
better-natured person; is better-natured

adjective plus participle   Use a hyphen in both the attributive and the predicative positions:

> hard-working employee; the employee is hard-working
> soft-spoken person; is soft-spoken

adverb plus participle   Do not use a hyphen with adverbs that end in *-ly:*

> rapidly growing deficit

Other adverb-participle combinations are hyphened in the attributive position and usually in the predicative position:

> broken-down car; the car is old and broken-down
> *but* the budget was broken down (verb) into two parts
> fast-acting drug; is fast-acting
> slower-moving traffic; is slower-moving
> well-intentioned person; is well-intentioned
> *but* well-known fact; is well known

Do not use a hyphen, even in the attributive position, if another adverb precedes:

> a very well known author

noun plus adjective; noun plus participle   Usage often governs whether hyphens are used. When a hyphen is appropriate, use it in both the attributive and the predicative positions.

> chlorophyll-rich food; the food is chlorophyll-rich
> colony-forming organisms; are colony-forming
> heat-resistant plastic; is heat-resistant
> trouble-free operation; is trouble-free

noun plus noun   Many noun forms, especially in technical material, are hyphened:

> boundary-value problem
> heat-transfer data
> slope-intercept form

Coequal proper nouns and combining forms of proper nouns used as compound modifiers are hyphened:

> Yale-Princeton game
> Franco-American relations

A proper noun consisting of more than one word retains its original form when used as a modifier:

Air Force regulation   Latin American countries
Blue Ridge Mountain trails   Winston-Salem area

Combinations of a proper noun and a common noun are normally not hyphened:

Ivory soap commercial

prepositional phrases Prepositional phrases used as modifiers are hyphened before a noun but not elsewhere:

off-the-record remark; this remark is off the record
an in-depth study; was studied in depth
up-to-date book; is up to date

Other Combinations
A foreign term retains its original form when used as a modifier:

a priori argument
pro forma invoice
trompe l'oeil painting

A compound modifier consisting of a number followed by a noun, typically a unit of measure, is hyphened (see also Chapter 3):

20-cent stamp
100-meter dash
but 10 percent discount

Compound modifiers consisting of a noun followed by a letter or a number are not hyphened:

grade B bonds
number 1 priority
Title IV grant

When a series of hyphened compound modifiers contains a common last word that is expressed only in the final modifier in the series, use a hyphen (sometimes called a *suspending hyphen*) after each of the incomplete modifiers:

short- and long-term notes (notice the space after the first hyphen)
5-, 10-, and 15-year intervals

En Dash in Compound Modifiers

An en dash, which is slightly longer than a hyphen (see Section 10-6), is used to join two unhyphened compound modifiers:

New York–New Haven route

or an unhyphened and a hyphened compound modifier:

New York–Wilkes-Barre route

or a one-word modifier and a hyphened compound modifier:

Philadelphia–Wilkes-Barre route

or an unhyphened compound modifier combined with a one-word modifier:

life insurance–oriented program
toluidine blue–stained sample
vitamin A–derived supplement

To join hyphened compound modifiers or a hyphened compound modifier combined with a one-word modifier, use an en dash if the linked terms are coequal:

first-in–first-out inventory system
salary–cost-of-living relationship

However, to join three or more words forming a single adjectival concept, use hyphens only:

control-group-based results   inner-city-oriented program
cost-of-living-related increase   three-year-old child
gas-liquid-interface temperature

Exceptions

Some compound modifiers that are in common use in a particular field form units that are easily recognizable; they are therefore often unhyphened:

accounts receivable entry
adult education course
birth control program
civil service reform
connective tissue proliferation
control system engineer
credit and collection department
data processing equipment
electron transport system
floppy disk storage
free enterprise system
health care team
internal combustion engine
junior high school teacher
liberal arts college
life insurance company
mental health clinic
per capita reserve

physical education teacher
polar coordinate system
profit and loss statement
profit sharing plan
public address system
public relations field
public school teacher
real estate tax
real number coefficient
second derivative test
serial access memory
sickle cell anemia
sine wave voltage
social service work
social studies class
subject matter areas
white blood cell count

However, in material meant for nonspecialists or presented at a low reading level, it may be desirable to use hyphens where they would ordinarily be omitted:

internal-combustion engine
profit-sharing plan
white-blood-cell count

Chemical terms, names of diseases, and common names of plants and animals retain their original form when used as modifiers:

amino acid polymer
carbon dioxide gas
spiny anteater skeleton

vitamin A deficiency
white pine production
yellow fever virus

Some terms contain no compound modifier, although the unwary might think that they do; the insertion of a hyphen in such terms would be incorrect:

grid bias voltage
grid leak bias
ground handling techniques
  (airport procedures)

parallel resonant circuit
peak inverse voltage
silicon controlled rectifier

1-3

ITALICS AND QUOTATION MARKS

For the use of quotation marks with extracts (quoted material), see Section 4-1.

Emphasis

Emphasized words and passages are set in italic type:

> The cover should *never* be removed except by a qualified
> service technician.
> *Proceed with caution.*

Defined Words and Special Usage

Words and passages that are to be emphasized are set in italic type. New terms may be italicized or enclosed in quotation marks at their first appearance. Words used in an unusual sense are enclosed in quotation marks. **Boldface** and CAPITAL LETTERS are avoided for these purposes because of their obtrusive appearance. Boldface is sometimes called for, however, to set off defined terms, especially in biology books.

Either italics or quotation marks may be used simply to call attention to a word or phrase or to part of a word; the device chosen should be used consistently throughout the book:

too many *and's*	the phrase "to mock up"
the word "tree"	adverbs ending in *-ly*
the word *atom* (from the Greek *atomos,* "indivisible")	anti*b*allistic *m*issile (ABM)

Irony, slang, coined expressions, and inexact usage are indicated on first occurrence by quotations marks rather than italics. (In books written in a colloquial style, quotation marks for slang are generally not necessary.)

> an "honest" thief
> an "exact" answer
> a "prestige" product
> *but* a so-called prestige product

In subsequent appearances such terms need not be set off by quotation marks except where required for clarity.

Titles

Book, periodical, and legal case titles are italicized in the text as well as in footnotes and bibliographies. (See Chapter 5.)

Titles of plays, films, long poems, paintings, and sculptures are italicized. Quotation marks are used for the titles of articles, short stories, essays, and short poems. Names of radio and television series and programs are italic, but the titles of individual episodes are set in roman type with quotation marks.

The Rivals	"A Dissertation upon Roast Pig"
Citizen Kane	"My Last Duchess"
Paradise Lost	*Upstairs, Downstairs*, "On with
Leonardo's *La Gioconda*	the Dance" (episode)
Michelangelo's *Pietà*	

Quotation marks are used for names of songs. Italic type is used for names of song cycles and other long compositions, except for titles designating the musical form, key, or number.

"Drink to Me Only with Thine Eyes"
Dichterliebe (Poet's Love) (roman type for translation of title)
Beethoven's Symphony No. 3 in E flat major; Third Symphony; *Eroica Symphony*
Sonata in A major for Violin and Piano, Op. 17
Mozart's Quintet in E flat major, K. 614, second movement
"Ach Golgotha" from the *St. Matthew Passion*
Mass in B minor, Kyrie I
Tristan und Isolde, Prelude to Act I

Italic type is used for individual names, but not for classes, of ships, planes, trains, and spacecraft:

the guided missile cruiser *Long Beach;* USS *Long Beach*	*Orient Express*
	Echo 2
the *Spirit of St. Louis*	an Atlas booster
a Piper Cub	

Foreign Words and Phrases

Roman type is used for foreign words and phrases that have been assimilated into the English language. Note also that assimilated German nouns are lowercased.

Because the extent of assimilation may vary from one context or discipline to another, the following list should be considered a general, rather than a rigid, guide:

ad hoc	*inter alia*
ad lib, ad libitum; to ad-lib	in toto
a priori	in vivo
art nouveau	laissez faire (no hyphen in n.
bourgeoisie	or adj.)
chargé d'affaires	modus vivendi
commedia dell'arte	ombudsman
coup d'état	op. cit.
de facto	per annum
élan	per se
elite	poseur
esprit de corps	pro forma
et al.	pro rata
ex ante	pro tem (but *pro tempore*)
ex officio	rapprochement
fait accompli	résumé
finca	sine qua non
gemeinschaft	sotto voce
Gemütlichkeit	status quo
gestalt	sub rosa
habeas corpus	vice versa
haute couture	vis-à-vis
ibid.	*Zeitgeist*
in esse	

The *Random House College Dictionary* is a useful guide to currently accepted forms for other foreign words and phrases.

Names of foreign institutions and organizations are usually set in roman type:

> Bibliothèque Nationale
> Banco de la República

For titles of reference materials in foreign languages, see Chapter 5.

Taxonomic Nomenclature
Combined Latin names of genera and species (binomials) are italicized, as is the name of a genus standing alone:

> *Lactobacillus acidophilus*
> but *L. acidophilus* (subsequent mention)
> *Lactobacillus* spp.
> a lactobacillus (roman type and lowercase in the vernacular)
> *Homo neandertalensis*
> Homo sapiens (in the general sense)

Any rank higher than genus is set in roman type and capitalized:

the order Rosales
the phylum Chordata

See Section 8-7 for a more detailed discussion and additional examples.

Letter Symbols

Letters of the alphabet used as mathematical symbols are italicized:

x children	line ac
nth	point (a, b)
sin x	$P(0,1)$

Roman type is used for chemical elements:

O_2
$CaCl_2$

Roman type is used also for arbitrary designations:

brand X
subject A

for letters indicating shape:

I beam
S-shaped curve

for abbreviations:

S-R (stimulus-response) connection

and for musical notation:

AABA; AAbA pattern	B minor; B flat minor
themes A and B	C clef; middle C

See Chapter 3 for the use of italic type with measurements and symbols; Chapter 7 for more information on italics in mathematics, electronics, and computer science; and Chapter 8 for usage in chemistry.

2

CAPITALIZATION

As used in this chapter, the term *capitalization* refers to special treatment of the names of places, people, organizations, objects, and ideas. It does not refer to style for symbols and abbreviations (covered in Chapter 3) or to the typographic treatment of displayed material, such as headings.

Rules for capitalization are difficult to devise because they are difficult to apply. In general, capitalization is used to distinguish unique and particular entities. But what is considered a specific name or part of a name in one context may not be so in another; conventions vary in different fields, and local usage is frequently at odds with the style guides. For that reason, capitalization is discussed here according to context, and more through examples and exceptions than through rules (although some short general rules are given).

One thing is certain, however: the trend is toward less rather than more capitalization, and that trend is reflected in the rules and examples that follow. Although the forms shown have wide acceptance, they may be modified to reflect level of readership, local custom, or usage in a particular field.

2-1

PLACE NAMES

General Rules

1 Proper names (specific names) of places are capitalized, except in certain derivative uses (see Section 2-12):

> Portland, Oregon   *but*   portland cement (a derivative term)

2   Generic terms (common nouns) are capitalized when they are an integral part of a proper name:

Elbe River

but are usually lowercased when they precede the specific name or stand alone in a subsequent reference:

the river Elbe
traffic on the river

3   Generic terms used alone are capitalized when they are widely recognized as a short or popular substitute for the full name:

Blériot flew across the Channel in 1909. ("English Channel" understood)
The princes were slain in the Tower. ("Tower of London" understood)

4   Descriptive terms (adjectives) are capitalized when they are an integral part of a proper name and in certain traditional contexts:

North America
Southern Conference

but purely descriptive terms are lowercased if they refer to a region with inexact boundaries, even in many familiar combinations:

continental Europe	deep south
corn belt	southeast Asia

Examples

divisions of the globe

Antarctic circle	polar regions
equator	tropic of Capricorn
international date line	the tropics
north pole	

For rules governing capitalization of the word *earth*, see Section 2-5.

physical geography

Great Artesian Basin; the basin
Suez Canal; the canal
Mojave Desert; the desert
Victoria Falls; the falls
Gulf of Mexico; the gulf
Leeward Islands; the Leewards; the islands
Rocky Mountains; the Rockies; the mountains

Atlantic Ocean; North Atlantic Ocean; the ocean
Pike's Peak; the peak
Mongolian Plateau; the plateau
Great Plains; the plains
Walden Pond; the pond
Great Barrier Reef; the reef
Missouri River; the river
East Siberian Sea; the sea
Death Valley; the valley

Widely accepted short or popular forms are capitalized:

Rock of Gibraltar; the Rock
Sierra Nevada; the Sierras (specific mountain chain)

A generic term preceding the specific name is often lowercased:

the forest of Arden
the river Danube

but when no other order of words is possible, the generic term is capitalized:

Lake Geneva	Mount Rainier
Mont Blanc	Strait of Gibraltar

A generic term used with more than one specific name is lowercased:

lakes Huron and Ontario
the Mississippi and Missouri rivers

For geologic terms, see Section 2-6.

descriptive designations   Although a descriptive term that does not refer to an exact region is usually lowercased:

new world; old world; third world	wild west
north temperate zone	winter wheat belt
the occident; the orient	

some local descriptive terms are traditionally capitalized:

Bay Area (San Francisco)
Lake District (England)

East, west, north, and *south* are capitalized as part of a proper name:

East Chicago
Union of South Africa

Otherwise they are lowercased:

the east; the west	north central states
east Africa	northern hemisphere
east coast; west coast	southeast Asia
eastern culture	southern states
middle west; midwest	western movie

continents and countries   Names of continents and countries are always capitalized:

Africa	People's Republic of China
Eurasia	Romania

smaller political divisions and neighborhoods

Back Bay
the Bronx; borough of the Bronx
the City of New York (official name); New York City; the city
Twin Cities; the twin cities of Minneapolis and St. Paul
county Cork; Queens County; the county
Foggy Bottom
Golan Heights; the heights
Cobble Hill
province of Quebec
the Riviera
New York State; state of New York; the state
Indiana Territory; the territory
Tobyhanna Township; the township
the village
but the Village (popular short form for Greenwich Village)

structures, monuments, sites

Houston Astrodome; the Astrodome
Brooklyn Bridge; Bridge of Sighs; the bridge
Empire State Building; the building
the state capitol; the capitol
the national Capitol; the Capitol (Washington, D.C.)
Cathedral of St. John the Divine; the cathedral
Boston Common; the common (*sometimes* the Common—see below)

> Avery Fisher Hall; the hall
> the Mall (Washington, D.C.)
> Hatfield House; the White House
> the opera house; the house
> Van Cortland Park; the park
> Statue of Liberty; the statue; statue of General Grant
> the Eiffel Tower; the tower

In some contexts, short forms may be considered widely accepted enough to be capitalized:

> the Bethesda Athletic Center; the Center
> Boston Common; the Common
> Madison Square Garden; the Garden

The English equivalent of a foreign generic term is used in subsequent references unless the original term is familiar in English:

> Palais Royal; the palace
> Plaza Mayor; the plaza

streets and roads

> Fifth Avenue; the avenue
> Pennsylvania Turnpike; the turnpike

Street names are handled in various ways in foreign languages; for guidance consult appropriate dictionaries or street maps:

> Autobahn   Mozartstrasse
> 34, rue Faubourg-St-Honoré   Via Nazionale

2-2

NAMES AND TITLES OF PEOPLE

General Rules

1   Specific names of groups of people and names of individuals are capitalized.

2   Titles are capitalized when they precede a person's name, but they are generally lowercased when they follow the name or stand alone in a subsequent reference.

Examples

nationalities, types, races

American   a mesomorph
Eurasian   blacks; whites
Spanish-speaking peoples

personal names, nicknames, sobriquets

William Cody
Buffalo Bill
Ethelred the Unready

international officials

Secretary General Waldheim; Kurt Waldheim, secretary general of the
United Nations; the secretary general

government officials   *President, Vice President, Commander in Chief*
(referring to the President), and *Chief Justice* of the United States are
exceptions to the general rule calling for lowercase when the title follows
the name. *Speaker of the House* is also often capitalized in that position.
Lowercase is used for adjectives derived from these titles, for general references to the office, and for plurals.

administrator of the Veterans Administration; the administrator
Ambassador Smith; the ambassador to the United Nations
chairwoman of the Council of Economic Advisers; the chairwoman
director of the Federal Mediation and Conciliation Service; the director
Governor Carey; the governor
Mayor Velez; the mayor
minority leader of the Senate
office of senator
President Reagan; President of the United States; the President
presidential candidate; presidential seal; the presidency
Prime Minister Thatcher; prime minister of the United Kingdom of Great
    Britain and Northern Ireland; the prime minister
Representative Jones; the representative from New York
Secretary Haig; the secretary of state
Selectman DeCosta; the first selectman
Senator Eagleton; the senator
the Speaker of the House; the Speaker
Vice President Bush; the Vice President

Judicial officials

> associate justice of the United States; Justice Marshall; the justice
> chief judge of U.S. Customs Court; Judge Re; the chief judge
> Chief Justice of the United States; Chief Justice Berger; the Chief Justice
> judge of the New York State Court of Appeals; Judge Marley; the judge
> justice of the New York State Supreme Court; Justice Hughes; the justice

Law-enforcement officials

> chief inspector of the New York Police Department; Chief Inspector Mederos; the inspector
> chief of detectives; Chief Smith; the chief
> an officer of the New York City Police Department; Officer Walker; the officer

Military officials

> General George C. Marshall, chief of staff; the general; the chief of staff
> General Ulysses S. Grant, commander in chief of the Union army; General Grant; the commander in chief; the general
> Sergeant Mary Ryan; the sergeant

nongovernment officials

Education

> Professor Williams
> chairman of the New York State Board of Education; the chairman
> lecturer in the department of physics

In formal lists, such as acknowledgments and lists of contributors, titles are usually capitalized following the name. Named professorships and fellowships are capitalized wherever they appear.

> Elizabeth Janeway Professor of English (named professorship)

Occupational titles

> John Doe, curator of the Peabody Museum (*not* Curator Doe)
> middle linebacker for the New York Giants

Political titles

> chairman of the Democratic National Committee; the chairman
> president of Americans for Democratic Action

Business titles

> chairman of the economic policy committee of New York's Citibank
> vice president, finance (of XYZ corporation)
> vice president of the Provident Bank of Philadelphia

Religious titles   Usage varies, depending on the religion and often on the denomination:

> Cardinal Cooke, archbishop of New York; the cardinal
> Pope John Paul II; the pope; the papacy
> the Reverend Ann White; Miss White (many Protestant denominations)
> the Reverend Thomas Kelly; Father Kelly (Roman Catholic Church)

Royalty and nobility

> Elizabeth II, queen of Great Britain and Northern Ireland and of her other
>   realms and territories (exact title); Elizabeth II, queen of Britain (short
>   title); Queen Elizabeth; the queen; the sovereign
> Prince Philip; His Royal Highness the Prince Philip; the duke of Edinburgh;
>   the duke
> Claude Victor Perrin, duc de Bellune; the duke
> Marie de Vichy-Chamrond, marquise du Deffand; the marchioness (the
>   English-language equivalent of the title is used when the title stands
>   alone)

2-3

NAMES OF ORGANIZATIONS

General Rules

1   Exact titles of organizations and parts of organizations are capitalized.

2   Generic forms (the association, the company) standing alone, even when referring to a specific previously mentioned organization, are lowercased, except for certain quasi-governmental international organizations, as illustrated below.

Examples

international organizations

> Alliance for Progress; the Alliance
> Common Market
> General Conference of the ITO; the Conference
> Economic and Social Council of the United Nations; the Council
> International Monetary Fund; the Fund
> General Assembly; the Assembly (League or UN)
> League of Nations; the League
> Organization of American States; the Organization
> Mandates Section of the League; the Section
> United Nations Security Council; the Security Council
> Universal Postal Union; the Union
> World Bank; the Bank

Short forms of less official kinds of international organizations are lowercased:

> International Philatelic Association; the association

government organizations

Legislative, administrative, and deliberative bodies Complete official titles of national, state, and local government bodies are capitalized. The word *committee* standing alone is capitalized in references to a noncongressional committee.

> Fillmore administration; the administration
> Central Intelligence Agency; the agency
> Federal Reserve Bank; the bank
> California State Highway Commission; Highway Commission of California; the commission
> Committee on Foreign Affairs; Foreign Affairs Committee; the committee (congressional)
> President's Science Advisory Committee; the Committee (noncongressional)
> Congress
> congressional
> Department of Agriculture; the department
> federal government; the government
> General Assembly of Illinois; the general assembly
> the Government (British party in power)
> House of Representatives; the House
> North Carolina House of Representatives; the house

U.S. Office of Education; the office
Parliament
Reichstag
Senate (United States)
Illinois State Senate; the state senate; the state legislature
Subcommittee on Appropriations; the subcommittee of the Appropriations
    Committee; the subcommittee

Descriptive terms are lowercased:

legislative and judicial departments
the lower house of Congress

Some short forms are capitalized to avoid ambiguity or because of long-standing tradition:

Federal Reserve Board; the Board
Bureau of the Census; Census Bureau; the Bureau
House of Commons; the Commons

Judicial bodies   The word *court* standing alone is capitalized only in references to the U.S. Supreme Court or to the International Court of Justice:

Appellate Division of the State Supreme Court (New York); the appellate
    division
Municipal Court of Chicago; the court
Arkansas Supreme Court; the supreme court; the court
United States Supreme Court; the Court
United States Court of Appeals for the Second Circuit; the court of
    appeals
First Judicial Department (of the New York State Appellate Division)

Lowercase is used for short forms and descriptive terms even when they refer to a specific court:

circuit court	family court
county court	municipal court
court of appeals	traffic court

Law-enforcement bodies

New York Police Department; the police department
New York State Police; the state police
Sheriff's Office of Cook County; the sheriff's office
the police force

Military services Short forms (air force, army, coast guard, etc.) are capitalized only in references to U.S. services:

Afrika Korps (German, World War II)
Army of Northern Virginia; the army
the British Army; the army
Eighth Air Force
Green Berets
the Royal Navy; the navy
U.S. Army; the Army
U.S. Marine Corps; U.S. Marines; the Marine Corps; the Marines
the armed forces
the paratroopers

nongovernmental organizations

Education

the Board of Regents of the University of California; the California board
of regents; the regents
Child Guidance Bureau (of the New York City Department of Education)
Educational Policies Commission (of the National Education Association);
the commission
Head Start
Urban School Services (of the New York State Department of Education)

Major divisions of educational institutions are capitalized:

Barnard College
Columbia University
Graduate School of Arts and Sciences (of Columbia University)
the Law School (of Columbia University)
Teachers College (of Columbia University)

but individual departments are lowercased:

the department of physics
the history department

Business Both full and shortened names of businesses and business organizations are capitalized. Words like *company* and *corporation* do not in themselves constitute a shortened title.

Bell Helicopter (of Textron)
the Bell System
the Book Company (of McGraw-Hill, Inc.)

Corporate Management Information Services (of McGraw-Hill, Inc.)
General Electric
New York Stock Exchange; the Stock Exchange
New York Telephone Company; New York Telephone; the company

Lowercase is used for inexact titles of divisions or departments and for descriptive or general terms. (If it is impossible to determine whether the name given to a division is the exact title, a descriptive term may be used.)

corporate finance area
the gas company
the jewelry division
research and development (R&D)

school publishing area
systems and programming
McGraw-Hill's corporate systems
unit

Associations and conferences   Full and shortened official names of teams, associations, unions, meetings, and conferences are capitalized. Words such as *association*, *society*, and *league* are lowercased when they stand alone.

American Podiatry Society; the society
American Society for the Prevention of Cruelty to Children; the society
Boston Chamber of Commerce; the chamber of commerce; the chamber
Girl Scouts of America; the Girl Scouts
the Grange
League of Women Voters; the league
Lions International; the Lions
National Maritime Union; the union
National Organization for Women
New York Jets; the Jets
New York Road Runners Club; the Road Runners

political parties and groups

International alliances

the Allies
Organization of American States

Central Powers
Triple Entente

Political organizations and their members   Note that the word *party* is not capitalized.

West Side Republican Club; the
club

Democratic National Committee;
the committee

Communist (member of the
  Communist party)
Fascist
Labour party (Britain)
Labourite (Britain)
the Left (parliamentary bloc,
  e.g., in France)
Opposition (British party out of
  power)
a Populist (member of the
  People's party)

Progressive party
a Republican
Republican National Committee
Republican party
South-West Africa People's
  Organization
Tammany Society; Tammany
a Tory
Wobbly (member of Industrial
  Workers of the World)

Ideologies and descriptive political terms are lowercased:

abolitionist
bolshevism
democracy
eastern bloc
fascism
independents
Jacksonian democracy

leftists
mugwumps
progressive movement
prohibitionist
right wing
socialist
third world

Rules for capitalization in various specific contexts follow.

2-4

ART, LITERATURE, MUSIC

Terms designating musical, artistic, and literary genres, movements, styles, and schools are generally lowercased:

art deco
ashcan school
baroque
Bloomsbury group
chamber music
classicism
cubism
dada
Dutch school
fauvism

gothic
impressionism
modern jazz
New York school of architecture
pop art
postimpressionism
realism
romanticism
surrealism
theater of the absurd

However, some terms are capitalized to avoid ambiguity:

International style
Perpendicular style

In the context of the arts, adjectives derived from proper names are usually capitalized:

Johnsonian wit
Shavian satire
Wagnerian opera

See Section 2-12 for the treatment of other derivative terms and Section 1-3 for the titles of works of art and literary and musical compositions. See also Chapter 5.

2-5

ASTRONOMY

In names of celestial objects and regions, only the proper nouns are capitalized:

Arcturus
Crab nebula
Halley's comet
the Hyades cluster
the Lesser Magellanic Cloud (full name of galaxy)
the Milky Way; the Milky Way galaxy

Generic and descriptive terms are lowercased:

black hole	solar system
cepheid variable	universe
galaxy	Van Allen radiation belt
pulsar	white dwarf

The words *sun* and *moon* are lowercased, even when they refer to earth's sun and moon. The word *earth*, designating the planet, is lowercased unless mentioned with the names of other planets or introduced by the word *planet*.

the moon	Venus, Mars, and Earth
the sun	the planet Earth
the earth	

2-6

GEOLOGY

Structural and Topographic Features
The generic part of the name is usually lowercased:

the Ortley anticline	south face
the Cincinnati arch	the San Andreas fault
the Pacific basin	the Rhine graben
the Idaho batholith	the Aar massif
the Atlantic coast	the Niesen nappe
western cwm	the Nazca plate
the California desert	the Blue Ridge uplift
the Blinman dome	the Ohio River valley

In geographic senses, however, a generic term such as *valley* is often capitalized (see Section 2-1):

Hudson Valley

Stratigraphic Terms
Formal divisions and subdivisions of time and time-rock (rock formed during a specified geologic time interval) are capitalized. To determine which units are considered formal, consult the *Code of Stratigraphic Nomenclature* of the American Commission on Stratigraphic Nomenclature or the table "Geologic Time and Formations" in *Webster's Third New International Dictionary.*

Ochoan Age	Early Devonian Period
Recent Epoch	Upper Devonian Period
Paleozoic Era	Ocoee Series
Paleozoic Erathem	

2-7

HISTORY

Periods
Lowercase is used for most historical (not geologic) periods, except for words designating a person or place:

ancient Greece	baroque period

bronze age	romantic period
colonial period	space age
eighteenth century	Sung dynasty
gay nineties	the twenties
ice age	Victorian age
iron age	Weimar republic

However, certain names of historical or cultural periods are capitalized because of long-standing tradition or when the designation might be confused with the term used in its general sense:

Age of Reason	Reformation
Eighteenth Dynasty (Egypt)	Renaissance
Fourth Republic	Third Reich
Middle Ages (*but* medieval)	

Events

Lowercase is used for most historical events, except for words designating a person or place:

California gold rush	industrial revolution
cold war	Norman conquest
Dreyfus affair	panic of 1837
the great depression	westward movement

Popular names of historical events are capitalized when necessary to avoid ambiguity or when the capitalized form is widely accepted:

Boston Tea Party	Prohibition
the Crusades	Reign of Terror
Custer's Last Stand	South Sea Bubble
New Deal	Whiskey Rebellion

wars and revolutions   Historically accepted full names of wars and revolutions are capitalized. Lowercase is used for short or inexact forms.

American Revolution; the revolution
French Revolution
Civil War (United States); War between the States
Korean war (inexact form)
Revolutionary War (American)
Vietnamese war (inexact form)
World War I; World War II; First World War; Second World War; the war;
   the two world wars

battles In names of battles, the word *battle* is lowercased:

> battle of the Bulge
> battle of Gettysburg

Treaties, Documents, Doctrines, Plans, Concepts

Full formal names are capitalized:

> Mayflower Compact; the
>   compact
> Declaration of Independence
> Monroe Doctrine; the doctrine
> Magna Charta
> Pact of Paris; the pact
> Marshall Plan; the plan
> Second Five-Year Plan; the plan
>
> New Economic Policy; the policy
> European Recovery Program; the
>   program
> Wilmot Proviso; the proviso
> Tonkin Gulf Resolution; the
>   resolution
> Treaty of Tordesillas; the treaty

Lowercase is used for most designations of general historical concepts and movements:

> civil rights movement
> energy crisis
> imperialism
> iron curtain
>
> lend-lease policy (*but* Lend-
>   Lease Act)
> open-door policy
> women's movement

Quotation marks may be appropriate for some historical concepts to avoid confusion with the terms used in their general sense:

> the "great society"
> the "new frontier"
> the "politics of joy"

2-8

LAW

Acts, Laws, Bills, Amendments

Full official titles or widely accepted short titles of acts and laws are capitalized and set in roman type without quotation marks. The words *act* and *law* are lowercased when they are used alone.

> the antitrust act
> the Civil Rights Act of 1965; the act

Emergency Petroleum Allocation Act; the act
National Bankruptcy Act; the bankruptcy act; the act
interstate commerce law
the Multiple Dwelling Law; the law

Lowercase is used for the parts of titles of bills and proposed constitutional amendments that are not proper names:

the equal rights amendment
the prohibition amendment
the Wagner housing bill; the Wagner bill; the bill

Full formal titles of enacted and ratified amendments to the U.S. Constitution are capitalized:

the Fifth Amendment
the Thirteenth Amendment

Inexact names of constitutional amendments are lowercased:

the income tax amendment
the prohibition amendment

Compilations

Exact names of compilations (bodies of law) are capitalized:

ABA Canons of Professional Ethics
Acts and Resolves of Massachusetts
Revised Statutes Annotated of the State of New Hampshire
Massachusetts Appeals Court Reports

Rulings

Judicial rulings are capitalized, except when the ruling is referred to only by number:

Rule against Perpetuities
Rule in Shelley's Case
rule 105-6

Legal Citations

In text, the following forms are used. See also "Legislative and Legal Citations" in Chapter 5.

Branzburg v. Hayes, 408 U.S. 665

Hotel Utica, Inc., v. Armstrong, 404 N.Y.S. 2d 455 (App. Div. 1978)
In re Mirvis, 309 F. 2d 5 (1st Cir. 1962)
Seto v. Muller, 395 F. Supp. 811 (D. Mass. 1975)
Voting Rights Act of 1965, Pub. L. 89-110, 79 Stat. 437

2-9

RELIGION

The guidelines given here may be varied to fit the needs or understanding of readers for whom a book is intended. Religious titles are included in Section 2-2; buildings, in Section 2-1. For the spelling of transliterated terms, follow the latest edition of *Webster's.*

Festivals, Holidays, Seasons
Religious festivals, holidays, seasons, etc., are capitalized:

Feast of Saint Michael and All Angels	Lent
Good Friday	Maundy Thursday
Hanukkah	Ramadan
Holy Week	Saint Cecilia's Day
	Yom Kippur

When the name of the festival, holiday, or season can stand alone, attached generic terms are lowercased:

Christmas; Christmas day	New Year's eve
Easter; Easter week	Purim; feast of Purim

Religions, Denominations, Sects, Cults, Orders, Congregations, Schools
Full official names of religions, denominations, sects, cults, etc., and their adherents are capitalized. Unless words like *sect, cult,* and *church* are part of the full official name, they are lowercased.

Baptists; Baptist
Buddhism; Buddhist
Catholicism; a Catholic; Catholic church
Christian Brothers
Christianity; Christian
Franciscan (Order of Friars Minor)
Gnosticism; Gnostic
Hinduism; Hindu
Islam; Moslem; Muslim

Jainism; Jain
Judaism; Jew
Methodism (or Methodists); Methodist
Mormon church (Church of Jesus Christ of Latter-Day Saints); Mormon
Shinto(ism); Shintoist
Society of Jesus; Jesuit
Taoism; Taoist
Yellow Hat sect

Rituals and Services

It is usually appropriate to use lowercase for religious services, rituals, and sacraments:

bar mitzvah	holy communion
confirmation	lauds
eucharist	mass
ghost dance	vespers

Objects and Symbols

Vestments, objects, and symbols are lowercased:

alb	shroud of Turin
ark of the covenant	star of David
paten	the true cross

Councils

The names of religious councils are capitalized. The word *council* standing alone is lowercased.

First Council of Constantinople; the council
First Lateran Council (*or* Lateran I)
Lambeth Conferences; the conferences

Deities and Revered Persons

Allah	Jehovah
the Archangel Michael	the Messiah (*but* a messiah)
Buddha (*but* a buddha)	the Virgin
Father, Son, and Holy Ghost	Zeus
God	

Descriptive appellations are lowercased:

earth mother

supreme being
water god

Although there is a growing tendency to lowercase pronouns referring to the deity, they are still generally capitalized in most religious contexts:

God . . . He
His word

Religious Writings
Sacred books, creeds, and prayers are capitalized. Adjectives derived from capitalized sacred writings are lowercased.

Apostle's Creed	Koran; koranic
the Athanasian Creed	Kyrie
Bible; biblical (*but* scripture;	Lambeth Quadrilateral
scriptural)	the Lord's Prayer
Book of Daniel	the Psalms
the Decalogue	Proverbs
Donation of Constantine	the Shema
Gloria	Talmud; talmudic
the Hexateuch	Veda(s); vedic

Events
Religious events are lowercased:

the ascension	hegira
the exodus	the second coming

If necessary to avoid ambiguity, quotation marks or italics can be used, or explanatory terms can be added:

the exodus of the Israelites from Egypt
the "great departure"
the last supper of Jesus and the disciples

Concepts
Lowercase is used for most religious concepts:

being	five pillars of Islam
first cause	the trinity

"Places" and States of Being
Terms referring to states of being are lowercased:

> heaven   nirvana
> hell   the "pure land"

Names of supposed places are usually capitalized:

> Valhalla

Translation of Capitalized Terms
If a term is used purely as a translation, it is placed within quotation marks and lowercased:

> Hinyana, the "small vehicle"

If the translated term is used as a name, it should be capitalized:

> Buddha, the Enlightened One

2-10

TESTS

Educational, Occupational, and Psychological Tests
Complete titles of tests and parts of tests are capitalized. Short or inexact forms are lowercased. An authoritative list is given in Buros, *Tests in Print.*

> McGraw-Hill's Prescriptive Mathematics Inventory (PMI)
> National Merit Scholarship Qualifying Test (NMSQT); the test .
> Occupational Interest Inventory; the inventory
> the Original Drawing Test (exact title, part of a test battery)
> a Rorschach inkblot test (inexact title)
> Thematic Apperception Test (TAT); TAT Summary Record Blank
> Torrence's Test of Creativity

Medical Tests
Only proper names are capitalized:

> Benedict's qualitative test
> latex fixation test
> VDRL (Venereal Disease Research Laboratory) test

2-11

TRADE NAMES AND TRADEMARKS

Trade names, such as names of companies, and registered trademarks are
capitalized:

a du Pont product	Pepsi-Cola; Pepsi
Bakelite	Kodachrome film

Many trademarks are listed in *Webster's New Collegiate Dictionary.*
However, the authoritative source for U.S. trademarks is the United States
Trademark Association (6 East 45th Street, New York, NY 10017), which
issues style sheets and may be consulted directly on a particular question.

Unless a reference to a particular company or a specific product must
be retained, use the generic name instead of a trade name or trademark:

facial tissue (*not* Kleenex)
heat-resistant glass (*not* Pyrex)
petroleum jelly (*not* Vaseline)

If a trade name or trademark must be used, couple it with the corresponding generic name whenever possible, especially where there might be
ambiguity (e.g., if a company is well known for more than one type of
product). In books it is customary to omit the registration mark (the superscript ®), since capitalization of a term identifies it sufficiently as a trademark.

Some former trademarks have passed into the public domain and
have become generic names. Such terms are lowercased:

cellophane	mimeograph
dry ice	thermos

The following list shows some commonly used—and misused—
trademarks:

Ace elastic bandages	Day-Glo paint
Bacardi rum	Disposall food waste disposers
Band-Aid adhesive bandages	Fiberglas (fibrous glass) textiles,
Birds Eye frozen foods	yarns, etc.
Coca-Cola *or* Coke beverage	Fig Newtons cakes
Contac decongestant capsules	Freon refrigerants
Con-Tact self-adhesive plastic	Hydra-Matic automatic
Dacron polyster fiber	transmissions

Jeep vehicles
Levi's jeans and sportswear
Masonite hardboard products
Mercurochrome antiseptic
Mystik tape
Naugahyde vinyl-coated fabrics
Neo-Synephrine nasal
  decongestant
Novocain anesthetic
Phillips screws and screwdrivers
Ping-Pong table tennis equipment
Plastic Wood filler

Plexiglas acrylic plastic
Pyrex brand heat-resistant glass
Qiana nylon fiber
Sanforized preshrunk fabric
Scotchgard stain repeller
Sheetrock gypsum wallboard
Tabasco pepper sauce
Touch-Tone pushbutton dialing
Ultrasuede fabric
Vaseline petroleum jelly
X-acto knife
Xerox copiers or duplicators

2-12

DERIVATIVE TERMS

Terms Incorporating Proper Names

In terms that incorporate proper names, the proper name is normally capitalized, but other parts of the term are not:

cedar of Lebanon
Rocky Mountain spotted fever
Savannah sparrow (named for the city)
but savannah hawk (named for its habitat)
Uganda kob

Eponymic terms—terms involving the names of persons—are usually possessive in form, although there are many exceptions:

Achilles tendon
Boltzmann's equation
Engelmann's spruce *or*
  Engelmann spruce
Folin and Wu's method

Graves' disease
Newton's second law
Traill's flycatcher
Vicq d'Azyr's tract

In terms with words such as *law, method, stain, syndrome,* or *test,* the possessive form is not used when the proper name is preceded by an article:

Coombs' test   *but*   an indirect Coombs test
Gram's stain   *but*   a Gram stain

The possessive is not used when two or more persons' names are joined by a hyphen or en dash:

> Ahumada–Del Castillo syndrome

but it may be used with a hyphened compound surname:

> Albers-Schönberg's disease (one person)
> Brown-Séquard's syndrome *or* Brown-Séquard syndrome (one
>   person)

An alternative style, used by some medical publications, eliminates the possessive from eponymic names of syndromes and diseases:

> Epstein-Barr virus
> Laurence-Moon-Biedl syndrome

Derivative nouns referring to processes or conditions and verbs derived from proper names are lowercased:

> d'arsonvalization (electrotherapy with d'Arsonval currents)
> parkinsonism
> *but* Darwinism, Lamarckism (doctrines, not conditions)
> pasteurize; pasteurization

Vernacular names based on genus names are lowercased (see Section 8-7):

> dahlia (genus *Dahlia*)
> giant sequoia (genus *Sequoia*)

but note that a genus name, as such, can modify a noun, e.g., *Cebus* monkeys.

Derivative Terms No Longer Capitalized

Many terms have lost their association with the person or place for which they were originally named and are therefore lowercased. A representative list of such terms follows; the list includes a few trade names that have become generic terms.

> anglicize   bessemer steel
> artesian well   bohemian set

bologna sausage
brazil nut
brussels sprouts
bunsen burner
cartesian coordinates
castile soap
chantilly lace
chesterfield
chinese blue
cordovan leather
coulomb attraction
derby hat
diesel engine
doppler effect
epsom salts
euclidean geometry
french dressing
gaussian
german silver (*but* German
  measles)
glauber's salt
hamiltonian
herculean task
india rubber
italic type
japan varnish
klieg light
kraft paper

lagrangian
lyonnaise potatoes
madras cloth
manila paper
mason jar
merino sheep
morocco leather
murphy bed
newtonian
nicol prism
oxford shoe
paris green
petri dish
plaster of paris
portland cement
prussian blue
pullman car
rochelle salt
roman type
siamese twins
stillson wrench
sweet william
thermos bottle
timothy grass
turkish towel
venetian blind
venturi tube
vienna bread

NUMBERS, MEASUREMENTS, AND ABBREVIATIONS

NUMBERS

General Rules

use of figures Numbers used as nouns are generally written as figures:

> the number 3.14159
> a factor of 4
> approaches 0 (*sometimes* zero)

Figures are almost always used with units of measurement, whether spelled or abbreviated:

6 cm	1 N·m
350 J	5 days
100 watts	5 s

Figures are also used for numbers to be manipulated:

> divide by ½
> 3 white and 2 red, or 3 + 2 = 5

In most technical books, numbers under 10 are spelled when used with a word that is not a unit of measurement:

> five atoms
> 15 tubes

In most nontechnical books, numbers under 100 are spelled when used with a word that is not a unit of measurement:

> sixty-five colleges
> 125 students

At the beginning of a sentence, the spelled form is generally used. In expressions containing both single- and multidigit numbers, both are treated alike.

> Ten to fifteen trials were run.
> Attendance ranged from 9 to 125 employees.

In definitions of units, both the numbers and the units are usually spelled:

> One pascal is the pressure resulting from the force of one newton applied to an area of one square meter.

Of two adjacent numbers, one should be spelled:

> ninety 10-gram weights
> 125 twenty-cent stamps

zeros   In numbers between −1 and 1, a zero is generally placed before the decimal point; however, in books with many statistical passages, zeros are often omitted throughout:

> 0.5
> probability of .5

Zeros are used for round sums in thousands:

> 100,000 errors

In text the words *million* and *billion* are substituted for zeros:

> 7 billion calculations

In comparisons, however, zeros should be used if any of the numbers over 1 million have significant hundreds or thousands digits:

> 27,000,000 as compared with 27,500,000
> *not* 27 million as compared with 27,500,000

multidigit numbers Four-digit numbers are usually set without commas or space:

3000

Commas have customarily been used in numbers of five or more digits, but the use of space is acceptable and is preferred in the SI metric system:

30,000   *or*   30 000

In columnar material containing both numbers with four digits and numbers with five or more digits, either commas or space should be used in the four-digit numbers:

3,000		3 000
	or	
30,000		30 000

When space is used to separate groups of three, digits are counted from the decimal point to the left or right; commas are never used to the right of the decimal point:

27 724.326 965   *or*   27,724.326965

binary numbers In binary numbers, neither commas nor spaces are used:

100001

fractions Simple fractional quantities are spelled out:

one-hundredth
two ten-thousandths
two-thirds of the distance

except in mixed numbers:

4½ times

and before units of measurement:

¼ mA

ordinal numbers   Simple ordinal numbers in text are spelled, except in heavily technical passages. Some forms are dictated by practice in a given field.

> fifth determination
> eighth century
> third step
> 14th percentile
> nth
> Eighty-first Congress (81st Cong. in footnotes and bibliographies)
> 38th parallel
> 4th trial of the 61st experiment

roman numerals   The seven roman numerals are:

I	1	C	100
V	5	D	500
X	10	M	1000
L	50		

From these numerals, any number can be formed according to rules of position. For example, 1984 is written MCMLXXXIV.

An overbar signifies multiplication by 1000:

$$\overline{X} = 10,000$$

The use of roman numerals is conventional in certain designations:

World War II	Louis XIV
Type II error (statistics)	quadrant IV
type II land	VIth cranial nerves

Lowercase roman letters (i, ii, v, etc.) are often used for page numbers preceding the arabic sequence in a book. They are also sometimes used in lists and enumerations.

other designations   Note the use of numbers in certain other designations:

generator 1	plane 1-2-*A*-3
method 2	line 1-2 (*but* line *AB*)
type 3	

Money

Figures are always used in writing sums of money:

5 cents; $0.05 (in business books)	Mex$200
	£5.31
7 million dollars; $7 million	6 francs; fr. 6
$200	1 lira; 2 lire
US$200	5 German marks; 5 deutsche
Can$200	marks; 5 DM

In ranges the dollar sign is repeated but the word *dollar* is not:

$2 to $3 million
25 to 30 dollars

Ages

Figures are generally used for ages of persons:

a 3-year-old child
a woman of 25
aged 40 (*but* in his forties)

Ratios

For numerical ratios, a colon, a hyphen, a slash, or the word *to* may be used:

a 10:1 chance; a 10 to 1 chance
a 4-1 vote; a 4 to 1 vote
10/3 (statistics)

Ratios made up of words are expressed by a slant bar, a hyphen, or the word *to:*

male/female ratio; male-female   signal-to-noise ratio
  ratio   odds of ten to one
ratio of men to women

Symbolic ratios are usually written with a slant bar:

the *a/b* ratio; the ratio *a/b*
but the ratio of *a* to *b*

The selected form should be used consistently throughout the work.

3-2

UNITS OF MEASUREMENT

For units of time, see "Time Measurements" in Section 3-3.

The International System of Units (SI)

SI is a practical, worldwide system of units of measurement. It was established by the General Conference on Weights and Measures to form a basis on which science, education, and international trade could transcend the barriers of language and spelling through the use of uniform, internationally accepted symbols and definitions for units of measurement. Although SI is a metric system, not all metric units used in the past are part of the SI system.

SI units are divided into three categories: base units, derived units, and supplementary units.

base units   The seven base units, which were chosen by the General Conference because they are well defined and dimensionally independent, are shown in Table 3-1.

derived units   The derived units are formed by combining base units algebraically through multiplication or division. They are expressed in terms of the base units (Table 3-2) or with special names (Tables 3-3 and 3-4).

supplementary units   There are two supplementary units, the radian and the steradian (Table 3-5).

TABLE 3-1   SI BASE UNITS

QUANTITY	NAME	SYMBOL
Length	meter	m
Mass	kilogram	kg
Time	second	s
Electric current	ampere	A
Thermodynamic temperature	kelvin	K
Amount of substance	mole	mol
Luminous intensity	candela	cd

TABLE 3-2   SOME SI DERIVED UNITS EXPRESSED IN TERMS OF BASE UNITS

QUANTITY	NAME	SYMBOL
Area	square meter	m^2
Volume	cubic meter	m^3
Speed, velocity	meter per second	m/s
Acceleration	meter per second squared	m/s^2
Wave number	1 per meter	m^{-1}
Density, mass density	kilogram per cubic meter	kg/m^3
Current density	ampere per square meter	A/m^2
Magnetic field strength	ampere per meter	A/m
Concentration (of amount of substance)	mole per cubic meter	mol/m^3
Specific volume	cubic meter per kilogram	m^3/kg
Luminance	candela per square meter	cd/m^2

TABLE 3-3   SI DERIVED UNITS WITH SPECIAL NAMES

QUANTITY	NAME	SYMBOL
Frequency	hertz (pl., hertz)	Hz
Force	newton	N
Pressure, stress	pascal	Pa
Energy, work, quantity of heat	joule	J
Power, radiant flux	watt	W
Quantity of electricity, electric charge	coulomb	C
Electric potential, potential difference, electromotive force	volt	V
Capacitance	farad	F
Electric resistance	ohm	Ω
Conductance	siemens (pl., siemens)	S
Magnetic flux	weber	Wb
Magnetic flux density	tesla	T
Inductance	henry (pl., henrys)	H
Celsius temperature	degree Celsius	°C
Luminous flux	lumen	lm
Illuminance	lux (pl., lux)	lx
Activity (of a radionuclide)	becquerel	Bq
Absorbed dose, specific energy imparted, kerma, absorbed dose index	gray	Gy

prefixes   The SI prefixes, which signify decimal multiples, are shown in Table 3-6.

Symbols and Abbreviations

In the U.S. customary system the shortened forms for units of measure are referred to as *abbreviations*, but in SI they are called *symbols*. Abbreviations and symbols for units are used without periods, with the occasional exception of *in.* for *inch* in elementary material. The rules that follow

TABLE 3-4   SOME SI DERIVED UNITS

QUANTITY	NAME	SYMBOL
Dynamic viscosity	pascal second	Pa·s
Moment of force	newton meter	N·m
Surface tension	newton per meter	N/m
Power density	watt per square meter	W/m^2
Heat capacity, entropy	joule per kelvin	J/K
Specific heat capacity, specific entropy	joule per kilogram kelvin	J/(kg·K)
Specific energy	joule per kilogram	J/kg
Thermal conductivity	watt per meter kelvin	W/(m·K)
Energy density	joule per cubic meter	J/m^3
Electric field strength	volt per meter	V/m
Electric charge density	coulomb per cubic meter	C/m^3
Electric flux density	coulomb per square meter	C/m^2
Permittivity	farad per meter	F/m
Permeability	henry per meter	H/m
Molar energy	joule per mole	J/mol
Molar entropy, molar heat capacity	joule per mole kelvin	J/(mol·K)
Exposure (x and γ rays)	coulomb per kilogram	C/kg
Absorbed dose rate	gray per second	Gy/s

TABLE 3-5   SI SUPPLEMENTARY UNITS

QUANTITY	NAME	SYMBOL
Plane angle	radian	rad
Solid angle	steradian	sr

apply to both symbols and abbreviations, but for economy of expression both are referred to as symbols.

Symbols are almost always used for units of measurement when they are directly preceded by a number or other symbol denoting quantity, but they are spelled out otherwise:

5 cm³   *but*   measured in cubic centimeters

singular and plural   Use the same symbol both for the singular and the plural of a unit of measurement:

1 kg
24 kg

Use the normal plural for spelled-out measurements unless the quantity is less than 1. (See Table 3-3 for irregular plurals.)

15 kilometers   0.9 ounce
³⁄₁₀ mile 3×10^{-19} volt

TABLE 3-6   DECIMAL MULTIPLES

MULTIPLE	SI PREFIX	SYMBOL
10^{18}	exa	E
10^{15}	peta	P
10^{12}	tera	T
10^{9}	giga	G
10^{6}	mega	M
10^{3}	kilo	k
10^{2}	hecto	h
10	deka	da
10^{-1}	deci	d
10^{-2}	centi	c
10^{-3}	milli	m
10^{-6}	micro	μ
10^{-9}	nano	n
10^{-12}	pico	p
10^{-15}	femto	f
10^{-18}	atto	a

Generally use a singular verb regardless of the quantity:

> 3 kg of calcium is added
> 6 million dollars was allocated

compound units   A center point in a compound unit indicates multiplication:

> Pa·s
> ft·lb

Either a slant bar or a negative exponent indicates division:

> 3 kg/m   *or*   3 kg·m⁻¹
> *but usually* 3 cm⁻¹ (*not* 3/cm)

The word *per* is generally spelled with spelled-out units of measure or when one of the items is not a unit of measure:

> 3 meters per second
> 3 threads per inch

Longer or more complex units may be set in one of several ways:

> 1500 J s⁻¹ m⁻² K⁻¹
> 1500 J/(s·m²·K)
> 1500 J/(s)(m²)(K)

Note the thin spaces instead of center points in the first example above. The following are *not considered good usage:*

> 1500 J per s per m² per K
> 1500 J/s/m²/K

For squared and cubed measurements, use exponents:

> 10 cm³
> 5 ft²

degree sign   The degree sign, rather than the spelled form or abbreviation, is used for angles and temperatures, except for temperatures measured in kelvins, where the degree sign is omitted:

90° angle
100°C (*also* 100 °C)
100 K

The symbols for minutes and seconds of arc are used only in combination with another symbol; otherwise they are spelled:

32°22′16″   22 minutes
N30°15′E   16 seconds

ranges   In text, use *to* in ranges of measurements:

12 to 14 months

In tables and footnotes, an en dash may be used:

12–14 months

Do not repeat units of measurement in ranges or series:

800 to 1000°C
1200, 1400, or 1600 MHz

measurements as modifiers   Simple measurements used as adjectives are hyphened; many complex measurements are not:

a 14-kg weight
a 1¾-in margin
a 5-ft 6-in board
a 4-mm-thick layer
but a 50 percent reduction
a 3.6 × 10⁵ light-year distance

percentages   The word *percent* is customarily spelled in text matter, but the percent sign is generally used in tables and equations to save space:

3 percent (text)
3% (tables and equations)

The percent sign is *always* used in certain chemical expressions:

a 40% solution
10% aqueous sodium hydroxide

3-3

ABBREVIATIONS

Initial-Letter Abbreviations

Many abbreviations consist of lowercase initial letters; periods are usually omitted unless the abbreviation forms a common word:

> bp (boiling point)
> df (degrees of freedom)
> emf (electromotive force)
> esu (electrostatic unit)
> gcd (greatest common denominator)
> i.f. (intermediate frequency)
> mmf (magnetomotive force)
> nmr (nuclear magnetic resonance)
> pdf (probability density function)
> qid (4 times a day)
> rms (root mean square)

Other initial-letter abbreviations are capitalized in accordance with usage in the field:

> AFL-CIO (American Federation of Labor–Congress of Industrial Organizations)
> AT&T (American Telephone & Telegraph)
> OD (outside diameter)
> PE (potential energy)

ac and dc   When used as nouns, *alternating current* and *direct current* are usually spelled out without hyphens, but as adjectives they are abbreviated:

> dc generator
> 25 V ac

i.e. and e.g.   To avoid confusion, *that is* and *for example* are spelled rather than abbreviated when they occur next to numbers or symbols; in regular text, i.e. and e.g. are readily understood.

business terms The following business terms are almost always abbreviated in text:

    COD *or* C.O.D. *or* c.o.d. (cash/collect on delivery)
    CPM (critical path method)
    EOM *or* eom (end of month)
    FOB *or* F.O.B. *or* f.o.b. (free on board)
    GNP (gross national product)
    LCL *or* lcl (less than carload lots)
    LIFO *or* lifo (last in first out)
    PERT (program evaluation and review technique)
    R&D (research and development)

For abbreviations of trigonometric functions and other mathematical entities, see Chapter 7.

Time Measurements
Units of time may be abbreviated or not, depending on context. In nontechnical contexts, as well as casual uses in technical books, the spelled forms are usually preferable. In technical material, small units are generally abbreviated:

    s (second)
    min (minute)
    h (hour)

Larger units, such as day (d), week (wk), and year (yr), are rarely abbreviated, even when used as a precise measurement.

Names of months are spelled in text. In reference footnotes, bibliographies, tables, etc., all except May, June, and July are abbreviated when followed by the day of the month. Days of the week are spelled out in text but may be abbreviated in tables.

    February 1, 1982; 1 February 1982
    March 15 (Mar. 15 in references, etc.)
    the January 1982 issue
    the January 18, 1982, issue
    Saturday, August 12

Time of day is expressed as follows:

    2 P.M. *or* 2:30 p.m. (small capital letters or lowercase)
    two o'clock

Decades and centuries may be expressed in numbers or spelled out as words:

> the 1930s; the thirties; the nineteen-thirties
> ca. 1300 B.C.; A.D. 1900 (small capital letters or capitals)
> *but* the year 1900 (omit A.D.)
> the 1800s; the fourth century B.C.; the nineteenth century (omit A.D.)

In ranges the full year is usually repeated. The word *to* is preferred to the en dash in text unless the range is in apposition to a word denoting a block of time.

> from 1850 to 1895 (1850–1895 in tables or parenthetical references)
> the period 1850–1895; the decade 1930–1940
> the school (or fiscal) year 1982–1983
> *but* 1982–83 sometimes in education and economics books

States

The name *United States* is spelled as a noun. As an adjective it may be spelled or abbreviated. The abbreviated form is customary in names of governmental departments, bureaus, and offices.

> in the United States
> United States government; U.S. government
> U.S. Army; United States Army
> U.S. Department of Agriculture (sometimes USDA)

Names of states, commonwealths, territories of the United States, and provinces of Canada are spelled in text. In footnotes, references, and tables they are abbreviated after the name of a city or county. Table 3-7 shows both the conventional abbreviations and the two-letter forms used with U.S. zip codes.

Courtesy, Honorary, and Designative Titles

Some titles are always abbreviated when they accompany a full name or surname:

> Dr.   Jr.
> Mrs.   Sr.
> Mr.   Messrs.
> Ms.

Other titles are abbreviated only before the full name (although in prefaces and acknowledgments it is also common practice to spell them before the full name):

Prof. Albert Braun   Col. Mary Smith
Professor Braun   Colonel Smith

Courtesy and professional titles are generally omitted for both women and
men when works or writings are cited:

Braun's findings prove . . .

TABLE 3-7   ABBREVIATIONS OF STATES AND PROVINCES

United States

Ala.	AL	Ky.	KY	Ohio	OH
Alaska	AK	La.	LA	Okla.	OK
Ariz.	AZ	Maine	ME	Oreg.	OR
Ark.	AR	Md.	MD	Pa.	PA
Calif.	CA	Mass.	MA	P.R.†	PR
Colo.	CO	Mich.	MI	R.I.	RI
Conn.	CT	Minn.	MN	S.C.	SC
C.Z.*	CZ	Miss.	MS	S.Dak.	SD
Del.	DE	Mo.	MO	Tenn.	TN
D.C.	DC	Mont.	MT	Tex.	TX
Fla.	FL	Neb.	NE	Utah	UT
Ga.	GA	Nev.	NV	Vt.	VT
Hawaii	HI	N.H.	NH	Va.	VA
Idaho	ID	N.J.	NJ	V.I.‡	VI
Ill.	IL	N.Mex.	NM	Wash.	WA
Ind.	IN	N.Y.	NY	W.Va.	WV
Iowa	IA	N.C.	NC	Wis.	WI
Kan.	KS	N.Dak.	ND	Wyo.	WY

Canadian Provinces

Alberta	Alta.	Nova Scotia	N.S.
British Columbia	B.C.	Ontario	Ont.
Manitoba	Man.	Prince Edward Island	P.E.I.
New Brunswick	N.B.	Quebec	Que.
Newfoundland	Nfld.	Saskatchewan	Sask.

*Canal Zone.

†Puerto Rico.

‡Virgin Islands.

Saint is usually abbreviated as a title and in geographic names. In surnames the person's individual preference is followed when known.

St. George
St. Petersburg, Florida
Robert de Saint-Loup

Other Abbreviations

DDT
EST (eastern standard time)
H-bomb
i.t.a. (international teaching alphabet)
M.A. (master of arts)
MA (mental age)
M.Ed.
no. (tables and references)
U.S.S.R.
versus *or* vs. (in text); vs. (in tables); *v.* (in legal citations)
WCBS-FM

Abbreviations for some common terms used in references are given in Chapter 5. The *MLA Handbook* is an excellent source for bibliographic abbreviations.

3-4

PLURALS

Plurals of Numbers

For plurals of numbers (numerals), add *s* without an apostrophe:

0s   50s
1s   100s

Plurals of Symbols and Letters

With mathematical symbols and with letters, use an apostrophe for clarity:

Symbols

O's θ's
I's q_i's
A's

Letters

O's
I's
A's
but Ss (subjects)

Plurals of Abbreviations

In general, the plural of a capital-letter abbreviation is formed by the addition of *s* without an apostrophe, and the plural of a lowercase abbreviation by the addition of *'s*:

IQs	Btu's
Ph.D.s	emf's
RNAs	

For the plurals of symbols for units of measurement, see "Singular and Plural" in Section 3-2.

4

EXTRACTS, LISTS, AND OTHER ELEMENTS OF THE TEXT

4-1

EXTRACTS

An extract is an excerpt or passage (sentence, paragraph, table, etc.) quoted from another printed source. Extracts may be either *displayed* (that is, set off from the main text by indention or smaller type) or *run in* (included within the text). If the extent of a quotation is not clear in the typescript, the author should indicate its length with a vertical line drawn in the left margin.

Displayed Extracts
Quoted material of more than a few lines (approximately seven typed manuscript lines) is usually displayed in small type and is not enclosed in quotation marks. Double quotation marks are used within a displayed extract for dialogue and set-off words.

Run-in Extracts
Shorter extracts are generally run in with the text. A run-in extract is enclosed in double quotation marks. Single quotation marks are reserved for use within an extract already set off by double quotation marks.

Closely related or adjacent extracts are often treated alike, regardless of length. For example, if there are two or three displayed extracts on a page as well as a short excerpt, consider displaying the short one as well.

Editing in Extracts
In general, quoted matter is edited only to correct obvious typographical errors and the improper use of ellipses and quotation marks.

Interpolations

Words or comments such as *sic* inserted by the author in a quotation are enclosed in square brackets: [ ]. Explanations such as "italics supplied" are added as footnotes or enclosed in square brackets at the end of the extract.

Ellipses in Extract Material

Ellipses are the dots *(points)* that are used to indicate omission in a passage. Some authors indicate omission by using asterisks or an indiscriminate number of points, not realizing, perhaps, that conventions exist for handling omissions with clarity and accuracy. The "original" passage below can be used to illustrate how various problems of ellipsis should be treated.

"original" passage

> When Wilson returned from the Paris Peace Conference, he was confident that the Senate would vote in favor of the Versailles Treaty and thus of American membership in the League of Nations. But Wilson was wrong.
>
> He failed to persuade the American people or the Senate that the League of Nations was an acceptable approach to American security.
>
> In the autumn of 1919 he suffered a stroke, brought on perhaps by the strain of a losing battle.

number of points   Always use three points to represent ellipsis. In the example below, a portion of the first sentence of the original passage has been omitted:

> When Wilson returned from the Paris Peace Conference, he was confident that the Senate would vote in favor of . . . American membership in the League of Nations.

If a sentence comes to an end within the omitted portion, show the terminal punctuation of the sentence by using a fourth point:

> When Wilson returned from the Paris Peace Conference, he was confident that the Senate would vote in favor of the Versailles Treaty. . . . But Wilson was wrong.

By scholarly convention, in the example above, there should be a small (thin) space between the first point and the word that precedes it ("Treaty . . . ."), because the sentence does not end with that word. But since publishers cannot undertake to verify quotations, they generally close up the first point ("Treaty. . . .") when four are used.

omission of whole paragraphs   Do not use a row of points or asterisks to indicate omission of one or more paragraphs. Terminal punctuation followed by three points suffices.

> But Wilson was wrong. . . .
>   In the autumn of 1919 he suffered a stroke, brought on perhaps by the strain of a losing battle.

omission at the beginning or end of run-in quotations   Do not use ellipses if the quoted passage is clear without them. For example, if a run-in quotation is a sentence fragment related syntactically to the parent sentence, its nature as both extract and fragment is clear from the quotation marks, and ellipses are not required.

> *Adequate:*
> Smith points out that Wilson "failed to persuade the American people or the Senate that the League of Nations was an acceptable approach to American security."

> *Unnecessary:*
> Smith points out that Wilson " . . . failed to persuade, etc."

omission at the beginning of displayed quotations   A new sentence simply starts with a capital letter, as in all the examples above. But if the extract begins in the middle of a sentence, there are three styles from which to choose.

1   The most common style calls for ellipses and lowercase:

> As Smith points out, Wilson
>   . . . was confident that the Senate would vote in favor of the Versailles Treaty, etc.

2   The quotation may start lowercase without ellipses:

> As Smith points out, Wilson
>   was confident that the Senate would vote in favor of the Versailles Treaty, etc.

3   If the quotation reads as though it were a complete sentence, the first letter may be capitalized even though it was lowercase in the original:

> According to Smith:
> He was confident that the Senate would vote in favor of the Versailles Treaty, etc.

In legal material, some authors prefer to use brackets for the editorial addition of a capital letter:

> [H]e was confident, etc.

Style 1 is preferable because it does not alter capitalization and because, in the absence of quotation marks, it alerts the reader to the fact that an extract is beginning.

Poetry

In general, poetry is displayed, and the original alignment is retained as nearly as possible. A row of dots, set to the width of the preceding line, is used to indicate omission of one or more lines of poetry. Asterisks are not used for this purpose.

> A raven sat upon a tree,
> And not a word he spoke, for
> His beak contained a piece of Brie,
> Or, maybe, it was Roquefort.
> We'll make it any kind you please—
> At all events it was a cheese.
>
> Beneath the tree's umbrageous limb
> A hungry fox sat smiling;
> . . . .
> "J'admire," said he, "ton beau plumage,"
> (The which was simply persiflage).

> Guy Wetmore Carryl (1873–1904)

When lines of poetry are run in, use slashes to indicate the end of each line. Note that each line retains the capitalization and punctuation of the original poem as follows:

> A raven sat upon a tree,/And not a word he spoke, for/His beak contained a piece of Brie,/Or, maybe, it was Roquefort.

Citing Sources

General rules for credit lines are given in Section 11-2.

4-2

LISTS AND OUTLINES

The typeface and indention chosen for lists and outlines may vary considerably from book to book, depending on the design chosen, but certain conventions are standard.

Lists

numbering   Lists may be numbered or unnumbered. Sometimes each item is introduced by a *bullet* (heavy black dot). Arabic figures (1, 2, 3) are preferred for numbered lists, with italic lowercase letters (*a, b, c*) for subitems.

style for run-in lists   When a numbered list is run into the text, the numbers are enclosed in parentheses:

> Computer science might be called the study of (1) machines that can hold data, (2) languages for describing data manipulation, (3) foundations that describe what kind of refined data can be produced from raw data, and (4) structures for representing data.

Parentheses are also used for lettered subitems that are run in, as in problem sections:

> 5-23. For the representation of exercise 5-22, write algorithms to (*a*) erase a matrix, (*b*) add two matrices, (*c*) multiply two matrices, and (*d*) print out a matrix.

style for displayed lists   Displayed lists (those which are set off from the text) are indented in one of three ways: paragraph style, hanging indention, and block style.

> *Paragraph style*
>   The first line of each item in the list is indented, and subsequent (turnover) lines are set to the left-hand margin. *(This item is set in paragraph style.)*

> *Hanging indention*
> Each item begins at the left-hand margin, and the turnover lines are indented. *(This item is set with hanging indention.)*

> *Block style*
> All lines align at the left, and some amount of extra space is used between items. *(This item is set in block style.)*

Long lists made up of very short items are generally set in two or more columns:

Baldwin	Great Neck	Roslyn
East Hills	Manhasset	Seaford
East Meadow	Massapequa	Syosset
Freeport	Plainview	Uniondale

punctuation in displayed lists   No punctuation is used after entries in a list composed entirely of nonsentence items. If nonsentence and sentence items are mixed, however, a period is used after every entry in the list. See Section 10-7.

Outlines

Outlines are displayed lists with two or more values.

numbering   The following numbering sequences are preferred:

Two values
1 . . .
   a . . .

Three values
1 . . .
   a . . .
      (1) . . .

Four values
I . . .
   A . . .
      1 . . .
         a . . .

Five values
I . . .
   A . . .
      1 . . .
         a . . .
            (1) . . .

indention   Outlines are usually indented in such a way that successive steps will be apparent:

1. Methods of composition
   a. Hot metal
      (1) Monotype
      (2) Linotype
   b. Film composition
   c. Electronic typesetting
2. Methods of printing
   a. Etc.

taxonomic keys   Taxonomic keys are outlines used for the identification of species. A key provides successively more detailed descriptions, each item leading to another part of the key until the name of the species is arrived at.

Key to Lactarius
1 *a* Fruiting body white, large (4–12 cm); latex white, unchanging, **2** *(The* **2** *means that if your specimen answers this description, you are to go on to item 2.)*
   b Fruiting body colored; latex white or variously colored, **4**
2 *a* Gills crowded, forked; cap glabrous, *L. piperatus (Here, the species is identified as L. piperatus.)*
   b Gills distant, not forked; cap finely tomentose (woolly), **3**
3 *a* Margin of young caps without a cottony roll, *L. vellereus*
   b Margin of young caps with conspicuous cottony roll, *L. deceptivus*
4 Etc.

lists and outlines in extracts   When lists or outlines occur in quoted matter, follow the original exactly for numbering and punctuation, but not necessarily for indention.

4-3

OTHER CHAPTER ELEMENTS

Especially in textbooks, handbooks, and certain other types of reference works, sections, paragraphs, and other elements of the text are often numbered. The choice of a numbering scheme depends on the complexity of the material and the degree to which specific cross-references are needed. In general, the simpler the numbering scheme, the better.

Sections
Major sections of a chapter may be double- or triple-numbered. See "Headings" in Section 11-1.

Illustrations
Illustrations may be numbered consecutively throughout the work (Figure 1, 2, 3, etc.) or double-numbered by chapter (Figure 2-1, 2-2, 2-3, etc.). Letters (*a*, *b*, *c*) are used to designate separate parts of illustrations and are often set in contrasting type (italic or boldface).

legends   Legends, or captions (the titles of illustrations), generally begin with a capital letter and end with a period. They should be as concise as possible.

   Credits are usually given in parentheses at the end of the legend and are often set in contrasting type. Credits for illustrations donated by private individuals include the words *courtesy of*; otherwise the name of the company or institution that provided the illustration is sufficient unless a specific wording was stipulated when permission for use was granted. The author is responsible for providing the correct wording of credit lines for illustrations. See also "General Rules for Credit Lines" in Section 11-2.

The examples that follow illustrate various acceptable styles for legends and credits:

> Figure 1   Symbolic representation of (*a*) a heat engine and (*b*) a refrigerator.
>
> Figure 2   Energy-level diagrams of a junction transistor. (*a*) Equilibrium with no applied voltage; (*b*) biased for use as amplifier or oscillator.
>
> Figure 7-4   (*a*) Network of capillaries in alveolar walls; (*b*) blood-filled capillary network in interalveolar septum of human lungs. X650. *(From Krahl, 1964.)*

The credit note in the example above refers to a bibliographic entry.

> Fig. 9.   Meristems. *Left,* longitudinal section through a seed; *right,* longitudinal section through a root apex. *(Courtesy of Dr. M. S. Fuller, University of California, Berkeley.)*
>
> Fig. 14.5   In a revolving-drum filter *A*, moist air is directed upward through adjustable grilles *B*. *(The West Bend Co.)*
>
> Fig. 4-11.   Schematic drawing of an end plate. [*R. Couteaux, in G. H. Bourne (ed.), The Structure and Function of Nervous Tissue, vol. 4, Academic, New York, 1972.*]

Tables
See Chapter 6.

Examples
Illustrative examples are often set off from the text by indention or smaller type or both. If the extent of an example is not clear in the typescript, the author should indicate its length with a vertical line drawn in the left margin. Examples are sometimes numbered, either by chapter or by section.

Problems and Exercises
Problems and exercises are usually placed at the end of a chapter and are set in type smaller than the text. They should be numbered, preferably

with double numbers for ease in identification. In books with numbered section headings, the heading "Problems" does not require a section number.

4-4

CROSS-REFERENCES

Whenever possible, avoid cross-references to specific page numbers in the same book, since their insertion in page proof involves expense and delay. Refer instead to the number of the item. Try also to avoid vague references to the location of tables, illustrations, and so forth, such as "See the table *above* (or *below*)," because in page makeup the item may not fall in that position.

Abbreviation and Capitalization

In nontechnical books, the names of parts of publications are usually spelled in text; in technical books, they are often abbreviated, although the spelled form is always used at the beginning of a sentence.

All names of parts of publications may be lowercased, as shown in Table 4-1, or they may be capitalized (Appendix A, App. A, etc.). Note that column (col.), footnote (fn.), and page (p.) are never capitalized.

Table 4-1 shows the most commonly used abbreviations. Additional abbreviations for parts of publications can be found in the *MLA* (Modern Languages Association) *Handbook* or other standard sources. Abbreviations for parts of publications in foreign languages are often not translated, since some of them have no ready equivalent in English.

Plurals

Plurals or plural abbreviations are used when more than one item is referred to:

> Chapters 2 and 3 discuss . . .
> . . . as explained in secs. 2-6 and 2-7
> Figures 2-1 and 2-2 show . . .
> *but* Figure 2-1*a* and *b* shows . . .

Ranges

Cross-reference to a range of items is made as follows:

> Tables 2-6 to 2-8 indicate . . .
> . . . Eqs. (2-10) to (2-13) prove . . .

4-5

RUNNING HEADS

The titles appearing at the top of each book page are called *running heads*. (If the design calls for them to appear at the bottom of the page, they are known as *running feet*.) In books divided into parts or units, the customary style calls for part (or unit) title on the left-hand page and chapter (or section or selection) title on the right-hand page. In books not divided into parts or sections, the chapter title may be used on both left- and right-hand pages, or the chapter number may appear on the left and the chapter title on the right.

TABLE 4-1   ABBREVIATIONS AND NUMBERING OF PARTS OF PUBLICATIONS IN TECHNICAL TEXT AND FOOTNOTES*

PART	ABBREVIATION	COMMONLY USED NUMBERING SYSTEMS
appendix	app.	A, I
article	art.	2-1
case	case	1
chapter	chap.	1
column	col.	1
equation	eq.	1, (2-1), 2-1
example	example	1, 2-1
exercise	exercise	1, 2-1
figure	fig.	1, 2-1
footnote	fn.	1 (or symbols)
page	page (in text), p. (in footnotes)	1
paragraph	par.	1, 2-1
part	part (in text), pt. (in footnotes)	1
problem	prob.	1, 2-1
section	sec.	1 (of book), 2-1 (of chapter)
table	table	1, 2-1
volume	vol.	1, I

*In nontechnical books, parts of publications, whether spelled or abbreviated, are often capitalized (Appendix A, Chap. 5, Fig. 26, etc.), with the exception of column (col.), footnote (fn.), and page (p.), which are always lowercased.

Other combinations are often more appropriate. In anthologies, for example, authors' names sometimes are given on the left and titles of selections on the right. In this style manual, chapter titles appear on the left and section numbers on the right. In dictionaries and encyclopedias, catchwords are used at the top of the page to indicate the first and last entries on that page; less commonly, there is only one catchword on the left-hand page and one on the right-hand page, representing the first entry on the left and the last entry on the right.

When titles are unusually long, the author may be asked to supply shortened versions for use in the running heads.

4-6

FRONT MATTER

Parts of a book that precede the beginning of the text are called *front matter* or *preliminaries*. Front matter is more than a collection of legalities, vanities, and inscrutable page numbers. It serves as a shop window for the book, telling readers what they'll find inside (table of contents) and guiding them to the best use of the facilities (preface).

In the past the table of contents was generally placed after the other prefatory material, where the reader or prospective buyer often had a hard time finding it. We recommend the practice of placing the table of contents where it will precede everything it lists.

Pagination

Table 4-2 shows the suggested sequence of front matter and some variant pagination systems. Few books, if any, will contain all the features shown in the table, but regardless of the number or length of front-matter items, the table can always be followed for the sequence of items and for new right-hand pages, with pagination changed accordingly.

The main text of a book usually starts on page 1. The use of roman numerals for page numbers in the front matter gives the publisher flexibility to expand, delete, or rearrange items as necessary. For this reason the second half title is here considered part of the roman-numeral sequence, although in some other systems it is considered arabic 1.

Blank pages are always counted in the numbering sequence. However, the folios (page numbers) for blank pages, and for certain other pages as well, are "blind," that is, not printed on the page.

An introduction that is prefatory is included in the preliminaries. An introduction that is part of the subject matter of the text itself is folioed arabic 1. Otherwise arabic 1 is usually the first page of Part 1, or Chapter 1, or whatever the first major division of the text happens to be.

TABLE 4-2   SEQUENCE AND PAGINATION OF FRONT MATTER

NORMAL SEQUENCE OF FRONT-MATTER ITEMS	IF NO FRONTIS-PIECE OR IF FRONTISPIECE IS AN INSERT	IF THERE IS A CARD PLATE[a] AND IF FRONTISPIECE IS ON TEXT STOCK	IF THERE IS NO CARD PLATE[a] AND IF FRONTISPIECE IS ON TEXT STOCK	IF INTRO-DUCTION BEGINS ON ARABIC 1
*Half title	(i)†	(i)	(i)	(i)
Card plate[a]	(ii)	(iii) ⎤		(ii)
or blank		(ii) ⎦ note		
Frontispiece		(iv)	(ii)	
*Title page	(iii)	(v)	(iii)	(iii)
Copyright page[b]	(iv)	(vi)	(iv)	(iv)
*Dedication[c]	(v)	(vii)	(v)	(v)
Blank	(vi)	(viii)	(vi)	(vi)
*Contents	vii	ix	vii	vii
Blank or continuation	viii	x	viii	viii
List of illustrations[d]	ix	xi	ix	ix
Blank or continuation	x	xii	x	x
List of tables[d]	xi	xiii	xi	xi
Blank or continuation	xii	xiv	xii	xii
*List of contributors	xiii	xv	xiii	xiii
Blank or continuation	xiv	xvi	xiv	xiv
*Editor's introduction	xv	xvii	xv	xv
Blank or continuation	xvi	xviii	xvi	xvi
*Foreword	xvii	xix	xvii	xvii
Blank or continuation	xviii	xx	xviii	xviii
*Preface to this edition	xix	xxi	xix	xix
Blank or continuation	xx	xxii	xx	xx
*Preface to previous edition	xxi	xxiii	xxi	xxi
Blank or continuation	xxii	xxiv	xxii	xxii
Acknowledgments[d,b]	xxiii	xxv	xxiii	xxiii
Blank or continuation	xxiv	xxvi	xxiv	xxiv

TABLE 4-2 SEQUENCE AND PAGINATION OF FRONT MATTER (*Continued*)

NORMAL SEQUENCE OF FRONT-MATTER ITEMS	IF NO FRONTIS-PIECE OR IF FRONTISPIECE IS AN INSERT	IF THERE IS A CARD PLATE[a] AND IF FRONTISPIECE IS ON TEXT STOCK	IF THERE IS NO CARD PLATE[a] AND IF FRONTISPIECE IS ON TEXT STOCK	IF INTRO-DUCTION BEGINS ON ARABIC 1	
*Introduction[e]	xxv	xxvii	xxv	1	
Blank or continuation	xxvi	xxviii	xxvi		
*List of abbreviations	xxvii	xxix	xxvii	xxv	note
Blank or continuation	xxviii	xxx	xxviii	xxvi	
*Second half title	(xxix)	(xxxi)	(xxix)	(xxvii)	
Epigraph[c]	xxx	xxxii	xxx	xxviii	

*Begins on right-hand (recto) page.

† Parentheses around page numbers indicate blind folios.

[a]And/or list of consultants. (Consultants may also precede list of contributors.)

[b]The page that backs the title page is still called the copyright page, even though the law no longer requires the copyright notice itself to be placed there. The notice may appear in any easily noticeable location. In addition to the copyright notice, other items usually placed on this page are the Cataloging in Publication (CIP) data, grouped credits for anthologies, and sometimes photo credits.

[c]Other placements are possible, as appropriate.

[d]Alternatively, may be run in after preceding material or may begin on left-hand (verso) page.

[e]If, as sometimes happens, the introduction is important enough to occupy page 1, it takes its place at the end of this list, and the roman numerals assume the sequence shown in the last column to the right.

Definitions. Card plate: a page listing other books in a series or by the same author. *Blind folio:* a page number that is not actually printed on the page but counts in the overall sequence. *Half title* (sometimes called *bastard title*): a page showing the title alone, without the name of the author or the publisher's imprint.

Cataloging in Publication (CIP)

Since 1971 publishers in the United States and elsewhere have been cooperating with the Library of Congress in its CIP program. The purpose of the program is to publish cataloging information on the copyright page of the book itself, so that librarians can process new acquisitions immediately for placement on the shelves.

Before publication of a book, the publisher sends information about it to the Descriptive Cataloging Division of the Library of Congress in Washington, D.C. There, catalogers determine the various subjects under which the book should be classified and return the following information to the publisher for inclusion on the copyright page: (1) author, (2) brief identifying title, (3) series statement, (4) any necessary notes, (5) Library of Congress (LC) subject headings, (6) added entries, (7) LC call number, (8) Dewey decimal classification number, and (9) LC catalog card number.

At the same time, the Library of Congress enters the information into its system, generating lists of forthcoming books for subscribers to its service. Thus many people benefit from the CIP system—librarians, book wholesalers (jobbers), booksellers, publishers, and private owners of cataloged collections.

4-7

BACK MATTER

The term *back matter* refers to all the parts of a book that follow the main portion of the text. The arabic page-number sequence that is used in the text continues through to the last page of the back matter.

Sometimes back matter is an integral part of the book, intended to be referred to frequently. For example, a reader may need to consult the glossary often or turn continually to an appendix of mathematical formulas. Other back-matter items merely provide additional information for those readers who want to pursue the subject further.

Because to some degree each book has an internal logic of its own, there is no one conventional arrangement for back matter. However, a *postscript* or a *conclusion* is normally placed immediately after the text, and the *index* (or subject index, if there is more than one index) is generally placed at or near the end, to make it accessible for frequent use. The placement of other items is variable, but the following list can be used as a general guide. In establishing the order in which to present the back matter, always keep the convenience and needs of the reader uppermost in mind.

> *Sequence of back matter*
> Conclusion (Summary)
> Postscript (Epilogue, Afterword)
> Appendix(es)
> Acknowledgments (Credits—sometimes continued from the front matter)
> Notes (Endnotes, References)
> Bibliography (Suggested Reading)
> Glossary
> Chronology
> Answers to Problems (Answers to Questions)
> Name Index, Map Index, or other special indexes
> Subject Index (General Index)
> About the Author (About the Editor, About the Contributors)
> Other Books in the Series (if not in a card plate in the front matter)

A brief explanation of these items may be useful here.

conclusion   The conclusion is either a summary or a statement of the inferences that the author has drawn from the information presented in the text.

postscript   A postscript, or epilogue, often carries the theme of a book a step further. It can offer a moral or a look to the future, or it can introduce a new philosophical insight. Sometimes it merely provides a trivial afterthought. ("The man in the trenchcoat? He got off the train at Stamford, and we never saw him again.")

appendixes   In one sense, anything added, or appended, to the main text is an appendix, and some people use the term to cover all end-of-book sections. However, the term refers generally to sections that supplement the text in a substantial way—periodic tables, useful formulas, or lists of pertinent organizations, for example.

acknowledgments   Credits that were not given in the front matter are often presented here. Sometimes credits are continued from the front matter, where a page reference to the back matter is provided: "Acknowledgments continue on page 567."

notes   Notes (endnotes, explanatory notes, references) are often grouped at the ends of chapters or at the back of the book to avoid cluttering the text with footnotes (and to avoid the problems of page makeup that accompany extensive footnotes). When notes are placed at the end of the book, take care to identify them properly. If such endnotes are few, consider numbering them consecutively throughout the book. (Although this system makes them easier to find in the back matter, it may create problems if the book is revised.) If endnotes are voluminous, number them by page, and list them in the back matter under their page numbers. Otherwise, simply list them by chapter. (See Chapter 5.)

When two types of notes (explanatory and reference) occur in the same list, it is not incorrect to use a single numbering sequence for both, to avoid a confusing system of dual numbering. In some works, however, it may be best to drop explanatory notes to the foot of the page with asterisks (see Section 5-1) and to place reference notes at the end of the book, with numerical referents.

bibliography   A bibliography is a list of related literature. It is generally alphabetized by authors' last names, and therefore the items need not be numbered.

glossary   A glossary is an alphabetized list of terms used in the field, with their definitions. Occasionally the glossary is combined with the index, which then does interesting double duty.

chronology   A chronology is a time line often used in histories, biographies, and works on music and art.

answers to problems   Sometimes all answers are provided, and sometimes only answers to odd- or even-numbered problems. In some works the answer section is considered so important, and is expected to be used so frequently, that it follows the subject index.

name index   A list of the persons who have been mentioned in the text generally precedes the subject index. It usually (but not always) precedes other special indexes.

other special indexes   Any index to special features or terms is given a special title (Index to Maps, Plant Names, Words, Key Concepts, etc.) and precedes the general subject index.

general subject index   This is the index that most people expect to find at the end of the book and to which they turn to find out where and in what depth a given subject is covered in the text.
See Chapter 13 for information on indexing.

about the author (editor, contributors)   Sometimes a brief biography is added after the index, if it does not appear in the front matter or on the book's jacket.

other books in the series   Although this information is more likely to appear as a card plate in the front matter or on the jacket, it occasionally is given at the very end of a book.

5

REFERENCE MATERIAL

Reference material consists of footnotes (foot of page), notes (end of chapter or end of book), and bibliographies (end of chapter or end of book). All reference material should be presented in a recognized and consistent bibliographic style, such as the McGraw-Hill style set forth here,[1-47,*] or any other widely accepted style, such as that of the American Medical Association,[48,49] the American Psychological Association,[50,51] or the Modern Languages Association.[52,53] Like the rest of the manuscript, references should always be typed double-spaced.

5-1

FOOTNOTES AND NOTES

Numbering

Use a consistent system of numbering. In books of general interest, footnotes or endnotes are usually numbered consecutively throughout a chapter. In scientific and reference books, they are generally numbered by page. Under certain circumstances, however, the use of reference symbols (*, †, ‡, §, ¶) is preferred to the use of numbers:

1   In a work in which footnotes may sometimes be dropped from mathematical symbols or abbreviations, use reference symbols rather than numbers throughout to avoid the possibility of confusion with exponents.

2   When two separate sequences are needed in a given work, one for bibliographic citations and one for informational footnotes (as on this page), use symbols for the footnote sequence.

*Superior numbers in this chapter refer to numbered examples in Section 5-2.

To avoid excessive renumbering, as when a new footnote is added near the beginning of a long sequence, it is permissible to use a lettered reference.[4a]

Authors' Names

Authors' first names may be spelled out or given as initials; both forms are acceptable in the same reference.[2] When joint authors have the same surname, repeat the surname (Helen Smith and John Smith). For works by three or more authors, list all authors or use "et al." Note that et al. stands for *and others* and should not be used for *and Associates* or *and Coworkers*.[2,3]

If the author is not given, the name of a sponsoring organization is shown in the author position when it differs from the publisher;[4a] otherwise it appears only as publisher.[5] (See also "Sponsoring Organization as Author" in Section 5-3.)

Titles of Publications and Their Parts

Wording, spelling, and punctuation of titles should be shown exactly as they appeared in the original work, including the use of colon or dash between title and subtitle.[2,11] Capitalization, however, may be altered as follows: Articles, prepositions, and conjunctions that appear in capital-and-lowercase titles are lowercased; however, the first word of a subtitle always begins with a capital letter.[3] In a hyphenated compound, the word after the hyphen is capitalized unless it is an article, preposition, or conjunction.[15,21,26] When a word has a hyphened prefix, the letter after the hyphen is not capitalized unless it is a proper noun or adjective (e.g., Anti-intellectual, *but* Anti-American).

book, volume, and series titles   These titles are italicized and set in capitals and lowercase.[1,4]

chapter and article titles   These titles are enclosed in quotation marks and set in capitals and lowercase.[6,14]

periodical titles   Periodical titles are italicized and usually spelled out, but when feasible they may be abbreviated. The ANSI (American National Standards Institute) abbreviations or another recognized style should be used as a standard.[12,13]

titles of proceedings   These titles are set in capital-and-lowercase italic, like book titles.[23]

thesis and dissertation titles   These titles are set in capitals and lower-case with quotation marks.[34,35]

names of published tests   Test titles are set in capital-and-lowercase italic.[46]

Publishers' Names

Publishers' names are always roman. Either the full official form of publishers' names (such as McGraw-Hill Book Company[4a]) or an acceptable shortened form (McGraw-Hill[1]) should be used consistently. For reprints, both the original publisher and the current publisher may be cited.[11]

Names of sponsoring organizations or institutions are often cited as publishers (see "Authors' Names" above); when a branch or subdivision is given, the larger organization usually precedes.[5] Reference to the Government Printing Office and Washington may be omitted for federal publications if their official nature is obvious from the title or the series designation.[19,22] Names of government departments or agencies are generally omitted preceding the names of well-known bureaus; instead, the abbreviation *U.S.* may be supplied.[19] Place of publication is customarily given for publishers of books, but not of periodicals. The name of the state or country is usually omitted after well-known cities, such as Boston.[11]

Edition, Volume and Issue, Pages, Date

books   The edition number directly follows the book title.[3] Use either roman or arabic numerals for volume and part numbers of books, as in the source.[1,4]

periodicals   Here are several recommended styles:

(3)**61**(4):99–100 (1976)
or ser. 3, vol. 61, no. 4, 1976, pp. 99–100

51:99–100 (1976)
or vol. 51, 1976, pp. 99–100

A261:198–203 (1977)
or ser. A, vol. 261, 1977, pp. 198–203

482 (1978)

Whichever style is used, the series, volume, issue, pages, and date of publication at the end of periodical references should be treated consistently. Arabic figures are customary for volume numbers, even though the periodical cited may use roman. For popular or semipopular magazines, the date rather than the volume number is given;[12,15] the date then precedes the page number.

Citing exact page numbers is preferable to using the abbreviations f. and ff. [meaning "and following page(s)"].

Serial Publications

yearbooks   The title of a series is set roman in capitals and lowercase; it follows the title of an individual publication in the series, which is italicized.[18] Article or chapter titles, if given, are treated as they are in periodicals.[18] If place of publication is cited, it follows the series designation.

bulletins, circulars, monographs, etc.   Titles of individual bulletins, circulars, monographs, and pamphlets are italicized, like book titles.[19,21] The series title is roman and follows or includes the name of the organization. Issue numbers, sometimes in the form of a date,[25] are run in without commas[19] unless the comma is needed for sense.[21]

Legislative and Legal Citations

congressional bills, resolutions, statutes, etc.   These are identified by Congress and session numbers, series designation and number, date, and sometimes pages.[26,27] Abbreviations are shown in the U.S. Government Printing Office *Style Manual* (an exception is the use of 2d as the abbreviation for *second:* 2d Sess., *not* 2nd Sess.). Similar identification is given for state documents.[28]

Hearings are identified by Congress and session numbers and by the number of the related bill or resolution and/or the title of the hearing.[29,30]

court cases and proceedings   Titles of legal cases, in the form *Plaintiff v. Defendant,* are italicized in both text and footnotes, as are the names of proceedings following *in re, ex parte,* etc. Spell out United States and the names of individual states in case titles, but other names such as those of companies may be abbreviated according to the recommendations of *A Uniform System of Citation.* The same authority is used for abbreviations of reports and reporters and for the order of items in the balance of the citation.[32,33]

law publications   In manuscripts with many references to law publications, the *Uniform System* may be followed regardless of the style used for other references in the book:

    1 STAN. L. REV. 587 (1949)

recurring references   For bills, hearings, cases, etc., shortened forms are acceptable.[31]

references to the Constitution   If there are few such references, footnotes citing the Constitution follow the longer form:

    U.S. Constitution, Art. 5, sec. 3, par. 1

Otherwise, the short form may be used:

    U.S. Const., Art. 5, §3, ¶1

Repeated References

Either "ibid.," "op. cit.," and "loc. cit." or an abridged version giving the author's surname and the title of the work (shortened if long)[10] can be used for footnote references repeated in whole or in part within the same chapter. If more than, say, fifteen manuscript pages intervene, the abridged version is preferable.

1   Ibid., meaning *the same,* is substituted for the author (if any) and title and as many of the other details as are identical with those in the *immediately preceding* footnote.[7] Ibid. may be used directly after an op. cit. or loc. cit. reference.

2   Op. cit., meaning *the work cited,* is substituted for the title and publishing data of a work by the same author cited earlier in the chapter but not in the immediately preceding footnote.[8] When op. cit. is used, the original footnote must include the author's name. When the author has been mentioned only in the text, the surname must be added to the first footnote reference if there are subsequent references in the chapter to the same citation. If the works of two authors with the same surname have been cited earlier, the given name or initials must be included when op. cit. is used. If no author has been cited, only the title is repeated, without op. cit. or publishing data. If two works by the same author have been cited earlier, the surname and title (shortened if long) without op. cit. must be used.

3   Loc. cit., meaning *the place cited,* is used instead of op. cit. when the page numbers referred to are the same.[9]

The less familiar "idem," "supra," and "infra" are not recommended.

Foreign-Language Citations

Titles of books and articles in foreign languages are capitalized as in the original language. In German titles, the first word, all nouns, and adjectives derived from the names of persons are capitalized, but all other words are lowercased. In Spanish, French, and Italian titles, the initial word and proper nouns are capitalized, as well as the noun following an initial article. In French, adjectives between the initial article and the noun are sometimes capitalized.

In typesetting, accent marks are omitted on capital letters if they are not available in the typeface selected.

Permission Footnotes

The information to be included in footnote acknowledgments of permission to quote from published works is usually prescribed by the copyright holder. As long as all the information is given, it is generally permissible to style the publishing data for italics, quotation marks, and order of items, as for other footnotes. The phrase "By permission from" or "Used by permission" is not necessary unless requested. In the absence of special requirements, a standard reference footnote is considered sufficient identification of the original source. (See also Section 11-2.)

5-2

EXAMPLES OF REFERENCE NOTES

Books

[1]Ferdinand P. Beer and E. Russell Johnston, Jr., *Mechanics for Engineers,* vol. 2: *Dynamics,* 3d ed., McGraw-Hill, New York, 1976, p. 486, fig. 12.19.

(References to figures, charts, plates, tables, etc., follow page numbers.)

[2]John Verhoogen, F. J. Turner, L. E. Weiss, Clyde Wahrhaltig, and W. S. Fyle, *The Earth—An Introduction to Physical Geology,* Holt, New York, 1970, chap. 2.

(Alternative style: John Verhoogen et al.)

[3]Douglas Greenwald and Associates, *The McGraw-Hill Dictionary of Modern Economics: A Handbook of Terms and Organizations,* 2d ed., McGraw-Hill, New York, 1973.

[4]Henri Focillon, *The Art of the West in the Middle Ages,* vol. 1: *Romanesque Art,* 2d ed., Jean Bony (ed.), Donald King (trans.), Phaidon Press, Ltd., London, 1969.

(When multivolume works have both author and editor, the editor's name follows the volume title. The translator's name, if given, precedes the publisher's name.)

[4a]Carnegie Commission on Higher Education, *Opportunities for Women in Higher Education,* McGraw-Hill Book Company, New York, 1973.

[5]*Schools for the 70's and Beyond: A Call to Action,* National Education Association, Center for the Study of Instruction, Washington, 1971, p. 124.

[6]Oliver Selfridge, "Reasoning in Game Playing by Machines," in Margo A. Sass and William D. Wilkinson (eds.), *Symposium on Computer Augmentation of Human Reasoning,* Spartan Books, Inc., Washington, 1965, pp. 1–12.

[7]Noah S. Prywes, "Browsing in an Automated Library through Remote Access," in ibid., pp. 105–130.

(Ibid. here refers to Sass and Wilkinson, *Symposium on Computer Augmentation . . . ,* in note 6.)

[8]Verhoogen, Turner, Weiss, Wahrhaltig, and Fyle, op. cit., p. 34.

(Alternative style: Verhoogen et al., op. cit., p. 34. The reference is to the work cited in note 2.)

[9]Selfridge, loc. cit.

[10]Beer and Johnston, *Mechanics for Engineers,* pp. 84–87.

[11]William James, *Human Immortality: Two Supposed Objections to the Doctrine,* Houghton Mifflin, Boston, 1898, p. 12; Dover, New York, 1956, p. 21.

Periodicals and Newspapers

[12]Bradford Perkins, "Planned Parenthood: How to Beget and Raise a Branch or Subsidiary," *Architectural Record,* August 1976, pp. 53–57.

[13]F. Buckens, "Basic Flow Analyses Used in the Study of Broad-Bank Noise in Compressors," *J. Eng. Power Trans. ASME* **A98**(1):23–28 (1976).

(As indicated in note 13, initial-letter abbreviations are used for well-known societies.)

[14]D. Shapiro, B. Tursky, and G. E. Schwartz, "Control of Blood Pressure in Man by Operant Conditioning," *Circ. Res.,* vol. 26, suppl. 1, 1970, p. 27.

[15]Arthur Levin, "The Swine-Flu Plan: A Health Program in Search of a Disease," *New York,* Apr. 26, 1976, p. 57.

[16]Jo Ann Lewis, "The African Roots of Modern Art," *The Washington Post,* Oct. 20, 1977.

(Column and page numbers may be omitted for newspapers having more than one edition.)

[17]Max Frankel, "Ho Hum, Another Last Hurrah," *The New York Times Magazine,* July 11, 1976, p. 10.

Serial Publications

[18]Theodore W. Schultz, "Education and Economic Growth," *Social Forces Influencing American Education,* NSSE Yearbook, pt. 2, chap. 3, 1961, pp. 46–88.

[19]"Educational Data: Spain," *Information on Education around the World,* U.S. Office of Education Bulletin 34, November 1959.

[20]J. Paul Leonard, "Recruiting Talent for College Teaching," *Expanding Resources for College Training,* American Council on Education Studies, ser. 1, vol. 20, no. 60, October 1956, p. 7.

[21]E. S. Miliaras, *Power Plants with Air-Cooled Condensing Systems,* Monographs in Modern Electrical Technology, no. 7, MIT Press, Cambridge, 1974, pp. 75–79.

(Alternative style: Mon. Mod. Elec. Tech.)

[22]"Land-Grant Colleges," *Education '65,* U.S. Department of Health, Education, and Welfare Publication OE-11006, 1966.

[23]Elliott I. Organick, "Computer Sharing," in Don Morrison (ed.), *Proceedings of the Ninth College and University Machine Records Conference,* Educational Data Processing Monograph 4, Educational Systems Cooperation, College Station, Tex., 1964, pp. 115–117.

[24]W. E. Parkins, "The Sodium Reactor Experiment," *Proc. Intern. Conf. Peaceful Uses At. Energy, Geneva,* vol. 3, Aug. 13, 1955, pp. 175–187.

[25]George A. Dale, *Education in the Republic of Haiti,* U.S. Department of Health, Education, and Welfare Bulletin 1959, no. 20, p. 21.

Legislative and Legal Citations

[26]*Proposing an Amendment to the Constitution of the United States Providing for Four-Year Terms for Members of the House of Representatives,* 89th Cong., 2d Sess., S.J. Res. 126, Jan. 20, 1966, p. B-1.

[27]*Title II: Controlled Substances Act,* 91st Cong., Pub. L. 91-513, Oct. 27, 1970.

[28]*Partial Report of the Senate Interim Committee on Adult Education,* California State Senate, S. Res. 185 (1951), 1953.

[29]*Events Following the Watergate Break-In, Hearings before the Committee on the Judiciary,* 93d Cong., 2d Sess., May–June 1974, pp. 1165–1167.

[30]*Hearings before the Subcommittee on Patents, Trademarks, and Copyrights of the Committee on the Judiciary on S. 597,* "Copyright Law Revision," Apr. 6, 11, and 12, 1967, 90th Cong., 1st Sess., pts. 3 and 4, 1967, pp. 989–1014.

[31]*Hearings on S. 597,* p. 990.

[32]*Brown v. Board of Education of Topeka,* 347 U.S. 483 (1954).

[33]*United States v. Eller,* 144 F. Supp. 384 (M.D.N.C.), *rev'd,* 208 F. 2d 716 (4th Cir. 1953), *cert. denied,* 347 U.S. 934 (1954).

Theses and Dissertations

[34]Patricia Alice McKenzie, "The Last Battle: Violence and Theology in the Novels of C. S. Lewis," Ph.D. thesis, University of Florida, Gainesville, 1975.

(Publishers usually follow the manuscript in the use of the terms *Ph.D. thesis, doctoral dissertation,* etc.)

Microfilms, Microfiches, and Mimeographs

[35]I. Adizes, "The Effect of Decentralization on Organizational Behavior," doctoral dissertation, Columbia University, 1971. (University Microfilms, Ann Arbor, no. 71-17,563.)

[36]"International Petrodollar Crisis," in *Abstracts of Congressional Publications and Legislative Histories,* H241-5, July 9, Aug. 13, 1974, 94th Cong., 1st Sess., CIS Annual, 1975, pt. 1, CIS/MF/6, item 1025-A.

[37]"Long-Range Business Outlook to 1995," McGraw-Hill Publications Company, Economics Department, New York, July 21, 1976. (Mimeographed.)

Reports

[38]"Quality in Health Care," *Report of the 1968 National Health Forum,* Los Angeles, Mar. 15–17, National Health Council, New York, 1968.

[39]U.S. Bureau of the Census, *Census in Housing: 1970,* vol. 7, pt. 8, *Cooperative and Condominium Housing,* 1973.

[40]U.S. Bureau of the Census, "Computer Mapping—Graphic Display of Data," in *Census Use Study: Health Information System II,* Rep. 12, Washington, 1971, pp. 29–49.

[41]U.S. Bureau of the Census, *Subject Reports: Earnings by Occupation and Education,* ser. PC(2)-8B, January 1973, pp. v–x.

Technical Reports

[42]Tech. Data Sheet PC-101, MacDermid Incorporated, Waterbury, Conn., Apr. 13, 1967, p. 2.

[Either conventional abbreviations or two-letter forms for states (Conn. or CT) are permissible. See Table 3-7. Most authors use the two-letter form for postal addresses only.]

[43]J. R. Nall and J. W. Lathrop, "The Use of Photolithographic Techniques in Transistor Fabrication," Diamond Ordnance Fuze Lab. Rep. TR-608, ASTI Doc. AD-159233, June 1, 1958.

Conferences and Symposia

[44]W. M. Moreau, *Reg. Tech. Conf. Photopolymers, Mid-Hudson Sect.,* Soc. Plast. Eng., Tech. Pap., 1970, p. 137.

[45]R. L. Hallze and J. H. Rizley, "Fused Silica as an Aerospace Material," *Symp. Newer Struct. Mater. Aerosp. Veh.,* ASTM Spec. Tech. Publ. 379, 1964, pp. 15–24.

Tests

[46]*Peabody Picture Vocabulary Test,* American Guidance Service, Inc., Minneapolis, 1959.

Patents

[47]Rainer Anton, Thermoelectric Matrix Printing Head, U.S. Patent 3,955,204, Sept. 25, 1974; German Patent 2,353,182, Oct. 24, 1973.

AMA Style

[48]Cogan DG: An introduction to eye movements, in Chase TN, Tower DB (eds): *The Nervous System.* New York, Raven Press, 1975, vol 2, pp 481–486.

[49]Bleifeld W, Mathey D, Hanrath P: Acute myocardial infarction: VI. Left ventricular wall stiffness in the acute phase and in the convalescent phase. *Eur J Cardiol* 2: 191, 1975.

APA Style

[50]Anthony, E. J. The behavior disorders of childhood. In P. H. Mussen (Ed.), *Carmichael's manual of child psychology* (2d ed.). New York: Wiley, 1970.

[51]Donley, R. E., & Winter, D. G. Measuring the motives of public officials at a distance: An exploratory study of American presidents. *Behav. Sci.,* 1970, *15,* 227–231.

MLA Style

[52]Henry James, *Parisian Sketches: Letters to the New York Tribune, 1875–1876,* ed. Leon Edel and Ilse Dusoir Lind (New York: New York Univ. Press, 1957), p. 15.

[53]Vladimir Nabokov, "On Translating Pushkin," *Partisan Review,* 22, No. 4 (1955), 18–21.

5-3

BIBLIOGRAPHIES

Resemblance to Footnotes

The style of the bibliography should match that of the footnotes, with two exceptions:

1   Names of authors are inverted in an alphabetized list; when a work has more than one author, only the name of the first author is inverted.

2   A colon rather than a comma usually separates the author's name (or authors' names) from the title.

Numbering

Bibliographies need not be numbered unless items are referred to by number. When they are numbered, text references to the numbers may be enclosed in brackets or parentheses or set as superior figures. When APA style is used, reference to the bibliography is made as follows:

Smith (1974) has stated . . .
. . . this theory (Smith, 1974) . . .
. . . according to Smith (1974, p. 38) . . .

Alphabetizing

An unnumbered bibliography is usually arranged alphabetically by author or, if no author is given, by title. When titles are alphabetized, initial articles (A, An, or The) are disregarded. Multiple works by the same author are listed alphabetically by title or chronologically, but a uniform arrangement should be followed throughout. In unnumbered bibliographies, a three-em dash is sometimes used instead of repeating the name of an author, with a separate dash for each coauthor.

Sponsoring Organization as Author

To give emphasis to an organization or department, a work sponsored by it may be listed with the name of the organization in the author position. In any one bibliographic list all items sponsored by a particular organization for which no individual's name is cited should be grouped together and the titles listed alphabetically.

5-4

EXAMPLES OF BIBLIOGRAPHIC ENTRIES

Arensberg, Conrad M., and S. T. Kimball: *Culture and Community,* Peter Smith Publisher, Gloucester, Mass., n.d.

——— and ———: *Family and Community in Ireland,* 2d ed., Harvard University Press, Cambridge, Mass., 1968.

——— and Arthur H. Niehoff: *Introducing Social Change: A Manual for Community Development,* 2d ed., Aldine, Chicago, 1970.

Jensen, Eileen: "Women's Fiction Today: It's a Fast Track," *Writer's Digest,* August 1976, pp. 22–23.

Onyx Group, Inc.: *Environment U.S.A.: A Guide to Agencies, People, and Resources,* Bowker, New York, 1974.

6

TABLES

6-1

TABLE DESIGN

A table is a visual presentation of related data, usually arranged in columns and rows and designed to be read both across and down, like a grid. Because the compressed information in a table must be readily comprehensible, any element of design that distracts or misleads the reader should be avoided. Although tables should be designed as consistently as possible throughout a book, the internal logic of each table must be considered in determining its setup, and often its typographic design as well. The examples in this chapter illustrate various styles for tables, with annotations describing many features that enhance readability. The forms shown can be applied quite generally, even for tables quoted or adapted from another source.

Numbering

Tables that are more than a few lines long should be numbered and referred to in the text by number (e.g., "see Table 23-4") rather than by location (e.g., "see the table below"), since when the book is paged, the tables may not fall exactly at the point shown in the manuscript. In the text, tables are often double-numbered by chapter.[1,*] In an appendix, tables are usually lettered (A, B, C or A-1, A-2, A-3, etc.).

Title

The table title should be brief but specific. A subtitle or headnote, often in parentheses, may be used for explanatory material that applies to the whole table.[2] Incidental short tabulations do not need titles.[30,31]

---

*Superior numbers in this section refer to numbered annotations next to the tables.

Rules

Horizontal rules are customary at the top and bottom of the table and under column heads. These three rules always extend the full width of the table. *Straddle rules* are a valuable device for separating and clarifying levels of column heads; a straddle rule extends only to the width of the columns that it straddles.[7] Horizontal rules are sometimes used also above and below horizontal crossheads that break the table into major divisions.[8] The first crosshead must appear *below* the column heads, not above them, unless new and different column heads are required after the second crosshead.

Occasionally, horizontal rules are necessary between rows containing mathematical or chemical expressions.[29] Space, instead of horizontal rules, may be used within a table to show minor breaks or groupings.[17]

Top and bottom rules are omitted in two-row and T tables.[30,31] Internal rules are generally omitted from word tables unless needed for clarity.[26]

A *total rule* is set to the width of the column totaled in ruled tables, to the width of the figures in unruled tables. The total rule is not extended through the stub or through columns in which no total appears.[12] A double total rule is often used below figures representing a grand total.[35]

Vertical rules between columns are occasionally needed for clarity;[15] with few exceptions, side rules are not used.

Doubled-Up Tables

Narrow tables are often arranged in two or more sets of columns to save space. Those with vertical rules require a double rule between the parts;

Table 6-1 Approximate Absorptivities of Various Surfaces
(Values at intermediate temperatures can be obtained by linear interpolation)

Material	Temperature range, °C	Absorptivity
Polished metals:		
Aluminum	250–600	0.039–0.057
Brass	250–400	0.033–0.037
Copper	100	0.018
Iron	150–1000	0.05–0.37
Filaments:		
Molybdenum	750–2600	0.096–0.29
Tantalum	1300–3000	0.19–0.31
Other materials:		
Asbestos	40–350	0.93–0.95
Ice (wet)	0	0.97

① *Double numbering: 6-1 signifies the first table in Chap. 6*

② *Headnote*

③ *Units of measure abbreviated in column heads and set off by comma*

4 *Indention of subitems*

⑤ *Ranges aligned on en dash and centered; single numbers aligned on units digit or decimal point and centered*

those without vertical rules need no rule if space between the parts is adequate.

Stub

The stub, usually the first column on the left, lists the items about which information is provided in the horizontal rows to the right. If the stub consists entirely of word items, they are set flush left, with turnovers indented.[21] If only numbers or symbols occur in the stub, they are aligned as appropriate (see "Alignment" below) and centered. If a stub contains both word items and numbers or symbols, all items begin flush left (see Table 6-7). Generally, only the first word of a stub entry is capitalized.

Column Heads

A column head (often called a *boxhead*) is supplied for each column. It defines the vertical entries in the table. The stub often has a column head (*stub head*), but if there is no useful definition for the stub items, no head is needed and the space may be left blank.[6] The first word of each column head is usually capitalized, and nouns are singular whenever possible.[20] Column heads generally align at the bottom (see Table 6-1).

Table 6-2   Typical Productivity of Various Cultivated and Natural Ecosystems*

	Net primary production, g/m^2	
	Per year	Per day
Cultivated		
Wheat	344	0.94 (2.3)
Oats	926	2.54 (6.2)
Corn	412	1.13 (2.3)
Hay	420	1.15 (2.3)
Potatoes	385	1.10 (2.6)
Sugar beets	765	2.10 (4.3)
Sugar cane (Hawaii)	3430	9.40 (9.4)
Noncultivated		
Giant ragweed	1440	3.95 (9.6)
Tall spartina salt marsh	3300	9.0 (9.0)
Forest, pine	3180	6.0 (6.0)
Forest, deciduous	1560	3.0 (6.0)
Tall grass prairies	446	1.22 (3.0)
Seaweed beds	358	1.98 (1.0)

*Values represent world average where crops are widespread, otherwise areas of highest yield. Values in parentheses are rates for growing season only.

(6) *Stub head blank*

(7) *Straddle rule separating levels of column heads*

(8) *Crosshead (does not apply to specific columns)*

(9) *Long explanatory note dropped from table title*

Table 6-3   Municipal Water Uses in the United States

| Use | Quantity, L/capita per day (gal/capita per day*) | |
	Range	Typical
Domestic	150–300 (40– 80)	250 (65)
Public†	60–100 (15– 25)	75 (20)
Commercial and industrial	40–300 (10– 75)	150 (40)
Total	250–700 (65–180)	475 (125)
Loss and waste‡	60–100 (15– 25)	75 (20)
Total	310–800 (80–205)	550 (145)

*Often abbreviated gpcd.
†Includes water required for schools, hospitals, street washing, and parks.
‡Includes leaks from the system, meter slippage, and unauthorized connections.
Source: Based on K. Sekiguchi and J. Fitzpatrick, Management of Water Resources, Byard, New York, 1979.

⑩ Dual measurements (here, SI units given first, U.S. customary units in parentheses)

⑪ Footnote symbols used with five or fewer entries (order of placement is across by row, not down by column)

⑫ Indention of Total; width of total rules

⑬ Grand total flush left

⑭ Source note

Table 6-4   Tankers and Carriers with a Draft of 60 ft (18.3 m) and Over
(In service, under construction, or on order—worldwide)

| Range of draft (1) | | Total ships (2) | | In service (3) | | Under construction or on order (4) | |
Feet	Meters	T	C	T	C	T	C
60–62	18.3–18.9	24	7	14	4	10	3
62–64	18.9–19.5	122	6	113	6	9	
64–66	19.5–20.1	213	....	125	....	88	
66–68	20.1–20.7	149	20	57	18	92	2
68–70	20.7–21.3	78	2	19	1	59	1
70–72	21.3–22.0	49	5	15	2	34	3
72–75	22.0–22.9	174	....	19	....	155	
75–80	22.9–24.4	13	....	....	....	13	
80–90	24.4–27.5	11	....	11			
90–100	27.5–30.5	6	....	2	....	4	
Tankers		839	....	375	....	464	
Carriers		...	40	....	31	....	9
Total ships		879		406		473	

Note: T = tanker, C = carrier.

⑮ Vertically   ruled table

⑯ Column numbers

⑰ Space used instead of rule for minor break in table

⑱ Leaders   (when used) in unfilled columns (no leaders if no item to the right)

⑲ Explanatory note when not dropped as a footnote from table title

Numbered Columns
Columns are sometimes numbered for ease of reference. The column numbers are placed above or below the column heads, in parentheses, and aligned horizontally.[16] Placement at top or bottom should be as consistent as possible throughout a book.

Abbreviations
Unless they stand alone as a heading (as in Table 6-4), units of measurement are given as symbols or abbreviations and are set off by commas in both stub and column heads.[3] They are set within the column when units vary and cannot logically be placed in the stub or head.[24] Abbreviations of units that are lowercased in the text are not capitalized in tables when they begin a column head. "Percent" and "percentage" may be spelled in column heads and stub where space permits, but the symbol % is used in crowded heads and within columns. Abbreviations for words as well as for units of measure are often necessary to save space, but they should be easily recognized and consistent within a table. "Number" may be abbreviated *no.* in a column head.

Punctuation
Regardless of the internal punctuation of a nonsentence table entry, no final punctuation is used.[28] In columns consisting of sentence items, final punctuation is used.

Indention
Subitems in the stub are indented beyond main items,[4] as are turnover lines in both stubs and table columns.[27] The word *Total* or *Average* is indented beyond the preceding entry,[12] except in a grand total[13] or in a column of centered items, where it is flush left. *Total* is not indented when it appears above the items added.

Table 6-5 Principal Radionuclides Induced in Soil

Isotope	Symbol	Half-life	Ci/Mt
Sodium 24	^{24}Na	15 h	2.8×10^{11}
Phosphorus 32	^{32}P	14 days	1.92×10^{8}
Potassium 42	^{42}K	12 h	3×10^{10}
Calcium 45	^{45}Ca	152 days	4.7×10^{7}
Manganese 56	^{56}Mn	2.6 h	3.4×10^{11}
Iron 55	^{55}Fe	2.9 yr	1.7×10^{7}
Iron 59	^{59}Fe	46 days	2.2×10^{6}

(20) *Singular nouns in boxheads*

(21) *Word column (as in stub) flush left*

(22) *Alignment on multiplication sign*

(23) *Symbols (as in second column) aligned left, then centered under column head*

(24) *Entries representing different units of measure (as in third column) aligned left, then centered*

Table 6-6 General Characteristics of Soils*

Soil	Profile	Native vegetation	Climate
Tundra	Dark brown peaty layers over grayish horizons mottled with rust. Substrata of ever-frozen material	Lichens, moss, flowering plants, and shrubs	Frigid humid
Podsol	A few inches of leaf mat and acid humus. A very thin dark gray A horizon, a dark brown B horizon. Strongly acid	Coniferous or mixed coniferous and deciduous forest	Cool temperate and humid
Gray-brown	Thin leaf litter over mild humus over dark-colored surface soil 2 to 4 in thick over grayish-brown leached horizon over heavy B horizon. Less acid than podsols	Mostly deciduous forest with mixture of conifers in places	Temperate humid
Laterites	Red-brown surface soil. Red, deep B horizon. Red parent material	Tropical savanna vegetation	Tropical wet-and-dry

*Based on Jones [34]. Used by permission.

(25) *Footnote reference dropped from table title, leading to bracketed number for full citation in bibliography*

(26) *Word table without internal rules*

(27) *Turnover lines indented*

(28) *Final punctuation not used with nonsentence items*

Leaders

Leaders (rows of dots leading the eye to the item on the right) are occasionally used after entries in the stub, unless the entries are centered. If leaders are extended across unfilled columns in unruled tables, they are normally set to the width of the widest entry in the column. In ruled tables, leaders often extend the width of the column.[18] Notice that leaders are not used when they do not *lead*, i.e., when there is no entry to the right.

Alignment

Columns of figures are usually aligned vertically on the decimal point or units digit. For appearance, however, figures that represent *different units of measure* are aligned at the left.[24] In columns combining numerical items with several worded items, all entries are aligned at the left (with turnovers indented as usual).

Dollar signs are aligned vertically within a column, clearing the widest figure[33] (see exception in sample column b in "Ranges," below). Positive and negative signs, in tables as in text, are set close to numbers. Columns of numbers expressed as powers of 10 should be aligned on the times sign only, with normal space next to the times sign.[22]

Ranges

Ranges of figures in stubs and columns may be aligned on the en dash (or preposition "to"), or they may be aligned at the left. See sample columns a and b below. When a column of figures representing like units of measure contains both ranges and single numbers, the ranges are aligned on the dash and centered; single numbers are aligned on the units digit or decimal point and centered.[5] (Exception: When items in ranges are to be added or subtracted, they are aligned on both the en dash and the units digit. An example of this rare occurrence is shown in Table 6-3.) Ranges in columns of figures representing unlike units are aligned at the left as in sample c below.

Over 500 000	None	Time, s	1.7–2
100 000–499 999	$1–$499	Length, cm	9.52–12
30 000–99 999	$500–$999	Depth, cm	15
10 000–29 999	$1000–$1999	Mass, g	2.4–2.5
2 500– 9 999	$2000 or more	Capacity, mL	100
2 499 and under	Total		
(a)	(b)	(c)	

Table 6-7 Results of Computations of Equivalent Rigidities for Example 1

Parameters and equivalent rigidities	Frame I	Frame II
$\dfrac{l^3(1 + 2k)}{96EI_t(2 + k)}$	$\dfrac{3.06^3(1 + 2 \times 1.51)}{96 \times 3 \times 10^6 \times 0.0452(2 + 1.51)}$ $= 2.70 \times 10^{-6}$	$\dfrac{3.06^3(1 + 2 \times 2.23)}{96 \times 3 \times 10^6 \times 0.069(2 + 2.23)}$ $= 1.88 \times 10^{-6}$
$\dfrac{3l}{8GA_I}$	$\dfrac{3 \times 3.06}{8 \times 10^6 \times 0.58} = 1.98 \times 10^{-6}$	$\dfrac{3 \times 3.06}{8 \times 10^6 \times 0.83} = 1.38 \times 10^{-6}$
Deflection of frame beam at center of span under action of unit force, m	$(2.70 \times 1.98) \times 10^{-6} = 4.68 \times 10^{-6}$	$(1.88 + 1.38) \times 10^{-6}$ $= 3.26 \times 10^{-6}$

(29) Math table with both vertical and horizontal rules

Mean length, cm	10	0.01	8	15
Area, cm²	4	4.04	2	6

(30) *Two-row table, untitled; items centered on each other*

φ	ψ
0°	180°
90°	0°
180°	−180°
270°	0°
360°	180°

(31) *T table (refers to shape); untitled*

Zeros

Zeros are used before decimal points unless the table is very crowded or the figures represent coefficients of correlation or zeros are otherwise not used in the text. Zeros are used after the decimal point in sums of money when other sums in the same or strictly comparable columns have digits in this position. Except with money, publishers usually follow the manuscript on the number of zeros after the decimal point (see Table 6-2).

To conserve space in the width of a crowded table, large numbers may be compressed by omitting zeros and adding an explanatory note to the table title or the column head ("in thousands," "in millions," "000 omitted," etc.).

BLAIR & BENSON
Balance Sheet
June 30, 19X9

Assets

(32) *Vertical arrangement of assets and liabilities; they may also be placed side by side*

Cash		$ 9,000
Receivables	$28,100	
Less: Allowance for uncollectible accounts	600	27,500
Inventories		28,500
Equipment	$60,000	
Less: Accumulated depreciation	26,000	34,000
Total assets		$99,000

(33) *Alignment of dollar signs*

(34) *Leaders extend to columns containing entries*

(35) *Double total rule*

Liabilities & Capital

Liabilities:		
Notes payable		$20,000
Accounts payable		15,000
Total liabilities		$35,000
Partners' capital:		
Blair, capital	$47,990	
Benson, capital	16,010	64,000
Total liabilities and capital		$99,000

Footnotes

Footnotes are set directly below the table, to the width of the page or table. They are referred to by symbols in the order *, †, ‡, §, ¶.[11] If there are more than five footnotes to a table, superior italic letters are used for all (^{a}, ^{b}, ^{c}, etc.). Table footnotes are styled like text footnotes (see Chapter 5), but they should be complete within themselves (that is, with no ibid. or op. cit. references to text footnotes or to other tables).

Source Notes

The footnote indicating the source is preferably last, without a symbol but with the label *Source*.[14] A system of references to the bibliography, if used in the text, may also be used in tables.[25]

Continued Tables

If a table is too long to fit on a single page, the number, title, and column heads are repeated as necessary on successive pages. The designation *(Continued)* is used after the title. Footnotes are repeated as needed. When a wide table is turned on a verso (left-hand) page and continues on the facing recto (right-hand) page, the title and headings are not repeated on the recto.

TECHNICAL
STANDARDS

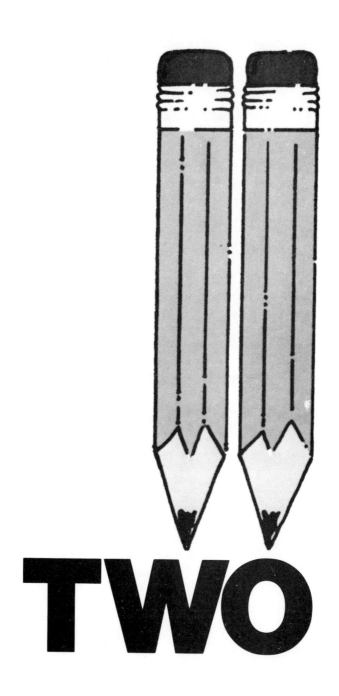

TWO

MATHEMATICS, ELECTRONICS, AND COMPUTER SCIENCE

This chapter presents standards for the visual appearance of technical notation in printed material. For chemical notation, see Chapter 8. Suggestions for preparing technical manuscripts are given in Chapter 11.

7-1

MATHEMATICAL NOTATION

Mathematical Symbols

Mathematical symbols are set in italic type:

$A; b$
$3x$

except in computer languages (see Section 7-3).

Abbreviations that are not variables (cannot represent more than one value) are set in roman type (for example, H for heads, S for spades). Letters indicating shape are set in roman type:

T network
S-shaped

Roman type is also used for abbreviations:

pH   Im
KE   sin

and for dimensionless groups:

pR   Re
Nu   Ma

The following equations illustrate various uses of italic and roman type:

$$I = \frac{E}{R} = 3.341 \text{ A} \tag{1}$$

$$\text{KE} = \tfrac{1}{2}mV^2 \tag{2}$$

$$W_{\text{rev}} = h_1 - h_2 = 264 \text{ J/kg} \tag{3}$$

Vectors, Phasors, Tensors

Vectors, which have both direction and magnitude (two dimensions), are usually set in boldface roman type:

A; **b**; τ

Avoid the use of arrows, dots, or bars over the symbol to indicate a vector.

In vector multiplication, dot products and cross products are indicated by boldface signs of operation if the vector symbols are set in boldface type:

$$\mathbf{A} \cdot \mathbf{B} \times \mathbf{C} = \mathbf{A} \cdot (\mathbf{B} \times \mathbf{C}) \tag{4}$$

Signs of operation other than those denoting vector multiplication are set in lightface type, as are subscripts and superscripts:

$$\mathbf{Q} = \mathbf{X}^T[\tfrac{1}{2}(\mathbf{A} + \mathbf{A}^T]\mathbf{X} \tag{5}$$

Boldface type may also be used in matrix notation [see Equations (31a) and (31b)].

Phasors, which have only magnitude (one dimension), are set in lightface italic type:

phasor A

Tensors, which have three dimensions, are set in a different typeface from the text (for example, in bold sans-serif type if the text is set in a serif typeface):

tensor **T**

Symbols in Apposition

Symbols used in apposition (that is, immediately after a descriptive word or phrase) are not set off by commas, parentheses, or other punctuation:

For any given vector **n**, the corresponding stress vector $\mathbf{s}_n$ is also known.

except to avoid ambiguity:

The ratio of the pressure gradients in the 16- and 18-in pipes, G/G_1, will be 1:8.

Other Alphabets

Greek Some Greek letters have alternative forms, as shown in Table 7-1. Wherever possible, the author should identify the form to be used.

TABLE 7-1 GREEK ALPHABET

LETTER	CAPITAL	LOWERCASE	LETTER	CAPITAL	LOWERCASE
Alpha	A	α (1) α (2)	Mu Nu	M N	μ ν
Beta	B	β	Xi	Ξ	ξ
Gamma	Γ	γ	Omicron	O	o
Delta	Δ	δ (1) ∂ (2)	Pi	Π	π
Epsilon	E	ϵ (1) ε (2)	Rho Sigma	P Σ	ρ σ (1) s (2)
Zeta	Z	ζ	Tau	T	τ
Eta	H	η	Upsilon	Υ	υ
Theta	Θ (1) Θ (2)	θ (1) ϑ (2)	Phi	Φ	ϕ (1) φ (2)
Iota	I	ι	Chi	X	χ
Kappa	K	κ	Psi	Ψ	ψ
Lambda	Λ	λ	Omega	Ω	ω

script Script capitals are sometimes used in advanced mathematical notation. Of the two styles shown here, the first is preferable if available:

$\mathcal{ABCDEFGHIJKLMNOPQRSTUVWXYZ}$

$\mathscr{ABCDEFGHIJKLMNOPQRSTUVWXYZ}$

Special Symbols

Mathematical and other technical notation may require accented letters, the most common of which are barred and dotted characters:

$$\bar{x}$$
$$\dot{x}$$

Where double or triple diacritical marks, such as $\bar{\bar{i}}$ or $\ddot{i}$, have been used, the author should be asked to provide simpler equivalents wherever feasible, since multiple marks are difficult to read and unusually sensitive to variations in printing.

A list of commonly used mathematical and logic symbols is given in Table 7-2.

TABLE 7-2   SIGNS AND SYMBOLS USED IN MATHEMATICS AND LOGIC

SIGN OR SYMBOL	DEFINITION	SIGN OR SYMBOL	DEFINITION
$\equiv$	Identical with	$\supset$	Contains
$>$	Greater than	$\subseteq$	Subset of
$\gg$	Much greater than	$\subset$	Proper subset of
$<$	Less than	$\cup$	Union
$\ll$	Much less than	$\cap$	Intersection
$\geq$ (or $\geqq$)	Greater than or equal to	$\vee$	Logic: *or*
		$\wedge$	Logic: *and*
$\leq$ (or $\leqq$)	Less than or equal to	$\exists$	There exists
$\sim$	Similar to, not, complement of	$\forall$	For all
$\approx$ (or $\simeq$ or $\cong$)	Approximately equal to	$\emptyset$	Null or empty set (phi is sometimes used in typescript)
$\leftrightarrow$ (or $\Leftrightarrow$)	Equivalent to	$\propto$	Proportional to (alpha is sometimes used in typescript)
$\rightarrow$	Implies		
$\in$	Member of (epsilon is sometimes used in typescript)	$\circ$, $\odot$, $\oplus$, $\otimes$, $\ominus$	Binary operations

Subscripts and Superscripts

Words, chemical formulas, and abbreviations in subscripts are set in roman type. Italic type is used for symbols and generally for single-letter abbreviations in subscripts.

$$V_{\text{flow}} \qquad\qquad V_{bc}$$
$$S_{\text{CO}_2} \qquad\qquad N_a$$
$$S_{\text{av}} \qquad\qquad V_{\text{in}} \text{ or } V_i$$
$$E_{\text{max}} \qquad\qquad V_{\text{out}} \text{ or } V_o$$

When a symbol carries two subscripts, a comma without space is generally used between them:

$$R_{1,\text{max}}$$

Subscript letter o (as in P_o) and subscript zero (P_0) are differentiated typographically, although the difference is often difficult to distinguish in typescript. The publisher generally assumes that the subscript is zero unless it is underlined to indicate the letter symbol o.

position of subscript and superscript In most modes of composition, subscripts and superscripts are vertically aligned:

$$D_{mn}^2$$

In an alternative style, used chiefly in hot-metal composition, the subscript precedes the superscript ($D_{mn}{}^2$) unless the superscript is a prime, a degree symbol, or an asterisk or contains three or more characters:

$$D_m' \qquad\qquad\qquad\qquad\qquad D_m^\circ$$
$$D_m^* \qquad\qquad\qquad\qquad\qquad R_{\text{opt}}^2$$

Where such alignment is not feasible, the subscript is placed to the *right* of the superscript (D'_m). In the following expressions, however, the sub- and superscripts always align:

refractive index, n_{D}^{20}
optical rotation, $[\alpha]_{\text{D}}^{20}$

Subscripts and superscripts do not always look distinctly inferior or superior to the basic symbol because of unavoidable typographic variations:

$$x^{a2} \qquad\qquad\qquad\qquad\qquad x^{ew}$$
$$a_w \qquad\qquad\qquad\qquad\qquad X^W$$
$$M^g \qquad\qquad\qquad\qquad\qquad B^R$$
$$x_{AT2} \qquad\qquad\qquad\qquad\qquad x_{A_B^2}$$

Wherever possible, levels of subscripts should be combined. Third-level subscripts are particularly difficult to distinguish:

$$W_{E_{A,av}} \quad not \quad W_{E_{A_{av}}}$$
$$W_{x1} \quad not \quad W_{x_1}$$
$$E_{o,rms} \quad not \quad E_{o_{rms}}$$

Symbols, Units of Measure, and Mathematical Abbreviations in Headings

Symbols, units of measure, and mathematical abbreviations are set in capitals or lowercase exactly as in the text. Except for boldface vectors, which are always set in boldface roman type, the use of boldface or lightface type for symbols should follow the style of the headings. Symbols that are italic in text should be italic in headings:

Treatment with SO_2Cl_2
Pressure p in a Cylinder
PRESSURE FOR A 30-mm HOSE

Other Abbreviations in Headings

In headings set in capitals and lowercase, abbreviations made up of initial letters are all capitals even though they may be lowercase in the text:

Other EMF Relationships (*not* **Emf**)
AC Systems (*not* **Ac**)

In headings set with only the first word capitalized, initial-letter abbreviations are treated as in text except that they are capitalized in full at the beginning of the heading:

Other emf relationships
AC systems

Fractions

symbolic fractions In displayed (separate-line) equations, symbolic fractions (that is, fractions that do not consist entirely of numbers) are normally *built up* (numerator over denominator):

$$r_p = \lim \frac{\Delta E_b}{\Delta I_b} = \frac{\partial E_b}{\partial I_b} \tag{6}$$

In the text, *shilling fractions* (numerator and denominator on the same line, as in $\partial E_b/\partial I_b$) are used for symbolic quantities unless the terms are particularly complicated or are not suitable in the shilling style. Shilling fractions are also generally used in the numerator and denominator of built-up fractions:

$$f = \frac{n/k}{n/(k-1)} \tag{7}$$

The shilling bar is used in exponents ($t^{(n-1)/2}$), but see Equation (36) for an exception.

conversion of fractions When shilling fractions are converted to the built-up style, parentheses that have become unnecessary are removed:

$$a/(b+c) \qquad becomes \qquad \frac{a}{b+c}$$

When a built-up fraction that contains a sign of operation is converted to the shilling style, signs of aggregation must be inserted:

$$\frac{1}{x+y} \qquad becomes \qquad 1/(x+y)$$

$$\frac{1}{x/y} \qquad becomes \qquad 1/(x/y)$$

$$2 + \frac{a+3}{b} + 4 \qquad becomes \qquad 2 + (a+3)/b + 4$$

If the converted fraction is followed by a letter symbol or a number, signs of aggregation must be inserted:

$$\frac{1}{x+y}abc \qquad becomes \qquad [1/(x+y)]abc$$

$$\frac{x}{y}c \qquad becomes \qquad (x/y)c$$

$$but \qquad c\frac{x}{y} \qquad becomes \qquad cx/y$$

A built-up fraction that contains no sign of operation can be changed to shilling without addition of parentheses unless a letter symbol or a number follows:

$$1 + \frac{x}{y} \qquad becomes \qquad 1 + x/y$$

$$a + \frac{3}{b} + 4 \qquad becomes \qquad a + 3/b + 4$$

In elementary texts, parentheses are sometimes added in other situations for pedagogical reasons; for example:

$$\frac{1}{2x} \quad becomes \quad 1/(2x)$$

numerical fractions   In typeset material, *special fractions* or *case fractions* are used for simple numerical quantities in text, in numerators and denominators of built-up fractions, in one-line-high displayed equations, and sometimes in exponents:

Special: $\tfrac{1}{2}x$; $t^{\frac{1}{2}x}$
Case: $\tfrac{1}{2}x$; $t^{\frac{1}{2}}x$

However, special and case fractions may be difficult to read in small type, and therefore shilling fractions are often used in exponents because they are more legible:

$x^{1/2}$
$t^{(1/2)x} \quad or \quad t^{x/2}$

A numerical fraction adjacent to a built-up fraction is also built up:

$$y' = \frac{1}{2}\frac{a+1}{b-1} \tag{8}$$

$$z_2 = -\frac{1}{2} + \frac{\sqrt{3}}{2i} \tag{9}$$

In other instances either built-up or case (or special) can be used:

$$y = \tfrac{1}{2}a + \frac{2A}{B} \quad or \quad y = \frac{1}{2}a + \frac{2A}{B} \tag{10}$$

Displayed Equations and Arrays

punctuation with equations   Punctuation is generally omitted after a displayed equation, even though the equation may end a sentence:

The corresponding phase constant β is

$$\cos \beta = \sqrt{\frac{R_2}{R_1}} \tag{11}$$

Punctuation is used before a displayed equation only if the grammatical construction requires it:

Under these conditions one has, referring to fig. 6-40d,

$$E_A - E_B = 2E'_g \tag{12}$$

arrangement of displayed equations Two equations on the same line are separated by extra space (2 ems) but no punctuation:

$$c_n = \sqrt{a_n^2 + b_n^2} \qquad \theta_n = \tan^{-1} \frac{b_n}{a_n} \tag{13}$$

Similarly, a 2-em space is used before and after *and* and *or* between two equations on the same line:

$$a_1 = \frac{\Delta P_1}{(T_a P_0)_1} \quad \text{and} \quad a_2 = \frac{\Delta P_2}{(T_a P_0)_2} \tag{14}$$

and to set off words following displayed equations:

$$Pg = E_{gm} I_c + 0.16 \cos \frac{\theta_c}{2} \qquad \text{for triodes} \tag{15}$$

and to separate an equation from its limiting term. A series of limiting expressions following an equation is aligned at the left:

$$\text{Re } Z(p) \geq 0 \qquad \begin{array}{l} \text{if } p \text{ is real} \\ \text{for Re } p > 0 \end{array} \tag{16}$$

When a displayed equation is broken at an equals sign or a sign of operation, the sign is placed at the beginning of the new line. (The opposite is true in text: the equation is broken after the sign.)

$$P(x, y, t + \Delta t) = s \, \Delta t \, P(x - 1, y, t) + \frac{(y + 1)P(x - 1, y + 1, t)va \, \Delta t}{h}$$
$$+ \frac{(y + 1)P(x, y + 1, t)\mu a \, \Delta t}{h}$$
$$+ \frac{(x + 1)P(x + 1, y, t) \, \Delta t}{h}$$
$$+ \left[1 - s \, \Delta t - y(\mu a + va)\frac{\Delta t}{h} - x\frac{\Delta t}{h} \right] P(x, y, t) \tag{17}$$

The sign is *not* used twice, that is, at both the end of the broken line and the beginning of the next.

A left-hand member common to a series of equations is ordinarily not repeated:

$$Q = 2 \int_0^{\pi r} \frac{c^3 p_0}{3\mu L} \cos^2 \alpha \, dx$$

$$= 2 \frac{c^3 p_0}{3\mu L} \int_0^{\pi r} \frac{L^2 \, dx}{L^2 + 4x^2} \tag{18}$$

If, however, the equations have limiting terms that vary from line to line, it is preferable to give the left-hand member once and to use only one equals sign followed by a brace:

$$W_{h(x)} = \begin{cases} B & \text{if } \varphi_x(x) \text{ divergent} \\ A \cup B & \text{if } \varphi_x(x) \text{ convergent} \end{cases} \tag{19}$$

Short transitional words between equations are set flush left, often on the same line as the second equation. The equals signs in a series of related equations are usually aligned.

Differentiating with respect to t yields

$$\frac{d(x^2)}{dt} + \frac{d(30^2)}{dt} = \frac{d(s^2)}{dt} \tag{20}$$

or $\qquad\qquad 2x \dfrac{dx}{dt} + 0 = 2s \dfrac{ds}{dt}$ $\qquad\qquad\qquad$ (21)

and so $\qquad\qquad x \dfrac{dx}{dt} = s \dfrac{ds}{dt}$ $\qquad\qquad\qquad\qquad$ (22)

Sometimes, as when space is at a premium, several equals signs may be run across the page:

$$b_n = \frac{1}{\pi} \int_{-\pi}^{\pi} x \sin nx \, dx = \frac{2}{n}(-1)^{n+1} \tag{23}$$

position of equation numbers   Equation numbers are usually set flush right in parentheses. When a displayed equation runs to two or more lines, the equation number appears on the last line of the equation [see Equation (17)]. A repeated or out-of-sequence equation number is indented from the right:

$$E_A - E_B = 2E'_g \tag{12}$$

When a single equation number is used to identify two or more equations, the equation number is centered on the group, without a brace:

$$e(t) = E_m \sin (\omega t + \theta)$$
$$A(t) = \frac{1}{R}(1 - \epsilon^{-Rt/L}) \tag{24}$$

Although in this manual all displayed equations have been numbered to illustrate the position of the number in various situations, it is not necessary to number all equations in every work. Many authors prefer to number only the equations that are actually referred to.

equations with units of measure Units of measure that follow a *symbolic* equation are separated from the equation by extra space (2 ems):

$$I = A_0 ST^2 \epsilon^{-bo/T} \qquad A \tag{25}$$

When the right-hand member is numerical, no extra space is used before the unit:

$$|E_R^+| = |E_s^+|\epsilon^{-al} = 3.06 \text{ V rms} \tag{26}$$
$$Z_s = 861 - j332 \ \Omega \tag{27}$$

words in displayed equations The first word of the left-hand member of an equation is capitalized (both numerator and denominator of a fraction); all other words are set in lowercase type:

$$\frac{\text{Downward force}}{\text{Upward force}} = \text{net effect} \tag{28}$$

However, abbreviations and units of measure that are normally lowercased remain lowercased:

$$\text{r/min} = \frac{120 \times \text{Hz}}{P} \tag{29}$$

Abbreviations such as const, vol, wt, no., and av are often used in displayed equations to save space.

defining lists following displayed equations   Lists defining more than two symbols used in an equation are set up as follows whenever the material is adaptable to such an arrangement:

$$dF = \frac{\mu_0 I_2 \, dl_2 \, I_1 \, dl_1}{4\pi r^2} \tag{30}$$

$$\begin{aligned}
\text{where } d\mathbf{F} &= \text{force on element 1, N} \\
\mu_0 &= \text{permeability of air, H m}^{-1} \\
dl_1, dl_2 &= \text{lengths of elements 1 and 2, m} \\
I_1, I_2 &= \text{currents in elements 1 and 2, A} \\
r &= \text{distance between elements, m}
\end{aligned}$$

Note that units are abbreviated and set off by commas and that unnecessary articles are omitted. Defining lists consisting of only one or two items are run into the text following the equation.

arrays   In a matrix or other array, the elements are ordinarily centered on one another within a column, and a 1-em space is used between columns. A column in which all elements are numbers is aligned on the units digit; if one column of an array consisting of numbers contains a minus sign, the space between other columns is increased to 2 ems. Omission of columns is indicated by three dots set horizontally; omission of rows, by three dots set vertically in a single-column array, and by a continuous row of dots in an $n \times m$ array. Matrices are sometimes enclosed in parentheses instead of brackets. For a determinant, vertical bars are used.

$$\begin{pmatrix} 10 & Y_a & 8.66 \\ 5 & -Y_{ab} & 1.2 \\ Y_a & 3 & Y_{ab} \\ -Y_{ab} & 4.2 & Y_a \\ 8.66 & Y & -Y_a \\ Y & 1.2 & 0.357 \end{pmatrix} \qquad \begin{vmatrix} 2 & -1 & 5 & 1 \\ 9 & 0 & 26 & 7 \\ 8 & 0 & 17 & 6 \\ 5 & 0 & 7 & 6 \end{vmatrix}$$

$$\qquad\qquad\text{MATRIX}\qquad\qquad\qquad\qquad\text{DETERMINANT}$$

$$\begin{bmatrix} 1 & -p & \cdots & 0 & 0 \\ -p & 1+p^2 & \cdots & 0 & 0 \\ 0 & -p & \cdots & 0 & 0 \\ \cdots\cdots\cdots\cdots\cdots\cdots\cdots \\ 0 & 0 & \cdots & -p & 1 \end{bmatrix} \qquad \begin{bmatrix} V_1 \\ 0 \\ \cdot \\ \cdot \\ \cdot \\ 0 \end{bmatrix}$$

$$\qquad\quad n \times m \text{ MATRIX}\qquad\qquad\text{SINGLE-COLUMN} \\ \text{MATRIX, OR VECTOR}$$

Column or row labels are set in small type:

$$A = \begin{bmatrix} \overset{s}{A_{11}} & \overset{s}{A_{12}} \\ A_{21} & A_{22} \end{bmatrix} \begin{matrix} r \\ r \end{matrix}$$ (31a)

Boldface zero is frequently substituted for the oversize zero or null sign:

$$p^{-1}tp = \begin{pmatrix} a_1 & & & & \\ & a_2 & & \mathbf{0} & \\ & & \cdot & & \\ \mathbf{0} & & & \cdot & \\ & & & & a_n \end{pmatrix}$$ (31b)

Mathematical Signs

times signs and other signs of multiplication   Multiplication may be indicated by times signs, center dots, parentheses or other signs of aggregation, or merely juxtaposition. No sign is needed for two built-up fractions that are to be multiplied:

$$\tan \theta = \frac{ML}{I} \frac{v_b^2 t_b}{6 v_a}$$ (32)

Center points between simple terms are usually eliminated by the publisher. Neither a times sign nor a center dot is used before d and delta combinations (except in vector products).

$$T = \tau_{\theta 2} r \int_0^a 2\pi r \, dr$$ (33a)

rather than

$$T = \tau_{\theta 2} \cdot r \int_0^a 2\pi r \cdot dr$$ (33b)

In the multiplication of numbers, any of three forms may be used:

2×3
$2(3)$
$(2)(3)$

The form $(2)3$ is not recommended.

Center points are used in factorial notation, and times signs are used with powers of 10:

$$10! = 10 \cdot 9 \cdot 8 \cdots 1$$
$$3.204 \times 10^{-22}$$

parentheses, brackets, braces   Except with special notation, the usual sequence, starting with the innermost element, is parentheses within brackets within braces within parentheses, etc.:

$$(\{[(\quad)]\})$$

Signs of aggregation in exponents are not considered part of the main sequence:

$$\chi(E) = \left\{ \sum_{i=1}^{\infty} z_i \int_0^{\infty} \overline{U_i(r)} \sin 2[kr + \delta(k)] \, dr \right\}^{-1}$$
$$m(e^{-p/(p+1)N} + g)$$

In some forms of special notation, the usual sequence is not used. Examples follow:

1   Brackets to indicate chemical concentration:

$$[S^{2-}]$$

2   Brackets (or alternatives as shown) in certain expressions with upper and lower limits:

$[\cos \theta]_0^{\pi}$ $\qquad\qquad\qquad\qquad$ $\cos \theta |_0^{\pi}$

$\cos \theta]_0^{\pi}$ $\qquad\qquad\qquad\qquad$ $(\cos \theta)_0^{\pi}$

3   Braces for Laplace transforms and sets:

$\mathcal{L}\{y\}$
$\{1, 2, 3\}$

4   Parentheses with functions:

$f(g(x))$

See also "Parentheses" in Section 7-3.

Superfluous parentheses, brackets, etc., are omitted since they take up valuable space and add to the compositor's work.

Superfluous	Preferred
$x = (y + 1)$	$x = y + 1$
$\dfrac{(p_0 - p)}{p_0}$	$\dfrac{p_0 - p}{p_0}$
$\dfrac{(x + 1)(x - 1)}{(x + 2)}$	$\dfrac{(x + 1)(x - 1)}{x + 2}$
$\left(\dfrac{1 + \alpha}{2}\right)\gamma$	$\dfrac{1 + \alpha}{2}\gamma$

The author should be consistent in the use of parentheses after derivatives:

$$\frac{d}{dt}\left(\frac{xy}{y^2}\right) \quad or \quad \frac{d}{dt}\frac{xy}{y^2}$$

ellipses   An ellipsis (dots used to indicate an omission) is shown by three low points in a series containing commas or semicolons:

$$(p_1, p_2, \ldots, p_n)$$

Space is used after punctuation between items in a series, whether or not the series is enclosed in parentheses.

Center points are used in all other series:

$$p_1 + p_2 + \cdots + p_n$$
$$\pi = 3.14 \cdots$$
$$a_1 a_2 \cdots a_n$$

If commas or signs of operation are used in a series, they should appear before the ellipsis, as well as after the ellipsis when the series continues. If plus and minus signs alternate in the series, however, no sign of operation is inserted after the ellipsis:

$$a + b - c + \cdots n$$

integral, summation, and product signs   Limits of integration are shown to the right of a single integration symbol and centered above and below two or more symbols. Indices to summation and product signs are usually set above and below the symbols.

$$\int_\theta^{2\pi} \quad \int_0^{\pi/2} \quad \int_0^2 \quad \iint_R \quad \sum_{i=1}^{k} \quad \prod_{i=1}^{k}$$

$$p(v_2) = \sum_l \frac{e^{v_2/\mu_l S_n}}{\mu_l S_n \prod_{k \ne l} (1 - \mu_k/\mu_l)} \tag{34}$$

When the signs appear in a line of text, the limits are sometimes set to the right to avoid excessive spreading of text lines, for example, $\Sigma_{i=1}^{k}$, $\Pi_{i=1}^{k}$.

Other Conventions

space in mathematical material It is standard practice to use a small space before and after d and delta combinations (dy, Δy, ∂y, δy, $d\omega t$, etc.):

$$\frac{\partial}{\partial t}\left[\left(\int_{T_R}^T cp\, dT\right) dx\, dy\, dz\right] = \frac{\partial}{\partial t}(cpT\, dx\, dy\, dz) \tag{35}$$

$\Sigma\, \Delta t$
$(a - bt)\, dy$
$x\, dx\, (but\ 3dt)$

Space is not required before letters representing functions or before the exponential e or ϵ:

$t = F(\tau)G(x)$
$2xf(y)\, dy$
$(T_2 - T_P)k_2 e^{-K2/4a_2}$

trigonometric functions and other mathematical abbreviations A small space is used around trigonometric functions (sin, cos, csch, cosh) and around log, Re, div, and the like:

$b \sin^2 \theta_2$ $y\, \text{Re}\, (E_m \epsilon^{j\omega t})$

$z\, \text{div}\, \mathbf{a}$ $\log \dfrac{a}{b}$

$x \ln (j\omega - s_1)$

Ambiguity in expressing the arguments of trigonometric functions is avoided by spacing:

$\sin \omega t \, \alpha$

or by inserting parentheses:

$(\sin \omega t) \, \alpha$

When an argument that appears as a built-up fraction is converted to the shilling style, parentheses are inserted where needed for clarity:

$$\log \frac{b}{a} = \log (b/a)$$

$$\ln \frac{b}{a+1} = \ln [b/(a+1)]$$

$$\frac{\tan 2\pi l}{\lambda} = (\tan 2\pi l)/\lambda$$

Some preferred forms for abbreviations are:

cot	*not*	cotan
csc	*not*	cosec
arctan	*not*	arc tan
arcsin	*not*	arc sin
log	*not*	$\log_{10}$
ln	*not*	$\log_e$

Both arctan and $\tan^{-1}$ are acceptable, but the negative exponent style is preferred for hyperbolic trigonometric functions ($\tanh^{-1}$). An author who wishes to capitalize Sin, etc., as a special distinction should alert the editor to this usage.

The exponential e is replaced by "exp" and the exponent is set on the line if it includes radical signs, integral or summation signs with limits, or special symbols not available in small type:

$$y = C_0 \exp \frac{\sqrt{a+b}}{4kt} \qquad not \qquad y = C_0 e^{\sqrt{a+b}/4kt} \qquad (36)$$

$$u = \theta \exp \left(-\int_0^t \psi \, d\tau \right) \qquad not \qquad u = \theta e^{-\int_0^t \psi \, d\tau} \qquad (37)$$

coordinate expressions   Space is used after a comma or semicolon separating two or more coordinate symbols or numbers:

$f(x, y)$ the point $(2, -3)$
$g(\mathbf{x}; \xi)$ the point x, y, z

7-2

ELECTRONICS

Abbreviations, Acronyms, Symbols

Some abbreviations and acronyms are associated almost exclusively with the field of electronics. They generally (but not universally) consist of capital initial letters, with periods omitted. With a few exceptions, their plurals are formed by the addition of a lowercase s without apostrophe. In mathematical material, these abbreviations are always set in roman type, even as subscripts. Always define them at their first appearance in the text. Table 7-3 lists some of the most common abbreviations.

types of semiconductor material   Types of semiconductor material are generally indicated either by lowercase italic letters or by roman capitals. When these letters are combined to indicate junctions, it is preferable not to use hyphens:

n material	*or*	N material
pn junction	*or*	PN junction
npn transistor	*or*	NPN transistor

R, L, C   The symbols R, L, and C (used as adjectives for resistive, inductive, and capacitive, respectively) are set in italic capitals:

RLC circuit
L/R time constant
RC coupling

dc and ac circuits   There is a common convention that for dc circuits capitals are used for such quantities as voltage, current, or resistance (V, I, R); for ac circuits, lowercase symbols are used (v, i, r). This convention is not, however, universally observed.

Electronics Jargon

Avoid field jargon in written text. For example, change *breaker* to *circuit breaker*, *scope* to *oscilloscope*, and *short* and *shorted* to *short circuit* and *short-circuited,* respectively. Use *capacitor* in preference to *condenser* except in the terms *bushing condenser, steam condenser,* and *synchronous condenser.*

TABLE 7-3   SOME ABBREVIATIONS AND ACRONYMS USED IN ELECTRONICS

ABBREVI- ATION	MEANING	ABBREVI- ATION	MEANING
A.A.	Angular aperture	N.A.	Numerical aperture
A/D	Analog to digital	N.F.	Noise figure
AES	Auger electron spectroscopy	PESIS	Photoelectron spectroscopy of inner-shell electrons
AGC	Automatic gain control		
AM	Amplitude modulation	PESOS	Photoelectron spectroscopy of outer-shell electrons
CMRR	Common-mode rejection ratio		
		PLL	Phase-locked loop
CRT	Cathode-ray tube	PM	Phase modulation
D/A	Digital to analog	RED	Same as RHEED
DFG	Diode function generator	RHEED	Reflected high-energy electron diffraction
DO	Data out		
emf	Electromotive force (Note: plural is emf's)	SC	Semiconductor
		SCR	Silicon controlled rectifier
EPR	Electron paramagnetic resonance	SEM	Scanning electron microscopy
ESCA	Electron spectroscopy for chemical analysis	SPST	Single-pole single-throw (switch)
FES	Field-emission spectroscopy	TED	Transmission electron diffraction
FET	Field-effect transistor	TEDCM	Transmission electron diffraction contrast microscopy
FM	Frequency modulation		
F.S.	Full scale		
IC	Integrated circuit	TEM	Transmission electron microscopy
i.f. or IF	Intermediate frequency	UAF	Universal active filter
ILF	Input load factor	UHF	Ultrahigh frequency
INS	Ion neutralization spectroscopy	UJT	Unijunction transistor
I/O	Input/output (or input-output)	UPS	Ultraviolet photoelectron spectroscopy
JFET	Junction field-effect transistor	VCCS	Voltage-controlled current source
LED	Light-emitting diode	VCO	Voltage-controlled oscillator
LF	Low frequency	VCVS	Voltage-controlled voltage source
LEED	Low-energy electron diffraction		
MDAC	Multiplying digital-to-analog converter	VFC	Voltage-to-frequency converter
MF	Multiple feedback	VLS	Vapor liquid solid
MOSFET	Metal-oxide semiconductor field-effect transistor	VOM	Volt-ohm-milliammeter
		XPS	X-ray photoelectron spectroscopy

7-3

COMPUTER SCIENCE

For a work containing many computer printouts, authors are usually asked to provide copies of the printouts suitable for photographic reproduction. When computer programs and statements are set in type, they are generally rendered in full roman capitals. The compositor will indent the lines as shown in the manuscript. Note, however, that vertical alignment of letters is generally not feasible:

```
  C   FIND THE GREATEST COMMON DIVISOR
      INTEGER A, B, Z
      FORMAT (2I5)
  1   IF (A .GE. B) GO TO 10
 10   Z = A − B * (A/B)
      A = B
      STOP
```

Space should be placed between the statement number and the statement itself. A thin space should be used on either side of the signs of operation $(+, -, =, \rightarrow, *)$ unless space is incorrect in a particular language. (The publisher usually relies on the author to indicate that space is not correct.)

Computer Languages

Some computer languages have special typographic and grammatical conventions. For example, when APL programs or statements are typeset, either the special APL font (if available) or italic type should be used. Reserved words in Cobol (words having a predefined meaning) are set in capital letters and underscored:

END-OF-PAGE
ZERO

Names of computer languages that can be read as a word are set in initial capital and lowercase letters or entirely in capital letters. The following list shows the most common languages and the terms from which their names are derived:

Algol *or* ALGOL	*Algo*rithmic *l*anguage
APL	*A* *p*rogramming *l*anguage
Basic *or* BASIC	*B*eginner's *a*ll-purpose *s*ymbolic *i*nstruction *c*ode

Cobol *or* COBOL	*Common business oriented language*
Fortran *or* FORTRAN	*For*mula *trans*lation
PL/1	*Programming language* 1
RPG	*Report program generator*

Numbers and Symbols
Figures are generally used with units of measure and for pure numbers:

5 binary units	logic 0 output
4 bits *or* 4 b	address 07
1024 bytes	the 2 decimal
integer 1	8 punch

No commas or spaces are used with binary numbers:

101011
10101.101

italic and roman notation   Mathematical symbols used in computer languages are usually set in roman capital letters both in running text and in programs:

variable X
the equation X * Y * Z = 6

Mathematical symbols used in a strictly algebraic sense and without reference to computer language are set in italic type:

variable X
the equation $XYZ = 6$

In a conversion between symbols used in a computer-language context and a standard mathematical context, each grouping remains typographically distinct:

The Fortran expression X = A + B/C − D ** 2 is converted into the formula

$$X = A + \frac{B}{C} - D^2$$

Other computer-language symbols are set in roman letters:

C bit   C'nn' (ASCII code character)
operand xxx   variable Fw.d

parentheses   Since brackets have a special meaning in some computer languages or are not used at all, multiple groupings of parentheses are generally used to indicate sequence of operations:

$X = ((A * B)/C) * D$

Capitalization

Initial-letter abbreviations in computer science are commonly capitalized:

CPU (central processing unit)
EBCDIC (extended binary-coded decimal interchange code)
RAM (random access memory)
ROM (read-only memory)
TTL (transistor-transistor logic)

As with languages, the names of computers are set either in initial capital and lowercase letters or in all capitals. If not pronounceable, they are set in all capitals.

Edvac *or* EDVAC   RCA Cosmac
Xerox Sigma   Intel 4004
Univac   XGP

The names of computer programs, subprograms, routines, algorithms, and statements are generally set in all capitals or small capitals:

algorithm ENTER
EDIT facility
PRINT statement
RESET line (*but* RESETs)
subprogram FREEFIELD

Instructions to the computer are set in all capitals, all small capitals, or capitals and lowercase:

ADD CARRY   *or*   Add Carry
INTERRUPT ENABLE   *or*   Interrupt Enable

STORE IN MEMORY	*or*	Store in Memory
WRITE	*or*	Write

Some common terms, including the names of logic gates, are set in all capitals or all small capitals:

ANDing
ANS Cobol
EXCLUSIVE-OR gate
MUL (mnemonic for multiplica-
tion)

NAND gate
ON state
OP code

8

CHEMISTRY
AND LIFE SCIENCES

This chapter covers many of the conventions that have been established for the representation of chemical notation in print and gives recommendations for usage in the various biological sciences and the health professions. To ensure accuracy, it is important to begin with a cleanly prepared and unambiguous manuscript. (Suggestions for preparing technical manuscripts are given in Chapter 11.)

8-1

CHEMICAL SYMBOLS

Some common rules are given here. See also the latest edition of *Directions for Abstractors*, published by the Chemical Abstracts Service of the American Chemical Society.

Elements and Compounds

The names of elements and compounds may be spelled out, shown as symbols, or abbreviated, but the treatment should be consistent within a passage:

> H *or* hydrogen
> CO_2 *or* carbon dioxide
> ^{235}U *or* uranium 235
> DNA *or* deoxyribonucleic acid
> 5-BU *or* 5-bromouracil

Note that symbols are set in roman type.

articles   The choice of indefinite article before a chemical formula is governed by the pronunciation of the symbol rather than the spelled name:

     an Na_2SO_4 system

Before the symbol for an element, however, the article may be governed by the pronunciation of the spelled name if the author prefers:

     a H atom *or* an H atom

numbers   Numbers under 10 are generally spelled out with atoms, electrons, and molecules, but numerals are acceptable in computational passages and may be used throughout the book.

indices   The four numerical indices around a chemical symbol represent the mass number (upper left), atomic number (lower left), ionic charge (upper right), and number of atoms (lower right):

     $^{40}_{20}Ca^{2+}$
     Cl_2

The mass number generally is shown only for isotopes. When a right-hand index on one symbol might conflict with a left-hand index on the succeeding symbol, the symbols are separated by a thin space:

     $H_2\ ^{18}O$

     For the treatment of more complex compounds, see "Isotopes" in Section 8-3.

valences   Valences are treated as follows:

     Cl^-
     TiO^{2+} *not* TiO^{++}
     N^{3-}

Note that the sign alone is used for monovalent elements or groups. In text discussions of valence, the order of the number and sign is inverted:

     a charge of $+2$
     a -1 charge

Unshared electrons or electrons in the bonding shell of an element are shown by boldface dots around a chemical symbol. A bar is sometimes used for a pair of electrons.

$$\begin{array}{cc} \text{H} & \text{H} \\ \quad\ddot{\text{O}}\text{--H} & \quad\underline{\text{O}}\text{--H} \end{array}$$

$$\text{CH}_3\cdot$$

$$\cdot\dot{\underset{\cdot}{\text{C}}}\cdot$$

chemical substances or substituents Letters representing chemical substances or substituents are set in roman type, even when they are used in subscripts:

A	acceptor *or* acid
B	base
D	donor
R	radical *or* organic substituent
M	metal
N	nucleophile
X	halogen *or* other chemical substituent
Me	methyl
Ph	phenyl
Ac	acyl
E_A	energy of acceptor *or* acid

subatomic particles Subatomic particles may be spelled out or abbreviated, but they should be treated consistently within a given passage:

e *or* e	electron
n *or* n	neutron
p *or* p	proton
β	beta particle *or* β particle
μ	muon
π	pion

phase states   Abbreviations for phase states following chemical symbols are generally set in lowercase italic type and placed in parentheses. Roman abbreviations in parentheses are an acceptable alternative:

    (*aq*) *or* (aq)   aqueous (*but always* aq NaOH)

    (*g*) *or* (g)   gas

    (*l*) *or* (l)   liquid

    (*s*) *or* (s)   solid

    (*c*) *or* (c)   macrocrystalline

    $NiS(s) + O_2(g) \rightarrow NiO(s) + SO_2(g)$

Vertical arrows are sometimes used to indicate that a substance is a precipitate ($\downarrow$) or a gas ($\uparrow$):

    $CaSO_4\downarrow$
    $O_2\uparrow$

Phase-state abbreviations and arrows should not both be used in the same discussion.

chemical concentration   Brackets indicate chemical concentration:

    $[HCO_3^-]$
    $[Cl_2O_7]$

Units of chemical concentration are italicized:

    1.0 *M* HCl (molar)
    0.5 *m* NaOH (molal)
    2.0 *N* H_3PO_4 (normal)

When concentrations are expressed as percentages, the use of the percent sign is preferable to the spelled form:

    4.0% Cr
    15% HNO_3

atomic orbitals   Orbital designations are italicized:

    3d, 6p, 8f, 2p_x orbitals
    sp^3 hybrid orbital

bonding orbitals   Bonding orbitals, when abbreviated, are represented by the lowercase Greek letters sigma and pi. Their nonbonding alternatives are designated by the addition of a superscript asterisk.

π bond
σ^* orbital

electron shells   Electron shells are designated by capital roman letters:

K, L, M shells

thermodynamic quantities   Symbols for thermodynamic quantities are set in capital italic letters (note in these examples that a degree sign is used for the superscript):

ΔH_0° *or* $\Delta H_0^{\circleddash}$
ΔG_f°
ΔS_{sys}

energy states of excited molecules   In photochemistry, energy states of excited molecules are represented by italic capital letters with numerical subscripts:

T_1 first triplet state

S_0 singlet ground state

V_1 first vibrational energy state

reaction types   Abbreviations for reaction types are generally set in roman type:

$S_N i$ substitution nucleophilic internal

$S_N 2$ substitution nucleophilic bimolecular

E1   elimination unimolecular

$A_{AC}1$ acid-catalyzed acyl-oxygen cleavage unimolecular

use of asterisks   Asterisks are frequently used to denote special atoms in chemical structures:

$C_4H_9Br^*$

position of element   The position of an element in a chemical structure is designated as follows:

F-6α	fluorine in the 6α position
C-6	carbon in position 6 (*or* carbon atom 6)
α carbon	carbon in the alpha position
the 6 nitrogen	nitrogen in position 6

designation of chain length and ring size   Numerals are customarily used to designate chain length and ring size:

a C_{16} fatty acid *or* a 16-carbon fatty acid
a 6-carbon ring

negative log expressions   In the following expressions, p is always set in lowercase roman type:

pH
pOH
pK_a

CHEMICAL ABBREVIATIONS

Common chemical expressions are generally spelled out, but abbreviations (see Table 8-1) may be used in problems, illustrations, tables, equations, and other situations where frequent use or space considerations dictate.

Many chemical abbreviations consist of lowercase initial letters:

uv	ultraviolet
ir	infrared
nmr	nuclear magnetic resonance
esr	electron spin resonance

Other initial-letter abbreviations are capitalized:

HOMO	highest occupied molecular orbital
LCAO	linear combination of atomic orbitals
USP	United States Pharmacopeia
NF	National Formulary

Units of Measurement

Some non-SI units are still occasionally used in the field:

Non-SI	*SI Counterpart*
atm	Pa
Å	nm
kcal	J
torr	Pa
mmHg	Pa

The preferred abbreviation for the unit *milliosmol* is mosmol, but mOsmol or mOsm is acceptable if used consistently. The accepted abbreviation for the unit *equivalent* is equiv, but the abbreviation for *milliequivalent* is meq.

The unit *svedberg* (S) is equivalent to 10^{-13} second:

30 S *not* 30S

See also Chapter 3.

TABLE 8-1   SOME ABBREVIATIONS USED IN CHEMISTRY

ABBREVIATION	MEANING	ABBREVIATION	MEANING
aq NaOH	Aqueous NaOH	mol %	Mole percent
anhyd $CH_3CH_2OCH_2CH_3$	Anhydrous $CH_3CH_2OCH_2CH_3$	vol %	Volume percent
		wt %	Weight percent
concd H_2SO_4	Concentrated H_2SO_4	% v/v	Percent volume per volume
concn	Concentration	% w/w	Percent weight per weight
dil HCl	Dilute HCl		
ppt	Precipitate	% w/v	Percent weight per volume
insol	Insoluble		
soln	Solution	MW *or* mol wt	Molecular weight
mp	Melting point	AW *or* at wt	Atomic weight
bp	Boiling point	FW	Formula weight
temp	Temperature	EW *or* equiv wt	Equivalent weight
sp gr	Specific gravity		

8-3

CHEMICAL NOMENCLATURE

Inorganic Nomenclature

compounds composed of two elements   Compounds composed of only two elements usually derive their names directly from the elements:

    sodium chloride   NaCl

    aluminum nitride   AlN

Prefixes such as *di-*, *tri-*, and *tetra-* are used to show that more than one atom of an element is present in a compound:

    iron trichloride $FeCl_3$

    carbon tetrachloride CCl_4

compounds composed of more than two elements   The names of compounds of more than two elements may contain prefixes such as *hypo-*, *aquo-*, and *per-* and suffixes such as *-ate*, *-ite*, and *-ide*, alone or in combination:

    sulfuric acid H_2SO_4

    sodium sulfate $NaSO_4$

    sodium hypochlorite $NaClO$

    sodium perchlorate $NaClO_4$

    hypochlorous acid $HClO$

oxidation numbers   A roman numeral is sometimes used to show the oxidation number of an element; it is placed in parentheses immediately after the name or symbol of the element:

    iron(II) chloride
    Cu(III)

For clarity in complex formulas, the roman numeral may be treated as a superscript to the symbol:

    $Pb^{II}_2Pb^{IV}O_4$

complex ions Complex ions have names derived from the various elements of which they are made up. These names are treated as one word:

dichlorotetraaquachromium(III)
$CrCl_2(H_2O)_4^+$

Organic Nomenclature

locants Locants are numbers or letters that designate the position of an atom or a group in a molecule. They precede the word or group they modify. Locants are separated from the word by hyphens and from each other by commas without space.

1,4-cyclohexadiene
$N,\alpha,4'$-trimethyldibenzylamine
α-oxoglutaric acid
O-(2,4-dinitrophenyl)-hydroxylamine
pent-1-en-3-yne

Some prefixes, such as *di-*, *tri-*, or *tetra-*, are combined with the compound name. Other prefixes, such as *bis-*, *tris-*, or *tetrakis-*, usually precede a group enclosed in parentheses or brackets.

1,2-dibromomethane
1,3,5-benzenetripropanoic acid
1,2-bis(trifluoromethyl)-1,2-dicyanoethene
tris[3-trifluoroacetyl-*d*-nopinonato]europium(III)
tetrakis(triphenylphosphine)palladium

Table 8-2 lists the most common locants and chemical prefixes and indicates how they are treated in various situations.

organic functional groups Suffixes such as *-ane*, *-ene*, *-ol*, *-al*, or *-yne* are used to denote the various organic functional groups:

butane	ethanal	ethane
butene	ethanol	ethyne

class names Class names are often, but not always, separated from the words preceding them. The same or similar names should be treated consistently throughout the text; it is the author's responsibility to determine

TABLE 8-2   LOCANTS AND CHEMICAL PREFIXES

COMBINING FORM		ADJECTIVE FORM	CAPITALIZATION IN LABELS AND AT BEGINNING OF SENTENCE
n-		normal	*n*-Butane
sec-		secondary	*sec*-Butyl alcohol
tert- or *t-*		tertiary	*tert*-Butyl alcohol
cis-		cis	
trans-		trans	
sym- or *s-*		symmetrical	
asym-		asymmetrical	
unsym- or *uns-*		unsymmetrical	
syn-		syn	Cis form
anti-		anti	*cis*-Cinnamic acid
endo-		endo	
exo-		exo	
erythro-		erythro	
threo-		threo	
meso-		meso	
scyllo-		scyllo	
gem-		geminal	Geminal form
vic-		vicinal	*gem*-Dimethyl
m- or *meta-*	Not invariably	meta	*p*-Aminobenzoic acid
o- or *ortho-*	abbreviated,	ortho	*para*-Chlorophenol
p- or *para-*	but should be consistent	para	
β-		*β* or beta (*β* oxidation)	*β*-Alanine
D-		D	D-Glucopyranose
D(+)-		D(+)	D(+)-*α*-Phenethyltri-
L-		L	methylammonium
DL-		DL	
d-		*d* or dextro	
l-		*l* or levo	*d*-Tartaric acid
dl-		*dl*	
(+)-		dextrorotatory	
(−)-		levorotatory	(−)-Ephedrine
(*R*)- (rectus)		*R*	1(*S*),3(*S*)-Dimethylcyclo-
(*S*)- (sinister)		*S*	hexane
(*E*)- (entgegen)		*E*	(*Z*)-1-Bromo-1,2,-dichloro-
(*Z*)- (zusammen)		*Z*	ethene
bis			
tris			
cyclo		cyclo	Tris(*p*-nitrophenyl)methyl
di			bromide
bi			Isovaleric acid
mono		mono	
iso		iso	
2,2-dimethyl-3-chlorobutane			2,2-Dimethyl-3-chlorobutane
bicyclo[2.2.1]heptane		bicyclo compound [2.2.1] system	Bicyclo[2.2.1]heptane
N-, *O-*, *S-*, etc. (substituent on nitrogen, oxygen, sulfur, etc.)		the *N* position	*N,N′*-Bis(*p*-hydroxyphenyl)-2-pentene-1,5-diimine

whether a class name should be combined with the words that precede it
or be separated from them.

aryl nitriles	thio amides
nitro paraffins	methyl ethers
ethyl ethers	α-keto acids
β-iodo azides	

Biochemical Nomenclature

amino acids and proteins The three-letter and one-letter abbreviations
for the common amino acids are as follows:

Ala, A	alanine
Arg, R	arginine
Asn, N	asparagine
Asp, D	aspartic acid
Asx	asparagine or aspartic acid, undefined
Cys-Cys	cystine
Cys, C	cysteine
Gln, Q	glutamine
Glu, E	glutamic acid
Glx	glutamine or glutamic acid, undefined
Gly, G	glycine
His, H	histidine
Ile, I	isoleucine
Leu, L	leucine
Lys, K	lysine
Met, M	methionine
Phe, F	phenylalanine
Pro, P	proline
Ser, S	serine
Thr, T	threonine
Trp, W	tryptophan
Tyr, Y	tyrosine
Val, V	valine

These abbreviations are used only for sequences of amino acids or residues of proteins:

When Pro is removed from Pro-Lys-Leu . . . .

They are not used for free amino acids:

The essential amino acids are alanine, leucine, and . . . .

In known amino acid sequences, the abbreviations are separated by hyphens. For unknown sequences, the abbreviations are enclosed in parentheses and separated by commas.

Lys-Asp-Gly
Lys-Asp-Gly-(Phe,Tyr,Thr)-Lys

Terminal residues in peptide chains are referred to as the NH_2-terminal or N-terminal residue and the COOH-terminal or C-terminal residue.

bases and nucleosides   The common purine and pyrimidine bases are denoted by the three-letter abbreviations listed below. (For convenience in discussions of base sequences in DNA and RNA, the single-letter abbreviations for ribonucleosides are sometimes used to denote bases.)

Ade	adenine
Cyt	cytosine
Gua	guanine
Pur	purine
Pyr	pyrimidine
Thy	thymine (5-methyluracil)
Ura	uracil

The three-letter and one-letter abbreviations used to designate common ribonucleosides are as follows:

Ado, A	adenosine
Cyd, C	cytidine
Guo, G	guanosine
Ino, I	inosine

Thd, T	ribosylthymine
dThd, dT	thymidine
Urd, U	uridine

The three-letter abbreviations are used for free ribonucleosides; the one-letter abbreviations are used for sequences or residues thereof only.

The letter p represents phosphate groups in sequences. No hyphens are required between abbreviations strung together to form a sequence, although arrows are sometimes used:

ApG
pUpG
pU ← pG

sugars and carbohydrates   A monosaccharide is denoted by an abbreviation composed of the first three letters of its name unless such an abbreviation can be confused with other existing abbreviations. For sequences, abbreviations for monosaccharides are joined by hyphens or closed up with short arrows to indicate arrangement and linking.

Fru	fructose
Rib	ribose
but Glc (*not* Glu)	glucose

enzymes   Either systematic or trivial names for enzymes should be used consistently:

Trivial	*Systematic*
β-galactosidase	β-D-galactoside galactohydrolase, EC 3.2.1.23
ferredoxin-NADP$^+$ reductase	NADPH: ferredoxin oxidoreductase, EC 1.6.7.1

For systematic names, *Enzyme Nomenclature 1978* lists the Enzyme Commission names and numbers. With a few notable exceptions (ATPase, DNase, and RNase), enzyme names should not be abbreviated. Enzyme Commission names do not necessarily follow the rules for nomenclature set forth by the International Union of Pure and Applied Chemistry (IUPAC).

TABLE 8-3 COMMON BIOCHEMICAL ABBREVIATIONS

ABBREVIATION	MEANING
A, C, G, T, U	Nucleotides: adenine, cytosine, guanine, thymine, uridine
ACG, AAG, ATC	Codons (groups of three nucleotides): adenine-cytosine-guanine, adenine-adenine-guanine, adenine-thymine-cytosine
ACh, AChE	Acetylcholine, acetylcholinesterase
$ACTH_{1-13}$ or 1-13 ACTH	Adrenocorticotropic hormone (adrenocorticotropin), the 1 to 13 sequence of amino acids
ADH	Antidiuretic hormone (vasopressin)
Ala, Gly, Phe, Trp	Amino acids: alanine, glycine, phenylalanine, tryptophan
Ala-Arg-Val-Leu	Protein (amino acid sequence): alanine-arginine-valine-leucine
ATP, ATPase	Adenosine triphosphate, adenosine triphosphatase
AMP, cAMP or cyclic AMP	Adenosine monophosphate, cyclic adenosine monophosphate
CPK or CK	Creatine phosphokinase or creatine kinase
DNA, DNase	Deoxyribonucleic acid, deoxyribonuclease
dns-	Dansyl [5-dimethylaminonaphthalene-1-sulfonyl (used only as substituent on nucleoside)]
EC 3.1.3.9	Enzyme Commission number: glucose-6-phosphatase
FSH	Follicle-stimulating hormone
G_{M1}, G_{M2}, G_{M3}	Gangliosides
GH	Growth hormone
GMP, cGMP or cyclic GMP	Guanosine monophosphate, cyclic guanosine monophosphate
GnRH	See LHRH
G6PD or G-6-PD	Glucose-6-phosphate dehydrogenase
HCG or hCG	Human chorionic gonadotropin
LATS, LATS-p	Long-acting thyroid stimulator, long-acting thyroid stimulator protector
LDL, VLDL	Low-density lipoprotein, very low density lipoprotein
LH or ICSH	Luteinizing hormone or interstitial cell-stimulating hormone
LHRH (or LHRF) or GnRh (or GnRF)	Luteinizing hormone-releasing hormone (or factor) or gonadotropin-releasing hormone (or factor)
MSH	Melanocyte-stimulating hormone
NSILA, NSILA-s	Nonsuppressible insulinlike activity: nonsuppressible insulin-like activity, soluble (in ethanol)
P_i, PP_i	Inorganic phosphate (orthophosphate), inorganic pyrophosphate
PGE_1, $PGF_{2\alpha}$	Prostaglandin E_1, prostaglandin $F_{2\alpha}$
PTH, pro-PTH, prepro-PTH	Parathyroid hormone, proparathyroid hormone, preproparathyroid hormone
hPTH, bPTH, pPTH	Human PTH, bovine PTH, porcine PTH
RNA, RNase	Ribonucleic acid, ribonuclease
mRNA, nRNA, rRNA, tRNA	Messenger RNA, nuclear RNA, ribosomal RNA, transfer RNA
SRIF	Somatotropin release-inhibiting factor (somatostatin)
T_3, T_4	Triiodothyronine, triiodothyroxine (tetraiodothyronine)
rT_3	Reverse triiodothyronine
TBG, TeBG	Thyroxine-binding globulin, testosterone-binding globulin
^{99m}Tc	Technetium 99m
tos-	Tosyl [tolylsulfonyl (used only as a substituent on nucleoside)]
TRH	Thyrotropin-releasing hormone
TRIS	Tromethamine [tris(hydroxymethyl)aminomethane]
TSH	Thyroid-stimulating hormone (thyrotropic hormone)

isotopes For the treatment of isotopes of simple compounds, see "Indices" in Section 8-1.

In the more complex compounds of biochemistry, the isotope symbol generally is placed in square brackets and precedes the name or part of the name to which it refers:

β-hydroxyl[^{14}C]aspartate
[^{14}C$_2$]glycolic acid
[α-^{14}C]urea
[*carboxy*-^{14}C]leucine
[3-^{14}C,2,3-D,^{15}N]serine
L-[1-^{14}C]leucine

Brackets are also used around the isotope symbol when the compound is denoted by a common abbreviation:

[^{32}P]AMP *not* AM^{32}P

other symbols and abbreviations used in biochemistry The following symbols represent some common chemical and physical quantities used in biochemistry:

K_m Michaelis constant

g acceleration of gravity

s sedimentation coefficient

D diffusion coefficient

α refractive index

Table 8-3 lists some common biochemical terms and their abbreviations.

8-4

CHEMICAL FORMULAS AND EQUATIONS

Linear Formulas

bonds Single bonds between atoms are usually not shown for linear formulas in text:

CH_3CH_2OH
NaBr

In discussions of bonding, however, a bond is used:

> the $C-O$ bond
> the $-OH$ group
> the $CoA-S-$ complex

Multiple bonds are usually shown in linear formulas:

> $BrCH_2CH=CH_2$
> $HC\equiv CH$

Lightface center dots without space on either side are used to show water of hydration:

> $Na_2SO_4 \cdot 10H_2O$

charges   In linear formulas, charges are shown to the right or left of atoms as superscripts:

> COO^-
> $^+H_3NCHRCOO^-$
> $NH_4{}^+$

Structural Formulas

bonds   Since the compositor follows the manuscript in setting structural formulas, it is essential for the author to represent all bonds clearly, position charges and subscripts correctly, and draw ring structures with symmetrical accuracy. Care should be taken to see that bonds connect the atoms that are bonded. Bonds should go to the centers of the letters representing the bonded atoms.

Structural formulas taking up more than three lines of text should be displayed to avoid excessive spreading of typeset text lines. When a structural formula is run in with text, the central portion of the formula aligns with the text line:

$$\ldots \text{the ketone } R-\overset{\overset{\displaystyle O}{\|}}{C}-CH_3$$

A series of dots or dashes is used to indicate hydrogen bonding in configurational displays:

$$
\begin{array}{c}
\text{H} \\
\quad \text{O}\cdots\text{H} \quad \text{H} \\
\text{H}
\end{array}
\quad or \quad
\begin{array}{c}
\text{H} \\
\quad \text{O}\text{---}\text{H} \quad \text{H} \\
\text{H}
\end{array}
$$

Compositors normally follow the manuscript on the use of single bonds between groups of a horizontal chain in structural formulas. Consistency of presentation is preferred but not mandatory.

$$
CH_3CH_2C\overset{\displaystyle O}{\underset{\displaystyle OH}{}} \quad or \quad CH_3-CH_2-C\overset{\displaystyle O}{\underset{\displaystyle OH}{}}
$$

Compositors also follow the manuscript in representing the interior bonds of a benzene ring. Consistency in presentation is preferred.

or

A solid and dashed double bond is used to show resonance bonding:

A hexagonal ring without interior bonds is not a benzene ring; compositors will follow the manuscript style:

cyclohexane   benzene

It is preferable to show bonds from the corners of a ring to substituent groups. Single bonds may be omitted to conserve space if it is necessary.

For three-dimensional structures, a wedge is used to indicate groups above the plane of the structure, a dashed line to indicate a group below the plane of the structure, and a wavy line to indicate a group of uncertain configuration:

The mark $\sim$ is used to denote high-energy bonds:

Take care to distinguish between the identity symbol and a triple bond; if necessary, label each instance in the manuscript:

charges   In structural formulas, charges may appear as superscripts to the right or left of atoms; they may also appear centered above or below atoms, between two atoms, or within a ring. Circles around charges are not necessary.

For partial charges the plus or minus sign is preceded by a lowercase delta:

$$\overset{\delta+}{H}-\overset{\delta-}{Cl}$$

numbering of rings and chains When numbers are assigned to the backbones of rings and chains, they are set in small type:

Equations

numbers Numbers in chemical equations are closed up to the symbols that follow ($8H_3O^+$). Space is used for clarity, however, when the number precedes an isotope and occasionally with complex structural formulas.

arrows In chemical equations, an arrow is used between the symbols for reactants and the symbols for products in nonreversible or nonequilibrium reactions:

$$2KClO_3(l) \rightarrow 2KCl(s) + 3O_2(g)$$

Arrows with single barbs are used for reversible or equilibrium reactions:

$$2CO + 2H_2 \rightleftharpoons CO_2 + CH_4$$

Double-headed arrows signify resonance:

When an equation runs to two or more lines, the equation is preferably split at the arrow, and the arrow is shown on the first line only:

$$5Fe^{2+} + MnO_4^- + 8H_3O^+ \rightarrow$$
$$5Fe^{3+} + Mn^{2+} + 12H_2O$$

Single- or double-barbed arrows are sometimes used in structural formulas to indicate the movement of groups or electrons during a reaction. A wavy line through a bond indicates that the bond is being broken.

descriptive words   Descriptive words beneath chemical formulas are set in small type, with the first word capitalized. Notation above and below arrows is set in even smaller type and lowercased.

Acetaldehyde

$$CH_2{=}CH{-}CH_3 + Cl_2 \xrightarrow{500{-}600\,°C} CH_2{=}CH{-}CH_2Cl + HCl$$
  Propylene   Allyl chloride

8-5

ABBREVIATIONS AND SYMBOLS IN THE LIFE SCIENCES

No single set of guidelines covering the use of abbreviations and symbols in the life sciences and medicine is universally accepted. The guidelines given here may be varied to fit the level of sophistication of readers for whom a book or article is intended.

Abbreviations
In general, try to avoid the overuse of abbreviations, particularly those which might be unfamiliar to the reader.

established abbreviations   Some abbreviations are well known in a given field and may be used in text without being defined at first mention:

AV	arteriovenous or atrioventricular
CT scan *or*	computerized (*or* computed) tomography *or*
CAT scan	computerized (*or* computed) axial tomography
CNS	central nervous system
CSF	cerebrospinal fluid
ECG (*not* EKG)	electrocardiogram (or -graph)
EEG	electroencephalogram (or -graph)
HLA	human leukocyte antigen
IgA	gamma A globulin
RBC	red blood cell
WBC	white blood cell

Many abbreviations that are characteristically used in writing prescriptions or in keeping medical records are appropriate in text if they are used consistently and are defined at first mention:

BP	blood pressure
D&C	dilatation and curettage
D_5W	5% dextrose in water
D/W	dextrose in water
GI	gastrointestinal
Hct	hematocrit
IM	intramuscular
IV	intravenous
NPO	nothing by mouth *(non per os)*
PO	by mouth, oral *(per os)*
SC	subcutaneous
SOAP	subjective, objective, assessment plan

Some abbreviations are acceptable when used with dosages, but should be spelled out otherwise:

ac, pc	before, after meals *(ante, post cibos)*
ad lib.	ad libitum (at pleasure)
bid, tid, qid	two, three, four times daily *(bis, ter, quater in die)*
hs	at bedtime *(hora somni)*
prn	given when necessary *(pro re nata)*
qd	every day or daily *(quaque die)*
qh, q 2 h	every hour (*quaque hora*), every 2 hours
qs	as much as will suffice *(quantum sufficit)*
stat.	immediately *(statim)*

There are a few abbreviations that should not be used unless the purpose is to illustrate a patient's chart:

c *or* c̄; s *or* s̄	with *(cum)*; without *(sine)*
Dx	diagnosis
Hx	history
Px	past history *or* physical examination
Rx	prescription *or* therapy
Sx	signs and symptoms

ad hoc abbreviations To avoid undue repetition of a long or cumbersome term, a suitable abbreviation may be supplied when the term is introduced and used thereafter for convenience. This type of shorthand notation usually consists of roman capital letters without periods. Combinations of upper- and lowercase letters, numerals, and other symbols may also be used. When such abbreviations are used, they should be easily traceable to the spelled-out form.

The eosinophil chemotactic factor of anaphylaxis (ECF-A). . . . ECF-A and NCF-A are stored in the cells.

The Rous-associated virus (RAV). . . . Several distinct RAVs have been identified.

A decrease in the forced vital capacity (FVC). . . . When there is a change in the FEV_1/FVC ratio. . . .

Red-absorbing (Pr) and far-red-absorbing (Pfr) forms of phytochrome. . . . Conversion of Pfr to Pr and vice versa. . . .

Symbols

Symbols are always used when they have no convenient verbal equivalent:

> an XY chromosomal constitution
> a rise in arterial P_{CO_2} (or P_{CO_2})

Some symbols, although appropriate in illustrations, equations, and tables, are generally avoided in text:

> Pelage is the same color in males and females (*not* in ♂♂ and ♀♀)
> Findings reveal increased SGOT (*not* ↑SGOT)

plus signs   Plus signs are often used to indicate rough quantifications—for example, test results or relative responses to drugs. In text, these should be styled as follows:

> +   3+
> 2+   4+

In tables and illustrations, the following forms are acceptable:

> +   +++
> ++   ++++

Table 8-4 lists other common abbreviations and symbols currently in use in the life sciences. For mathematical notation, see Chapter 7. See also "Biochemical Nomenclature" in Section 8-3.

number   *Number* may be abbreviated *no.* or spelled out, but use of the symbol # is not acceptable:

> no. 12 *or* number 12 French catheter
> *also* 12F catheter
> no. 5-0 *or* number 5-0 suture
> no. 22 *or* number 22 needle

Greek letters   For the spelling of names of chemical compounds that include Greek letters, consult *The Merck Index*.

> β-alanine
> betanaphthol

**TABLE 8-4   COMMON LIFE SCIENCES ABBREVIATIONS
AND SYMBOLS**

ABBREVIATION OR SYMBOL	MEANING
	Cardiology
S_1, S_2, S_3, S_4	First, second, third, and fourth heart sounds
A_2, P_2	Aortic and pulmonic components of second heart sound
aV_L, aV_R, aV_F, I, II, III	Electrocardiograph limb leads
V_1, V_2, . . . , V_6	Electrocardiograph chest leads
P, Q, R, S, T, and U waves	Electrocardiogram waveforms
PR interval, QRS complex, ST segment, ST-T interval	Electrocardiogram segments
a, c, and v waves; x and y waves (*or* descents)	Jugular venous pulsation waveforms
	Hematology
A_1, A_2, B, A_1B, A_2B, O, O_h	Phenotypes (blood types) of the ABO system
anti-A, anti-B	Antibodies of types B and A blood, respectively
Le(a+ b−)	Phenotype of Lewis system
Le^a, Le^b	Antigens of Lewis system
Rh_0, rh′, hr″	Antigenic determinants of Rh system
A^1A^2	Genotype of the ABO system
Hb M	Hemoglobin M
Hb M Boston ($\alpha_2^{58His \rightarrow Tyr}\beta_2$)	Subtype of hemoglobin M with substitution of tyrosine for histidine at the fifty-eighth position in the α_2 chain
HbO_2	Oxygenated hemoglobin (oxyhemoglobin)
factors I to XIII	Coagulation factors
	Genetics
A to G	Chromosome groups
1 to 22	Autosome numbers
X, Y	Sex chromosomes
+21; −13	Additional chromosome 21; missing chromosome 13
p+ ;q −	Larger than normal short arm of a chromosome; smaller than normal (or deletion of) long arm of a chromosome
C6	Chromosome 6 of group C
46,XX	Karyotype of a normal female
46,XX,5p−	Karyotype of a female, indicating deletion of the short arm of chromosome 5 (cri-du-chat syndrome)
46,XX,del(1)(q21q31)	Karyotype of a female, indicating deletion of the long arm of chromosome 1 between bonds 21 and 31
46,XY,t(2;5)(q21;q31)	Karyotype of a male, indicating reciprocal translocation between the long arm of band 21 of chromosome 2 and the long arm of band 31 of chromosome 5

TABLE 8-4   COMMON LIFE SCIENCES ABBREVIATIONS AND SYMBOLS (*Continued*)

ABBREVIATION OR SYMBOL	MEANING
Genetics (Continued)	
SeSe, Sese, sese	Genotypes: capitalization indicates dominance; lowercase indicates recessiveness
P_1, F_1	First parental generation, first filial generation
Immunology	
B cells, T cells	Bursa- and thymus-derived lymphocytes
C1, C4, C2, C3, C5, . . . , C9	Components of human complement in order of reaction
C1q, C1r, C1s	Subcomponents of C1
C3a, C3b	Minor and major fragments of cleavage of C3
$C\overline{42}$	Activated complex of C4 and C2
HBsAg	Hepatitis B surface antigen
HLA	Human histocompatibility leukocyte antigen
HLA-A, HLA-B, HLA-C, HLA-D	HLA loci
HLA-B27, HLA-Dw3	Specific HLA antigens
IgG, IgA, IgM, IgD, IgE	Classes of immunoglobulins
IgG1, IgG2, IgG3	Subclasses of IgG
Anatomy and Physiology	
C_{in}	Clearance rate of inulin
ED_{50}, LD_{50}	Median effective dose, median lethal dose
C7, T12, L5, S5	Vertebrae: seventh cervical, twelfth thoracic, fifth lumbar, fifth sacral
MV_{O_2} *or* MV_{O_2}	Myocardial oxygen ventilation rate
P_{O_2} *or* P_{O_2}	Partial pressure of oxygen
Pa_{O_2} *or* arterial P_{O_2}	Partial pressure of oxygen in arterial blood
PA_{O_2} *or* alveolar P_{O_2}	Partial pressure of oxygen in alveolar blood
$\dot{V}_{O_2 \, max}$ *or* maximum $\dot{V}_{O_2}$	Maximum ventilation rate of oxygen
$t_{1/2}$	Half-life

In other terms that include Greek letters, the name of the letter may be spelled, or the letter itself may be used. Whichever style is chosen should be used consistently throughout a manuscript.

> beta-adrenergic *or* β-adrenergic
> alpha 1 receptor *or* alpha$_1$ receptor *or* α_1 receptor
> beta lipoprotein *or* β-lipoprotein
> *but* abetalipoproteinemia

8-6

UNITS OF MEASUREMENT IN THE LIFE SCIENCES

For basic information about units of measurement, see Chapter 3. The International System (SI) is generally recommended for use in the life sciences. Whether non-SI units should be converted to their SI counterparts depends on the nature of the book and on developing practice in the field.

molecular weight and mass   *Molecular weight* is a dimensionless, pure number; *molecular mass* may be measured in *daltons* (a unit used by biologists, but not recognized by any international scientific union):

> molecular weight of 260,000 *or* molecular mass of 260,000 daltons
> *not* molecular weight of 260,000 daltons

The symbol M (for molar) should not be used for mole:

> 3 M HCl (molar)
> 3 mol of ribulose 5-phosphate (moles)

unit   When used in a general sense, *unit* is sometimes abbreviated U:

> 50,000 units of vitamin D   *or*   50,000 U vitamin D

International units (IU), *Medical Research Council* units (MRC units), and *United States Pharmacopeia* units (USP units) indicate the amount of a substance (commonly a vitamin, hormone, enzyme, or antibiotic) that produces a specified biological effect. These units have been accepted internationally as a measure of the activity or potency of a substance. These units are sometimes equivalent to one another for a given substance, but not always.

> Calciferol contains 40,000 USP units or IU per milligram.
> One milligram of purified intact bovine parathyroid hormone is the equivalent of 2000 to 4000 USP or MRC units.

g % and similar terms   Because of their ambiguity and imprecision, the abbreviations g %, mg %, and μg % are unacceptable. Usually, they are equivalent to g/100 mL, mg/100 mL, and μg/100 mL, respectively, but mg %, for example, can also be interpreted as mg/100 mg or mg/100 g. Therefore, when a substitution is made, take care to verify that the correct equivalent is used. The following examples show the different possible interpretations of 20 mg %:

20 mg/100 mL *or* 20 mg/dL *or* 0.2 kg/m³
20 mg/100 mg *or* 200 g/kg
20 mg/100 g *or* 200 mg/kg

Note that 20 mg/dL and 0.2 kg/m³ are variant forms that are exactly equivalent to 20 mg/100 mL, but 20 mg/100 mg and 20 mg/100 g are *not* equivalent to 20 mg/100 mL.

beats per minute and similar terms   The units *beats per minute, breaths per minute,* and *respirations per minute* should be spelled out. An exception may be made to conserve space in tables, where bpm and rpm may be used if there will be no confusion about their meaning.

8-7

TAXONOMIC NOMENCLATURE

Latin genus and species names are always italicized. Genus names are capitalized; species epithets are lowercased:

Drosophila
Drosophila melanogaster
Ursus americanus
Homo sapiens (*but* Homo sapiens in a general sense)

A subspecific or varietal epithet is styled in the same way as a species epithet:

Passer domesticus niloticus

but any category designation introducing it is set in roman type:

Viola tricolor var. *hirta*

The name of the author of a species is set in roman type and may be included with the Latin name at first mention:

Magnolia grandiflora Linnaeus   *or*   *Magnolia grandiflora* Linn.

If the species has been transferred to another genus since its original description, the original author's name may be inserted in parentheses:

Streptococcus pneumoniae (Klein) Chester

Nomenclature for hybrids and other distinctive types varies. Some typical examples follow:

$\times$ *Triticosecale* (intergeneric hybrid)
Betula $\times$ *sandbergii* (collective epithet for interspecific hybrid)
Camellia japonica $\times$ *C. saluensis* (intergeneric hybrid, both species named)

The abbreviation sp. may be used with genus names to indicate that the species has not yet been named or to refer loosely to some or all species of the named genus:

Proteus sp. (singular or plural)
Proteus spp. (explicitly plural)

Abbreviations used to designate a new genus, new species, new variety, etc., may be given either in the Latin order (for example, gen. n., sp. n., var. n.) or in the English order (n. gen., n. sp., n. var.):

Sonoraspis californica sp. n.

Names of cultivated varieties of plants are capitalized, set in roman type following the Latin name, and enclosed in single quotation marks:

Saintpaulia ionantha 'Calico'

The genus in a binomial species name should be spelled out at first mention; thereafter it is generally abbreviated with the initial capital letter and a period:

Escherichia coli; then *E. coli*
Streptococcus faecalis; then *S. faecalis*

If necessary, longer abbreviations can be used to avoid confusion:

Streptococcus pyogenes and *Staphylococcus aureus;* then *Strep. pyogenes* and *Staph. aureus*

Taxonomic names of higher rank than the genus (family, order, class, phylum, etc.) are capitalized but not italicized:

Hominidae   Mammalia
Primates   Chordata

These higher taxa are treated as plurals except when accompanied by their category designation:

The Hominidae are . . . .
The family Hominidae is . . . .

In some cases a Latin taxon and a vernacular name are very similar in appearance; care should be taken not to confuse them:

Vertebrata; vertebrate(s)
Primates; primate(s)
Protozoa; protozoon, protozoa
Streptococcus; streptococcus, streptococci

The taxonomy of viruses is still evolving. When two or more forms are in use simultaneously, one should be chosen for consistency:

coxsackievirus   *or*   Coxsackie virus

Viruses are often referred to by nontaxonomic names:

T-even bacteriophages   echoviruses
group A arboviruses   Victoria type A (influenza virus)

Specific viruses are often denoted by letters and numbers:

X174; X 174; ϕX174
cyanophage LPP-25PI
coxsackievirus A15

8-8

DIRECTIONAL TERMS USED IN ANATOMY

Two sets of directional adjectives are in common use. The corresponding terms are not synonymous, and how they correspond depends on the "standard posture" of the animal in question. For example, in human anatomy the dorsal aspect of the body (the back) is also the posterior (hind, rear) aspect, but for quadrupeds the dorsal aspect (the back) is the superior (upper) aspect.

Posture-based terms

anterior	fore; nearer the front
posterior	hind; nearer the rear
superior	upper; nearer the top
inferior	lower; nearer the bottom

Region-based terms

cranial; cephalic	nearer the head
caudal	nearer the tail end
ventral	nearer the belly side
dorsal	nearer the back

Subject matter or context will often determine which term or set of terms is more appropriate, but if context provides no clue, the copy editor may choose either system to be used consistently. Some examples from human anatomy follow:

the superior (*or* cranial) vena cava
the inferior (*or* caudal) vena cava
the anterior (*or* ventral) column
the posterior (*or* dorsal) column
The retroduodenal fossa lies dorsal (*or* posterior) to parts of the duodenum, and ventral (*or* anterior) to the aorta.

Anatomic directional adverbs are formed by replacing the adjectival suffix (*-al, -or, -ic*) with the suffix *-ad,* meaning *-ward:*

superiad	upward
laterad	sideward
cephalad	headward; toward the head
orad	toward the mouth

The *-ad* forms are used in the same kinds of construction in which *-ward* forms are used:

moving ventrad   project superoposteriad
farther caudad   a craniad extension

When the ordinary -ly adverb or the adjective itself has been used correctly, the -ad form should not be substituted:

an anterior projection
extending caudally from the brainstem
passing lateral to the aorta (i.e., passing on the lateral aspect of the aorta)

8-9

PHARMACEUTICAL NOMENCLATURE

In the United States, official nonproprietary names of drugs are those which appear as monograph titles in the *United States Pharmacopeia* and the *National Formulary*. Drug names may be checked there or in the latest edition of *The Merck Index* or of the *Physicians' Desk Reference*.

A drug often has more than one name. If there is a question about which name to use, or if a manuscript has been inconsistent, choose the name under which information about the drug is given in *The Merck Index:*

aspirin (*rather than* acetylsalicylic acid *or* 2-acetyloxybenzoic acid)
levodopa (*rather than* L-dopa *or* levodihydroxyphenylalanine)

The preferred name for a drug is usually a simple nonproprietary (generic) name. Although numbers or letters distinguishing isomers may be included in a name as cited in *Merck*, they may be omitted unless they are needed for clarity:

furoic acid (*or* 2-furoic acid)
androstenedione (*or* 4-androstene-3,17-dione)

The nonproprietary name of a drug should normally be used throughout a manuscript, but at first mention a trade name may be placed in parentheses after it, if necessary:

First mention
. . . is sulfobromophthalein (Bromsulphalein, or BSP)

Subsequent mention
When using sulfobromophthalein . . . .

In exceptional cases (e.g., studies in which a specific formulation was used) a trade name may be more accurate:

> Our series of Bromsulphalein liver function tests showed . . . . *(specific reference)*

The symbols ® and ™ need not be used, since proprietary names are sufficiently identified by being capitalized.

8-10

SPELLING PREFERENCES IN THE LIFE SCIENCES

Check spelling first in the latest edition of *Webster's New Collegiate Dictionary*. For words not listed in the *Collegiate*, consult the latest edition of the *Gould Medical Dictionary*. For words not listed in either, use *Webster's New International Dictionary*, third edition, which is not as recent. A limited number of special terms are spelled in accordance with accepted practice in the literature, rather than according to these dictionaries.

Currently preferred forms for some commonly used terms are listed below. When no clear preference exists between two alternatives, both are given. An asterisk indicates that a term is an exception to *Webster's*.

> anulus* *or* annulus
> arenavirus (*not* arenovirus)
> blastodisk* *or* blastodisc
> curette *or* curet
> disk *or* disc
> endoderm *or* entoderm
> *Entamoeba** (not *Endamoeba*)
> fresh water (n.), *but* a freshwater (n., meaning a freshwater pond, lake, stream, or river)
> mamilla,* mamillary,* mamillated* *or* mammilla, mammillary, mammillated
> mollusk
> neurilemma
> oogonia, ootid, ootype (*not* oö-)
> pygmy (*not* pigmy)
> rhabdom *or* rhabdome
> technique (*not* technic)
> tendinitis (*not* tendonitis—exception to *Gould*)
> uvulae (muscle of the uvula)
> viricide *or* virucide
> workup (n., a diagnostic investigation)

Compound Nouns
To determine whether a compound should be one word, two words, or hyphened, consult the dictionaries listed above. If the term does not appear in any of them, it should be spelled as two words. Some examples follow:

bloodstream	end bulb
braincase	end plate
brainstem*	foot plate
chickenpox*	gallbladder
collarbone	hindbrain
cross section	kneecap
earlobe	shoulder blade
endbrain	taste bud

digraphs *ae* and *oe*   As a general rule, use the simplified spelling with e instead of the digraphs ae and oe:

asafetida	estrus
esophagus	hemophilia
estival	

In taxonomic nomenclature, however, the Latin spelling must be used:

Amoeba
Ferula assafoetida
Haemophilus
Haemosporidia

In terms derived from taxonomic forms, ae and oe are ordinarily retained:

amoeba; amoebic (*but* amebiasis; amebic dysentery)
haemosporidian
polychaete (*but* spirochete *or* spirochaete)

As a general rule, use the digraph in the combining form -coel- ("cavity," "hollow"), but use -celi- for "abdominal cavity." These forms should not be confused with the word root -cel- ("hernia," "tumor").

celiac	gastrocele (gastric hernia)
celiotomy	gastrocoel *or* gastrocoele
coelenteron	(gastrula cavity)
coelom	

The digraph is generally kept in the following terms:

aecium; aecial	gynoecium
androecium	ooecium
autoecious; dioecious;	paedogenesis
heteroecious; monoecious	paedomorphic
coenocyte; coenocytic	zooecia
coenurus; coenurosis	

Plural Forms

When a dictionary gives equal weight to alternative plurals, choose the first form shown. In the examples that follow, and in Table 8-5, asterisks indicate a preference that is contrary to *Webster's* or *Gould*.

With few exceptions, a regular English plural is preferred for names of the larger or more complex kinds of organisms, even if the name is Latin or Greek in form:

delphiniums (*but* cacti, gladioli)
mantises
octopuses

A regular English plural is generally used with the names of conditions, processes, and types of disease, except for those ending in -*um* (replaced in the plural by -a) and in -*is* (replaced by -es):

Singular	Plural
anemia	anemias
delirium	deliria*
impetigo	impetigos (*rather than* impetigines)
lupus	lupuses
mitosis	mitoses
schistosomiasis	schistosomiases

Medical terms ending in -*itis* take the plural form -*itides:*

Singular	Plural
dermatitis	dermatitides*
neuritis	neuritides

For medical terms ending in -*oma*, the English plural -*s* is preferred to the Greek -*ta*:

Singular	*Plural*
atheroma	atheromas (*rather than* atheromata)

In Latin phrases, only the proper Latin or Greek forms are acceptable, even if some of the individual words have English plurals when used separately:

Singular	*Plural*
adventitia	adventitias
but tunica adventitia	tunicae adventitiae
condyloma	condylomas
but condyloma latum	condylomata lata
extensor	extensors
but extensor digitorum	extensores digitorum

Some Commonly Occurring Affixes, Stems, Roots, Combining Forms

-agogue The -*a*- is an integral part of this combining form; -*ogogue* is incorrect:

lymphagogue
sialagogue

ante- Spell *ante-* solid:

antepartum

leuk(o)-, leuc(o)- The *k* spelling is preferred in such medical terms as names of diseases, conditions, processes, and operations, and in *leukocyte* and words related to it. The *c* spelling is generally preferred elsewhere and is obligatory in taxonomic names and their derivatives.

leukocidin*	leucoriboflavin
leukocytosis	leucocytozoan (from the
leukoderma	genus *Leucocytozoon*)
leukotomy	*Leuconostoc*
leucoplast	

**TABLE 8-5   PREFERRED SINGULAR AND PLURAL FORMS
OF SOME LIFE SCIENCE TERMS**

SINGULAR	PLURAL	SINGULAR	PLURAL
acetabulum	acetabula*	femur	femora or femurs
alga	algae	fibula	fibulae or fibulas
amoeba or ameba	amoebas or amebas	fistula	fistulas
		flora	floras
anlage	anlagen	focus (of disease)	foci*
aorta	aortas or aortae	foramen	foramina or foramens
arrector pili	arrectores pilorum		
bacterium	bacteria	fundatrix	fundatrices
bacteroides	bacteroides	fungus	fungi
biceps	biceps*	ganglion	ganglia
blastula	blastulae or blastulas	gastrula	gastrulae or gastrulas
bursa	bursas or bursae	genu	genua
calix or calyx (of kidney, etc.)	calices or calyces*	glomus	glomera
		gumma	gummas
calyx (of flower)	calyxes	histoplasma	histoplasmas
cambium	cambia*	hydra	hydras
centrum	centra*	klebsiella	klebsiellas or klebsiellae
chromonema	chromonemata		
chrysalis	chrysalides but chrysalid, pl. chrysalids	labium majus, minus	labia majora, minora
		lentigo	lentigines
coccidioides	coccidioides	meatus	meatuses
comedo (not comedone)	comedones	meatus acusticus	meatus acustici
		medusa	medusae
condyloma acuminatum	condylomata acuminata	morula	morulae or morulas
cornu	cornua	mycoplasma	mycoplasmas
corpus albicans	corpora albicantia	nautilus	nautiluses
corpus cavernosum	corpora cavernosa	nucleus pulposus	nuclei pulposi
crus cerebri	crura cerebri	ocrea	ocreae
ductus deferens	ductus deferentes	osculum	oscula*
epididymis	epididymides	patella	patellae or patellas
facies	facies	pedipalp	pedipalps but pedipalpus, pl. pedipalpi
fascia	fasciae		
fauna	faunas		

TABLE 8-5 PREFERRED SINGULAR AND PLURAL FORMS OF SOME LIFE SCIENCE TERMS (*Continued*)

SINGULAR	PLURAL	SINGULAR	PLURAL
pelvis (of body)	pelvises *or* pelves	shigella	shigellae *or* shigellas
pelvis (of kidney)	pelves *		
placenta	placentas	spermatozoon (*not* spermatozoan)	spermatozoa
plasmodesma *	plasmodesmata	stamen	stamens
plexus	plexuses (*not* plexi)	sterigma	sterigmata
proboscis	proboscides *	stigma (of flower)	stigmas *
prodrome	prodromes *but* prodroma, *pl.* prodromata	stigma (all other uses)	stigmata
		stoma (surgical)	stomas *
		stoma (all other uses)	stomata
proglottid	proglottids *but* proglottis, *pl.* proglottides	streptococcus	streptococci
		strobila	strobilae
pronephros	pronephroi *	strobilus	strobili
protonema	protonemata	taenia coli *or* tenia coli	taeniae coli *or* teniae coli
protozoon	protozoa *but* protozoan, *pl.* protozoans	thrips (*not* thrip)	thrips
		tibia	tibiae *or* tibias
rachis	rachises	ulna	ulnae *or* ulnas
reticulum	reticula *	vagina	vaginas *
rickettsia	rickettsias *or* rickettsiae	vagina dentis	vaginae dentium
rouleau	rouleaux *	varix	varices
salmonella	salmonellae *or* salmonellas	varix lymphaticus	varices lymphatici
		vas deferens	vasa deferentia
scapula	scapulae *or* scapulas	vas rectum	vasa recta
		vena cava	venae cavae
scolex	scolices	vertebra	vertebrae
sequestrum	sequestra *	viscus	viscera
serum	sera *or* serums		

*Indicates McGraw-Hill's preference regardless of the first form shown (or regular plural implied) in *Webster's Collegiate* or *Gould.*

-logue, -log   The shortened spelling is not recommended for life science or medical terms:

  analogue
  homologue

-physeal, -physial Both spellings are common. Whichever form is chosen should be used consistently throughout a manuscript.

> epiphyseal   *or*   epiphysial
> hypophyseal   *or*   hypophysial

post- *Post-* is solid as a prefix, but open in Latin adverbial phrases. In English adverbial phrases, replace *post* with *after.*

> postmortem (adj. and n.) *but* post mortem (adv. phrase)
> posttreatment (adj.) *but* 3 weeks after treatment
>   (*not* post treatment)

-trop- The word root *-trop-* means "tendency," "affinity," or "effect." It, rather than *-troph-*, is preferred in spelling names of hormones. (A hormone has an effect on, or an affinity for, its target organ.)

> gonadotrope
> phototropic (light-seeking; tending toward the light)
> somatotropin
> thyrotropin

-troph- The word root *-troph-* means "nourishment" or "metabolism":

> autotroph (*not* autotrophe)
> phototrophic (utilizing light in metabolism)
> trophoblast

8-11

HYPHENATION IN THE LIFE SCIENCES

Although the general rules of hyphenation in these fields are essentially the same as those given in Section 1-2, many of them are repeated here to provide examples specific to the life sciences.

Clarity is the goal. If a hyphen resolves ambiguity in a compound modifier, it should always be used:

> large-bowel obstruction
> superficial-muscle involvement

Many terms used as compound modifiers in the life science and medical fields are in common use and need not be hyphened:

bone grafting techniques	oat cell carcinoma
bud scale scars	sickle cell anemia
connective tissue proliferation	tobacco mosaic virus

A phrase that is hyphened in an introductory text—because it is presumably unfamiliar to the reader—may not require a hyphen in advanced works:

dark-field microscopy; dark field microscopy
giant-cell tumor; giant cell tumor

Noun-adjective or noun-participle combinations are hyphened, both before a noun (attributive position) and after a noun (predicative position):

blight-resistant varieties; is blight-resistant
calcium-rich diet; is calcium-rich
colony-forming organisms
melanocyte-stimulating hormone
mosquito-borne virus; is mosquito-borne
mucus-coated epithelium; is mucus-coated

Modifying phrases consisting of coordinate nouns or adjectives are hyphened:

anatomic-physiologic unit
antigen-antibody complex
blood-brain barrier

Phrases consisting of a single letter or symbol followed by a word are generally hyphened as modifiers:

D cells; D-cell adenoma
X chromosomes; X-chromosome defect
γ chain; γ-chain polypeptides

When the letter or symbol comes after the word, however, it remains unhyphened:

coenzyme A; coenzyme A synthesis
factor VIII; factor VIII deficiency
vitamin B complex (*but* B-complex vitamins)

For classes of compounds, enzymes, proteins, etc., in which a Greek letter is part of the name, a hyphen is used after the symbol but not after the spelled form of the letter:

> α-fetoprotein *or* alpha fetoprotein
> α-globulin *or* alpha globulin
> β-hemolysin *or* beta hemolysin

The hyphen is not used with nouns derived from terms designating classes of compounds, enzymes, proteins, etc., except when the Greek letter is part of a locant indicating position:

> α hemolysis *or* alpha hemolysis
> β oxidation *or* beta oxidation
> *but* 11β-hydroxylation (hydroxylation at the 11β position)

The hyphen is not used with other terms including Greek letters:

> α granule *or* alpha granule
> β cell *or* beta cell
> β chain *or* beta chain
> β streptococci *or* beta streptococci
> β thalassemia *or* beta thalassemia

8-12

WORD USAGE IN THE LIFE SCIENCES

Synonyms

There is often more than one acceptable term for the same entity. In some cases, it may be appropriate to introduce important synonyms at first mention of a term, and then use one of the terms exclusively thereafter:

> *Axons* (*axis cylinders*) are present in all neurons. . . . The Schwann cells ensheath the axons.

In other cases, alternative terms can be introduced together, and either one used thereafter:

> . . . the *hypophysis,* or *pituitary gland,* . . . .
> . . . *erythrocytes,* or *red blood cells,* . . . .

When an eponymic term is synonymous with a descriptive term and equally appropriate, choose one to use consistently throughout a passage or work:

> calcaneal tendon *or* Achilles tendon
> citric acid cycle *or* Krebs cycle
> islets of the pancreas *or* pancreatic islets *or* islets of Langerhans
> Mongolian wild horse *or* Przewalski's horse
> trisomy 21 syndrome *or* Down's syndrome (*not* mongolism or mongoloid
> idiocy)
> uterine tube *or* fallopian tube

Commonly Confused Terms

Some of the pairs of terms given in Table 8-6 have closely related or associated meanings, creating recurrent problems of usage. Other pairs, although unrelated in meaning and normally not associated with one another, nevertheless invite typographic or editing errors in certain contexts.

Medical Jargon

Imprecise or elliptical expressions characteristic of medical jargon should be avoided if possible:

> left ventricular failure (*not* left heart failure)
> normal individuals, subjects (*not* normals)
> serological findings (*not* serology)
> test the patient's urine with a Clinitest reagent strip (*not* clinitest the
> patient's urine)
> 24-h urine samples (*not* 24-h urines)

Symptomatology, etiology, and *pathology* should not be used for *symptom, cause,* and *disease* or *abnormality* in referring to particular phenomena, as opposed to the general phenomena, of a disease:

> The patient's symptoms (*not* symptomatology) suggested anemia.
> Coronary atherosclerosis is the most common cause (*not* etiology) of angina
> pectoris.
> No abnormality (*not* pathology) was found on biopsy.

case, client, patient Do not refer to a person as a case. A *case* is the instance of disease, not the person afflicted. A *patient* is a person under medical care. In nursing practice, the term *client* is sometimes preferred to *patient*, especially when the term refers to an outpatient.

TABLE 8-6 SOME COMMONLY CONFUSED TERMS

TERM	MEANING OR USE	EXAMPLES AND COMMENTS
Adrenalin	a pharmaceutical trademark for epinephrine	
adrenaline	the colloquial American and official British name for epinephrine	
albumen	egg white	
albumin	a type of protein found in egg white and elsewhere	
calix, calyx	a cuplike structure	renal calix *or* calyx
calyx	the outer sheath of a flower; the sepals	
chitin	a constituent of arthropod exoskeletons	
chiton	a kind of mollusk	
cyst(o)-	bladder	cystoscopy (examination of the urinary bladder)
cyt(o)-	cell	cytoscopy (examination of cells)
dilatation	a dilated condition or structure	dilatation of the pupil (condition) a venous dilatation (structure)
dilation	the process of dilating or becoming dilated	dilation of the pupil (process) *but* dilatation and curettage [process (exception)]
facial	of the face or facies	
fascial	of a fascia	
-gram	a recording	electrocardiogram
-graph	a recording apparatus	electrocardiograph *but* photograph, radiograph (exceptions)
ileum	part of the small intestine	
ilium	part of the hipbone	
insulin	a pancreatic hormone	
inulin	a plant polysaccharide used in medical tests	inulin clearance test
malarial	of or pertaining to malaria	malarial mosquitoes, malarial fever
malarious	infested or infected with malaria	malarious regions, malarious populations
mucus	noun	
mucous	adjective	mucous glands, mucous membrane, mucous secretion (a secretion containing mucus) *but* mucus secretion (the process of secreting mucus)

TABLE 8-6   SOME COMMONLY CONFUSED TERMS (*Continued*)

TERM	MEANING OR USE	EXAMPLES AND COMMENTS
osteal	of bone	often in combination, e.g., periosteal
ostial	of an ostium	
palpation	examination by touch	
palpitation	rapid throbbing or fluttering	
renin	a renal proteolytic enzyme	
rennin	an enzyme from calf's rennet	
-stomy	the operation of forming an opening, or stoma, into a part of the body	appendicostomy, colostomy, tracheostomy
-tomy	the operation of cutting, or making an incision, into a part of the body	appendectomy, colotomy, tracheotomy
tubercular	of a tubercle	
tuberculous	of tuberculosis	
-urea	a specified kind of urea	nitrosourea (urea with an —NH group)
-uria	a urinary condition	nitrituria (nitrites in the urine)
vesical	adjective: pertaining to a bladder	
vesicle	noun: a small sac or blister (adjective: vesicular)	

GRAMMAR, USAGE, AND PUNCTUATION

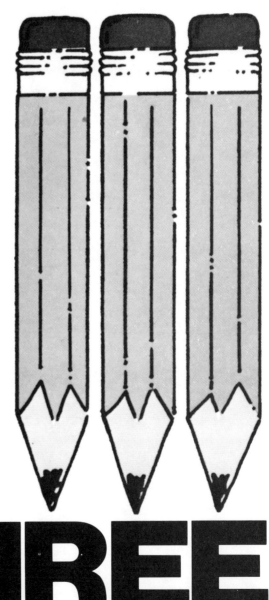

THREE

9

GRAMMAR
AND USAGE

This chapter illustrates the problems of grammar, syntax, word usage, and spelling that seem to occur most frequently in written text. No matter how skillful and literate the author or how painstaking the copy editor, scarcely a manuscript goes to the compositor without some form of language-related error in the text. Some errors are oversights caused by fatigue or haste; others are deliberate infractions (occasionally used for effect); but often an error is the result of misinterpretation or misapplication of a rule.

The word *rule* in this context is misleading: literary style is not established by fiat. Rather, language is governed, at any period in its history, by certain widely accepted *conventions* that have been found to improve the precision and clarity of communication between writer (or speaker) and reader (or listener).

Because language is subject to differences of opinion and taste, some of the recommendations in this chapter may seem controversial, especially to readers who believe that infinitives must not be split or that *however* must not be used at the beginning of a sentence. Nevertheless, the standards set forth here reflect contemporary preferences and are presented with what we hope are convincing arguments in their support.

For information on the mechanics of writing—organizing the material, constructing paragraphs, holding the reader's attention, and so forth—consult the bibliography.

a/an Words beginning with a vowel or an unsounded *h* are preceded by *an:*

    an igloo
    an hour
    an honorary degree

177

Words beginning with a consonant, a sounded *h,* or a *u* sound are preceded by *a:*

a test	a utility
a hierarchy	a European
a historical novel	

An historical is an archaism to be avoided. One is not tempted to write *an horse.*

-able/-ible and other troublesome endings　Is it contempt*able* or contempt*ible?* Pench*ant* or pench*ent?* There's no need to overload your memory circuits with these minor spelling variations. Keep a dictionary at hand, and use it.

accommodate　This is one of the most commonly misspelled words in the language; watch for the two *m*'s.

adverbs without -ly　There is a commonly held misconception that an adjective can become an adverb only by the addition of *-ly.* Even if that were so, the rule would not apply to idioms and aphorisms; you would never think of saying "playing fast and loosely." *Loose* has its own dictionary entry as an adverb and is used in many familiar combinations: *loose-fitting clothes, loose-woven fabric.*

　　Many other adverbs are identical in form to adjectives. We say hit *hard,* traveling *light, wide*-ranging. As Follett (*Modern American Usage*) points out, those who disapprove of the road sign *drive slow* would never say *widely awake.*

　　See also "Linking Verbs" below.

affect/effect　As a verb, *affect* means to call forth a response from or have a result on, and *effect* means simply to cause or produce:

> Bad weather may *affect* the outcome of the game. (Bad weather may *have a result on* the outcome.)
> A high-pressure area over the Great Lakes may *effect* a change in the weather. (A high-pressure area may *cause* a change in the weather.)

As a noun, *effect* means result. The noun *affect* is used chiefly in medicine and psychology to mean an emotional state.

age bias ("ageism")　See Section 12-6.

all are not/not all are

>   *Wrong:* All juveniles are not delinquent.
>   *Wrong:* All flowers do not thrive in full sunlight.

These sentences illustrate a common misconstruction. They are factually incorrect. *All* juveniles (or flowers) means *every* juvenile (or flower), and so these sentences are saying that no juvenile is delinquent and that no flower thrives in full sunlight. But of course some juveniles *are* delinquent and some flowers *do* thrive in full sunlight. "All are not" doesn't mean "not all are," and a thoughtful person will make the distinction.

alternate/alternative   *Alternate* implies a taking of turns in succession. *Alternative* carries the implication of choice. Odd and even numbers occur *alternately,* but a problem that can be solved in more than one way has *alternative* solutions. As an idiomatic exception, two roads leading to the same place are generally referred to as *alternate* routes.

among/between   A frequently cited "rule" states that *between* cannot be used for more than two items. Changing *between* to *among* is not always preferable, however. Consider, for example, the expression "quarrels between family members." If that means quarrels between brother and sister, aunt and grandparent, or any other twosome within the group, it would be incorrect, or at least not entirely accurate, to speak of quarrels *among* the members. Use *between* whenever you want to stress one-to-one relationships, no matter how many members are in the set.

appraise/apprise   To *appraise* means to evaluate; to *apprise* means to inform:

>   *Wrong:* Managers were *appraised* of the company's new policy on absenteeism.
>   *Right:* Managers were *apprised* (informed) of the company's new policy on absenteeism.
>   *Wrong:* Managers are *apprised* on their ability to meet company objectives.
>   *Right:* Managers are *appraised* (evaluated) on their ability to. . . .

Note the prepositions: appraised *on,* apprised *of.*

as to   *As to* is often used at the beginning of a sentence ("As to the results of the experiment, . . ."), but it should be removed or replaced by a single word when it appears elsewhere:

> *Poor:* He was asked *as to* why the balloon had drifted off course.
> *Preferred:* He was asked *why* the balloon had drifted off course.
> *Poor:* We wondered *as to* the outcome of the tests.
> *Preferred:* We wondered *about* the outcome of the tests.
> *Poor:* Their belief *as to* the divine right of kings. . . .
> *Preferred:* Their belief *in* (or *about,* depending on meaning) the divine right of kings. . . .

at this point in time　　This verbiage is a variation on the shorter but also wordy *at this time,* which is used in place of *at present,* which simply means *now.*

basic fundamental　　*Basic* and *fundamental* are synonyms. The expression *a basic fundamental* is redundant.

belabor/labor the point　　*Belabor* means to beat or strike repeatedly and by extension to attack verbally. *Labor* means to go into elaborate detail. Yet people often write "belabor the point" when the sense of the expression clearly calls for "labor the point." Belabor their knuckles!

Bureau of Standards　　The official name is the National Bureau of Standards, not the U.S. Bureau of Standards.

but as a negative

> *Wrong:* The building affords an impressive performance facility, which cannot *but* encourage. . . .

But in the sense of *only* is itself a negative (here implying *can do nothing but*). It should not be preceded by another negative. Change *cannot but encourage* to *can but encourage* or (better) *can only encourage.*

carat/caret/karat　　A *carat* is a unit of measurement for precious stones. A *caret* is the inverted V used in editing and proofreading to indicate the location of an addition. The *karat* (a variation of *carat*) is a measure of the purity of gold.

cement/concrete　　Even professionals sometimes confuse *cement* with *concrete. Cement,* as the name implies, is an adhesive. One doesn't build anything of cement. The structure would crumble.

center around　　A center is a point or innermost area; to center *on, in,* or *at* something means to concentrate on a point. The expression *center* *around* is merely an inexact way of saying *center on, in,* or *at,* some dictionaries notwithstanding. If one of those terms is not apt, *center around* should probably be changed to *revolve around.*

centigrade/Celsius   These two names represent the same temperature scale, but Celsius is now the preferred term. The Celsius scale is in wide general use, but for scientific work, temperature is measured in kelvins rather than degrees Celsius.

classic/classical   As an adjective, *classic* is generally used to describe something of great and continuing value, a standard of excellence:

> a classic example
> a classic novel

Classical refers to languages, works, or events characteristic of certain periods in history or to those who study them:

> classical Greek
> a classical scholar

collective nouns   One of the most prevalent misconceptions about the English language is that a noun which is not clearly plural (ending in s or some other evidently plural construction) must take a singular verb. But consider the following sentence:

> A number of terms (e.g., foliation, flow cleavage, slaty cleavage) are used to designate special types of rock cleavage.

Some writers would be uncomfortable with *are* in that sentence and would change it to *is,* on the assumption that *number* is singular. But *number* is really a collective noun, and it can be singular or plural as required by sense. Collective nouns are singular if the total group is stressed, but plural if the individuals making up the group are stressed. A good rule to remember is: "*the* number *is,* a number *are.*"

Among the many nouns that can be considered either singular or plural are *army, audience, average, couple, family, group, majority, number, pair, set,* and *variety.*

> An average of 7600 annual openings *are* expected in the social service field over the next five years.

It is the *openings* that are expected—the plural concept takes a plural verb.

> An average of six hours *is* required for construction of the model.

An *average time span* is required—singular concept, singular verb.

> Sharon's family *lives* in San Francisco.
> Sharon's family *are* always squabbling among themselves.

Members of Sharon's family are squabbling.

> This variety of apple *is* sour.
> A variety of apples *are* grown in the Hudson Valley: Jonathans, Cortlands,
>   Miltons . . . .

compare to/compare with   Use *compare with* for comparison of similarities and differences:

> Jones compared her research findings *with* those of her associates.

Use *compare to* for analogy, that is, for saying that one thing is like another:

> Smith compared his boss *to* Machiavelli.

A colleague of mine once put it succinctly: You can compare Brussels with Paris, but Paris only to heaven.

compares favorably   If A compares favorably with B, is A almost as good as B, equal to B, or better than B? The answer is yes to all three. By rights, "A compares favorably" should imply that A has the advantage. But who has not heard a sales pitch that goes something like this: "Here is our genuine plastic reproduction of a Dresden shepherdess. It compares very favorably with the old porcelain model." In other words, A is as good as can be expected.

And there are instances in which the advantages and disadvantages of A and B seem to cancel out and a sort of equality is achieved: "A has fewer speeds and a less convenient control panel, but for the price it compares favorably with B."

Writers who know what they mean should be able to find a less ambiguous way to express comparison.

comprise/compose   You won't confuse these two words if you think of *comprise* as coming from the same root as *prison*. It means "contain, include, embrace." In this sense it is incorrect to say that "spruce, fir, and pine comprise the forest." It is the forest that comprises (contains, includes) the trees. The whole *comprises* the parts; the parts *compose* or *constitute* the whole.

Dictionaries give *comprise* a secondary meaning of "constitute," as in "the chapters that comprise Part 3," but many language authorities consider this usage incorrect. On the other hand, the passive construction, "Part 3 is comprised of seven chapters," seems to have become acceptable, and thus it may not be long before *comprise* loses its distinctive meaning.

consensus of opinion   *Consensus* alone means agreement, or meeting of minds. *Consensus of opinion* is therefore redundant. Use *consensus* alone, and watch the spelling: one *c*, three *s*'s.

continual/continuous   *Continuous* can refer to either time or space, but *continual* denotes only time. For example, one does not speak of a continual line or a continual expanse.

Continuous means uninterrupted or unbroken: a continuous wave, a continuous line, a machine continuously in operation (i.e., running all the time). *Continual* means recurring frequently or at intervals: continual delays, continual interruptions. *Continual* can imply a recurring sequence stretching on in time: continually falling in love, continually smoking cigars.

A person who is *continually* hungry wants to eat frequently. A person who is *continuously* hungry will die of starvation.

correlative conjunctions   *Either/or, neither/nor, not only/but also,* and similar paired expressions are called *correlative conjunctions*. The word *pair*, of course, implies a matched set of two. One of the most common errors in writing is the mismatching of a pair.

Writers sometimes forget that the item following *or* must be parallel to, or cast in the same grammatical mold as, the item following *either*. In short, a pair must match.

Wrong: The motor will either stop or the feed mechanism will jam.

Here the word following *either* is *stop*, a verb. The expression following *or* is a whole clause, or statement: *the feed mechanism will jam*. The reader expected a pair—another verb: either *stop* or *do what?* Rearrange the sentence:

> *Right:* Either *the motor will stop* or *the feed mechanism will jam.*

Now the items following *either* and *or* are parallel in construction.

> *Wrong:* The first microscopes revealed not only the unseen world of single-celled organisms and bacteria, but also sounded the death-knell of the semimagical theories which sought to explain living processes in terms of nitro-aerial spirits.

The words following *not only* ("the unseen world") and *but also* ("sounded") are not parallel. A small transposition solves the problem:

> *Right:* The first microscopes not only *revealed* . . . but also *sounded.* . . .

By the way, it is not true that *not only* must always be complemented by *but also. But* alone or *but . . . as well* is also correct.

> *Right:* Not only Syria but the entire Middle East was affected by the decision.
> *Right:* Erasmus Darwin not only had an extraordinary fondness for food, but was fond of sacrificing to Bacchus as well.

> *Wrong:* We are neither in favor nor are we opposed.
> *Right:* We are neither in favor nor opposed.

In favor and *opposed* are parallel. For another discussion of parallelism, see "Unparallel Series" below.

dangling participles   See "Unattached Modifiers" below.

data are/data is   When *data* is used as the plural of *datum*, it generally takes a plural verb:

> Many data *were* obtained.

In the computer age, however, the word has come to mean a collection or mass of information and, in that sense, has lost its plural connotation:

> Data *is* stored for retrieval.

definition style   *A definition must be phrased in such a way that it rep-resents the same part of speech as the word defined*—a simple rule, frequently violated.

> *Wrong:* **Decompose.** A chemical and physical material breakdown.

Decompose, being a verb, must be defined as a verb: "to break down." The definition above is correct only for the noun: *decomposition.* Here are some other faulty definitions, all culled from the same glossary.

> *Wrong:* **Deflashing.** Covers the range of finishing techniques used to remove flash.

That is not even a definition. It should have been reworded altogether: "Removing flash by any of several finishing techniques."

> *Wrong:* **Foreign object.** Particles that occur as impurities in the material.

Here a singular was defined as a plural.

> *Wrong:* **Isotropic.** Material having the same properties in all directions.

An adjective was defined as a noun.
   To make sure that you have defined a word properly, try substituting the definition for the defined term in a sentence. Both should fit:

> There is a *foreign object* in my soup.
> There is a *particles* (?) in my soup.

dehumanizing language   Try to avoid categorizing people by their age or afflictions. Do not use terms such as *the blind, the deaf, a diabetic, the elderly, an epileptic, the mentally retarded, a terminal case, the young.* Refer instead, if possible, to *blind people, deaf people, person (or patient) with diabetes,* etc.

different from/different than   In comparing one noun form to another, prefer *different from* to *different than*:

> *Right:* Reich's findings were different *from* Adler's.

dilemma   A dilemma involves a choice between equally unpleasant alternatives. The word should not be used to express the mere existence of choice. If you are asked to choose between prison and exile, you probably have a true dilemma; if the choice is between vanilla and strawberry, you haven't.

disability bias ("handicapism")   See Section 12-6.

disbursement/dispersement   *Disbursement* is the paying out of money (from the same root as *bursar* and *la bourse*). *Dispersement* is an act of scattering, although the more usual noun form is *dispersion*. Always take a second look at these two words. Sometimes the two are oddly combined in "dispursement"—there's logic at work there, if not orthographic sophistication. (See "Sound-Alikes" below.)

discreet/discrete   *Discreet* means prudent. *Discrete* means separate or distinct. Many an inexperienced copy editor unfamiliar with *discrete* has changed it to the more familiar *discreet,* with devastating effect. (See "Sound-Alikes" below.)

double entendres   Be alert to words and word combinations that have another meaning in a different context. They are often unintentionally funny:

> Above is a picture of a cart drawn by a horse.
> Cook the rhubarb until tender. Serve it warm with cold cream.

Abbreviations and chemical symbols are sometimes a source of humor too:

> It was known that He is always present in radioactive materials.
> Na has a lower melting point than I.

electric/electrical   Use *electric* in describing anything that produces, carries, or is activated by an electric current:

> electric appliance
> electric charge
> electric circuit

Use *electrical* in describing things that pertain to but do not contain or carry electricity:

> electrical analog
> electrical engineer

enormity/enormousness   Enormity means outrageousness; enormousness refers to size.

ensure/insure/assure   Ensure is used in the general sense of *to make sure.* Insure means to protect financially against loss, as of life or property. Assure, although often used in place of the other two words, means to give confidence to or to state that a thing is certain or true and usually has one or more persons or a personal pronoun as its object.

> We took the car to a friend's repair shop to *ensure* a good job.
> The mechanic *assured* us the transmission was fixed.
> Fortunately, the car was *insured.*

extent of emphasis   The following sentence contains a minor but common inconsistency:

> If educators really believed in teaching "the individual pupil," there would be no need for separate emphasis on the "different pupil."

Two parallel terms are set off in quotation marks in this sentence, but the amount of material inside the quotes differs. There is no reason to include the article *the* in the first set of quotation marks.

As a general rule, when emphasizing a word or phrase, italicize or use quotation marks for the term only, not its article:

> known as a "bender"
> called a *flip-flop*
> The report recommends a "systematic changeover."

When emphasizing a full clause or sentence, include the article:

> The report concludes that *a lengthy period of transition will be required.*

These are minor points, to be sure, but consistency in minor details is often the difference between a good book and an excellent one.

extra syllables   Do not let an extra syllable (usually an extra *i*) slip into words. Classic examples are "mayorality" (for *mayoralty*) and "Westminister" (for *Westminster*).

farther/further   In general, use *farther* for distance, *further* for time or quantity:

Rose traveled *farther* than Felix.
He studied the subject *further*.

fewer/less   *Fewer* is used for a number of things, and *less* is used for a
single amount or a mass:

To lower cholesterol, eat *fewer* eggs and *less* saturated fat.

The misuse of *less* in advertising copy ("New! Contains less calories!") is
tiresome. Note, however, that quantities expressed with a unit of measurement are usually thought of as singular (see "Singular and Plural" in
Section 3-2), and thus the following constructions are correct:

less than 10 kilometers
less than 10 years

flaunt/flout   *Flaunt* means to wave or display. *Flout* means to make a
mockery of. Those who speak of "flaunting the law" are therefore flouting
the precepts of good usage.

focus on/focus around   To *focus* is to converge on a point. *Focus around*
is therefore a contradiction in terms. One focuses *on*, not *around*, the subject or job at hand.

forego/forgo   To *forego* means to precede or go before. To *forgo* means
to abstain from or give up (something). (See "Sound-Alikes" below.)

foreword/forward   A common error is the use of *forward* for *foreword*
(and the astonishing compromise *foreward*). The *words* be*fore* the text are
the *foreword*. (See "Sound-Alikes" below.)

fortuitous/fortunate   A fortuitous result may indeed be fortunate, but not
necessarily. *Fortuitous* means accidental, and the outcome may be lucky
or it may not. The word should not be used as a synonym for *fortunate*.

gamut/gantlet/gauntlet   These three words aren't used much these days
in their original senses; perhaps that is why, as the stuff of metaphor, they
are so widely abused.
    A *gamut* is a musical scale. By extension it is a range of anything
from one extreme to another. A person who has "run the gamut" can be
said to have covered the range of activities designated.
    Gantlet describes an old form of punishment in which the victim was

forced to run between two rows of people wielding clubs. To "run the gantlet," therefore, is to be severely criticized or to undergo an ordeal.

A *gauntlet* is a glove. To "throw down the gauntlet" is to challenge someone or something. To "take up the gauntlet" is to accept a challenge. So what does "He ran the gauntlet from A to Z" mean? Nothing. Fix it.

To confuse the issue, *gantlet* and *gauntlet*, according to some dictionaries, have interchangeable spellings. But their derivations are not interchangeable, and experts on usage prefer to keep the words distinct: *gantlet* for the ordeal, and *gauntlet* for the dueler's glove and the challenge.

To further confuse the issue, a maverick word appears in these expressions from time to time: If you listen closely, you may hear "run the *gambit*."

gender-related bias ("sexism")   See Section 12-6.

graduate   A person graduates *from* school or college. A school or college graduates the person.

> *Wrong:* Dr. Brucale graduated college in 1967.
> *Right:* Dr. Brucale graduated from college in 1967.
> *Right:* Dr. Brucale was graduated in 1967.

Grecian/Greek   Generally, use *Greek* except in idiomatic expressions such as *"Grecian* urn" and *"Grecian* sandals."

historic/historical   *Historic* is preferred in the sense of momentous or famous:

> historic occasions
> a historic speech

Historical means related to history:

> historical accuracy

historical present   See "The Universal Present."

hopefully   There are two points of view about this word, and both are presented here.

Argument 1   Since *hopefully* means "in a hopeful manner," it should not be used when the intended meaning is "it is hoped that."

Right: Hopefully, he waited for his agent's call.

That sentence is correct because he (the subject) waited in a hopeful manner.

Wrong: Hopefully, profits will be up next year.

That sentence is incorrect because profits are not hopeful—people are.

Argument 2 *Hopefully* has gone the way of certain other unattached adverbs and is now widely used in the sense of "it is hoped that." It does not have to modify anything, but rather expresses a point of view. "Hopefully, profits will be up" is no less correct than the following examples:

Fortunately, the lab was insured.
Regrettably, Dunphy's horse lost.

We hope you will subscribe to argument 1, but can't blame you for giving up and accepting argument 2.

however at the beginning of a sentence *However* indicates contrast between two ideas. *It belongs wherever sense requires it,* and often that is smack at the beginning of a sentence:

The service was unusually slow. However, I did not complain.

Moving *however* to any other part of this sentence tends to create false emphasis because the contrasted elements are no longer clear:

I, however, did not complain. (Implies that someone else did—undue emphasis on *I.*)
I did, however, not complain. (Places awkward emphasis on *did.*)
I did not, however, complain. (Implies that you thought I did, or that I should have—emphasis on *not.*)
I did not complain, however. (Implies that I did something else—emphasis on *complain.*)

In a long sentence especially, the connective word should be placed where it helps the reader the most.

immortal Always look twice at the spelling of this word, especially when you are proofreading. It lends itself to printer's error, as in "the immoral poetry of Emily Dickinson."

imply/infer These words are not synonymous. To *imply* is to suggest or signify. To *infer* is to deduce or guess.

> In *Testament of Youth*, Britton *implied* that war is cruel and futile. One *infers* from reading it that the author was a pacifist.

its/it's One of the most common errors in written English is the misuse of *it's* as a possessive.

> *Wrong:* The starling intimidated the smaller bird with it's bulk and made swiping attacks with it's bill.

Its (no apostrophe) is the possessive of *it* (*its* bulk; *its* bill). *It's* is a contraction of *it is* or *it has.*

> *Right:* It's a nice day. (It is a . . . .)
> *Right:* It's been an interesting trip. (It has been an . . . .)

The error often has nothing to do with illiteracy but is merely the result of carelessness. (See "Sound-Alikes" below.)

knot A knot is one nautical mile per hour and thus a measure of speed. "Knots per hour" is incorrect.

lay/lie There seem to be no good mnemonics for these words. One simply has to memorize the correct forms. The intransitive verb is *lie:*

> We *lie* in the sun now.
> We are *lying* in the sun.
> We *lay* in the sun yesterday.
> We have *lain* in the sun.

The transitive verb is *lay:*

> We *lay* the package on the desk now.
> We are *laying* the package on the desk.
> We *laid* the package on the desk yesterday.
> We have *laid* the package on the desk.

like as a conjunction The use of *like* as a conjunction is now widespread, although deprecated by many.

> *Poor:* The results were inconclusive, *like* they had been before.
> *Preferred:* The results were inconclusive, *as* they had been before.

> *Poor:* He ran *like* he had wings on his feet.
> *Preferred:* He ran *as though* (or *as if*) he had wings on his feet.
> *Poor:* The car rattled *like* an old jalopy does.
> *Preferred:* The car rattled *like* an old jalopy.

From these examples, it should be clear that a thing can be like another *thing,* but not like another thing *is.*

like (and *unlike*) **in invalid comparisons**   Careless writers often use *like* and *unlike* to create apple-and-orange comparisons:

> *Wrong:* Unlike the nineteenth century, workers today have formed strong unions to protect their rights.

Workers can be neither like nor unlike the nineteenth century.

> *Wrong:* Like bees attracted to nectar, the lure of gold brought swarms of prospectors into the Yukon.

The lure of gold is neither like nor unlike bees.

Bring the comparison into focus by locating the true subject and recasting the sentence:

> *Right:* Unlike laborers in the nineteenth century, workers today have formed strong unions to protect their rights.
> *Right:* Like bees attracted to nectar, prospectors swarmed into the Yukon.

linking verbs   Which is correct: "I feel bad" or "I feel badly"? "She looks happy" or "She looks happily"? Most people instinctively say the right thing ("I feel bad"; "She looks happy") but feel uncomfortable about it. They probably remember something about an adverb's being needed to modify a verb. *Feel* is a verb; surely it must always be modified by an adverb: *badly. Look* is a verb, and so *happily* must be right. Wrong.

In these constructions *bad* and *happy* are adjectives describing the condition of the subject. The verbs *feel* and *look* are not being modified. Instead they link the adjective (or other complement) to its subject; they are called *linking verbs.* Other linking verbs are *be, keep, remain, prove, become, get, grow, turn, act, appear, seem, taste, smell,* and *sound.*

Use an adverb if you want to say how an action is performed:

A willow grows quickly.

But use an adjective if you want to describe a condition:

> A willow grows beautiful with age.
> Roses smell good.
> Keep your work station clean.

literally   Do not say *literally* unless you mean "as actually meant or described by the words." The humor in mistaken uses—which seem more prevalent than correct ones—is evident from the following examples:

> Mammalogy courses increased in number gradually until after World War II, when they literally exploded.
> His performance literally brought the house down.
> The thought of growing begonias from seed literally scared me to death. (From an article in a gardening journal—literally a ghost-written article?)

loathe/loath   *Loathe* is a verb meaning "to detest":

> Felix *loathes* broccoli.

Loath is an adjective meaning "unwilling, reluctant":

> Felix is *loath* to eat broccoli.

The two words are not interchangeable. You can remember the verb form more easily by recalling that soft *-the* is a common verb ending: *bathe, breathe, writhe.*

manner born/manor born   A good way to lose a bet is to put your money on "to the *manor* born." It's "to the *manner* born" (*Hamlet*, act 1, scene 4).

metaphors and similes   A *simile* is a figure of speech in which one thing is likened to another. Most similes contain the word *like* or *as.*

> *Simile:* Her eyes as stars of twilight fair . . . . (Wordsworth)

A metaphor, on the other hand, likens by asserting that one thing *is* another:

> *Metaphor:* Eyes are the windows of the soul.

At their worst, similes and metaphors are the stuff of cliché:

> *Similes:* He had a voice like thunder.
>   She was fit as a fiddle.
> *Metaphors:* His life was an open book.
>   Her contribution was a drop in the bucket.

At their best, similes and metaphors are powerful devices in the hands of a good writer:

> London was like some huge prehistoric animal, capable of enduring terrible injuries, mangled and bleeding from many wounds, and yet preserving its life and movement. (W. S. Churchill)
> To the south and east the double islands watched silently the double ship that seemed fixed among them forever, a hopeless captive of the calm, a helpless prisoner of the shallow sea. (Conrad)

Mixed metaphors Hackneyed expressions are often used without thought to their literal meaning; when they occur in tandem, the images sometimes fail to correspond. Try to keep related metaphors in the same family; don't, for example, mix a nautical expression with a baseball cliché:

> Steer a straight course or you'll strike out.

Sometimes three or more unrelated images are ludicrously combined:

> The shifting sands of political opinion had produced a new tidal wave of grass-roots reaction.

militate/mitigate Because they sound somewhat alike, *militate* and *mitigate* are often confused, as in the following example:

> *Wrong:* Several factors *mitigate against* the accurate perception of self.

To *mitigate* means to alleviate or become milder. To *militate* means to have an effect (on a fact or a conclusion) and is generally used in a negative sense with *against*. The sentence above surely does not mean that accurate perception becomes "milder" as a result of certain factors; it means that those factors interfere with or distort (have a negative effect on) the perception. The author must have intended to say *militate against*.

minority-group bias ("racism")   See Section 12-6.

none   *None* is one of many words that can be construed as either singular or plural, depending on the meaning to be conveyed.

> *Right:* He looked for solace, but none was forthcoming.

The singular intention is clear—there was no solace.

> *Right:* He looked for his friends, but none were there.

The plural intention is clear—his friends were not there. A writer wishing to emphasize the singular could write "but not one was there."

The argument that *none* was originally a contraction of *no one* or *not one* is not reason enough to insist on a singular interpretation forever. Respected writers have used *none* with a plural verb for centuries.

In the construction *none of . . .* , the object of the preposition generally determines the verb:

> *Right:* None of the wood (singular) *has* warped (singular).
> *Right:* None of the buildings (plural) *are* fireproof (plural).

parenthetical cross-references   In referring to an illustration, some authors always run the parenthetical element into the sentence:

> . . . is called a *sprocket thumper* (see Fig. 3-1).

Some always treat it as a separate item:

> . . . is called a *sprocket thumper.* (See Fig. 3-1.)

And some use both methods, cleverly allowing the sense of the reference to dictate its form.

The run-in reference is appropriate only when Fig. 3-1 actually illustrates a sprocket thumper or is otherwise directly related to the sentence to which it is attached. It is *not* appropriate when the figure illustrates more than one sentence, perhaps even a paragraph or more. Thus it is possible for both styles of reference to occur quite properly in the same book.

The same general rule applies, of course, to references to other parts of a book (chapter, table, equation, etc.).

Style note: When the reference is run in, lowercase the *see* and place the final punctuation outside the closing parenthesis. When the reference stands alone, capitalize *See* and place the period inside the closing parenthesis.

phenomenon/phenomena   The singular is *phenomenon;* the plural is *phenomena.*

> *Wrong:* A volcano is a thermal phenomena.
> *Right:* A volcano is a thermal phenomenon.
> *Right:* Volcanoes are thermal phenomena.

prepositions mistaken for conjunctions   *In addition to, along with, as well as, together with,* and similar terms are prepositions, not conjunctions. These terms do not alter the number of the verb; in other words, they do not create a compound subject.

> Authority as well as responsibility *rests* with the president.
> Accuracy, together with high sensitivity, speed, and wide range of applicability, *makes* spectroscopy a useful analytical approach.
> Interest in another's point of view, along with the ability to resist interrupting, *is* characteristic of a good listener.

Sometimes a writer who is given to wordiness uses these longer expressions merely to avoid writing *and,* with which a plural verb would be correct. When you mean *and,* why not say it?

quite   This word suffers from having two irreconcilable meanings. "Quite full" can mean either "completely full" or "almost but not completely full." The meaning "almost but not completely" seems to be more prevalent these days—"quite a good game" is something less than "a very good game." The original meaning comes across, however, in phrases such as "you are quite mistaken," which means, of course, that you are totally mistaken. When you use *quite,* make certain that its meaning is not ambiguous.

redundancy   Wordiness wastes valuable space on the printed page and puts the reader's mind to sleep. Here are some examples of saying the same thing twice (in each example the italic word is redundant):

> increasingly *more* complex
> were combined *together*
> reset it *back* at zero
> The two researchers *both* discovered it simultaneously.

relation/relationship   In the following expressions, *relation* is used correctly:

>the relation of music to mathematics
>trade relations between Europe and Latin America

Relationship is usually applied to personal association or kinship:

>the relationship between teachers and students
>Sara and Joanna are probably distant cousins, but their relationship isn't clear.

say   The word *say* (meaning "for instance" or "approximately") is followed by a comma when it introduces a complement, but not when it introduces an appositive:

>a balloon containing, say, helium
>any gas, say helium, . . .

scan/skim   To *scan* is to read or examine closely. To *skim* is to read quickly or lightly. These two words are often confused.

shall/will   Conventional grammar teaches that the auxiliary verbs *shall* and *will* are used like this to express futurity:

>I shall   we shall
>you will   you will
>he, she, it will   they will

To express strong determination or requirement, the auxiliary verbs are reversed:

>I *will* have a tantrum.
>You *shall* leave at once.

There's an old story about a despondent Victorian gentleman who, as he was about to go under, cried out, "I will drown! No one shall save me!" Respecting his wishes, no one did. Today, of course, he would be in danger of rescue, because his chances of being overheard by a conservative grammarian are slim.

The distinction between futurity and emphasis seems to have been lost in casual speech, although the emphatic form survives vigorously in codes, standards, legal documents, and commands:

Rivets shall show a maximum hardness of Rockwell B 60 as measured on
the side of the shank.

The bearing surface shall be at right angles to the body within 2 degrees.

Thou shalt not kill.

so   Two informal uses of the word *so* are generally edited out of formal
writing.

1   When *so* introduces a clause of purpose or result, change it to *so
that*:

Two distinctive patterns of shading should be used *so that* the difference
will be apparent.

2   When *so* has the meaning of *therefore*, many writers prefer to say
and so:

This requirement is seen to be contrary to the ideal conditions for high
breakdown voltage discussed above, *and so* some compromise is necessary.

In informal writing there is no reason not to use plain *so* for both these
meanings.

sound-alikes   Some words lend themselves to spelling errors. Consider
how often *their* and *there*, *its* and *it's*, *brake* and *break* are confused in the
work of even the most careful authors. They know how to spell; the problem is that they skip past sound-alike words, accepting what they hear
instead of what they see. There is no moral here except to exhort writers
and editors to look twice at any word that sounds like another word. It may
turn out to be another word.

split infinitives   *To understand* is an infinitive. *To better understand* is a
"split" infinitive, because a word has been inserted between *to* and *understand*. Many people have been led to believe that splitting an infinitive is
wrong, and they will distort both syntax and meaning to avoid violating
this arbitrary rule. But consider the sentence:

To better understand the complexities of twentieth-century harmony, the
student of musical theory must realize that tonality, as generally understood in the eighteenth and nineteenth centuries, has outlived its usefulness.

Is there a graceful way to avoid the split infinitive in that sentence? *Better
to understand the complexities* sounds strained. *To understand better the*

complexities sounds unnatural. *To understand the complexities of twentieth-century harmony better* places *better* a long way from the word it modifies. The sentence as originally written seems compact and sensible in comparison with its alternatives.

Good writers use the split infinitive freely. Fowler *(Modern English Usage)* and other authorities agree that there is no grammatical basis for the stricture against splitting infinitives. Let's not perpetuate an ill-founded rule, but be guided in all instances by sound and sense.

subject and complement

> *Right:* Computers programmed to draw perspectives are a useful tool in architectural design.

Thinking that a complement must be plural if the subject is plural, some people would mistakenly change *a useful tool* to *useful tools* in that sentence. Although it is true that a verb must agree in number with its subject *(computers are)*, there is no rule, written or unwritten, that the complement *(a useful tool)* must also agree. Many things may be one thing, and one many.

According to Fowler *(Modern English Usage,* under "Number"), we may say "Our only guide was the stars" or "The stars were our only guide." Fowler does not even vaguely suggest revising a sentence when subject and complement are of different number. Follett *(Modern American Usage),* however, advises writers to avoid disparity in number if they are made uncomfortable by it. "No one," says Follett, "has to write a construction and like it just because it is demonstrably correct."

Many unnecessary and even ill-considered rules for "good" writing exist. Writers and editors who reword to avoid nonagreement of subject and complement are imposing an arbitrary rule where none is needed or desirable. Literary precedents abound:

> Literary men are . . . a perpetual priesthood. (Carlyle)
> Fools are my theme. (Byron)
> The ornament of a house is the friends who frequent it. (Emerson)

the subjunctive   Except in certain idiomatic expressions and in poetry, the traditional uses of the subjunctive mood have dwindled. There are now only two general constructions that regularly require the subjunctive.

1 *Hypothesis contrary to fact*   In sentences of the "If I were king" variety, it is customary to use the subjunctive. Compare these two sentences:

> If it was an order, it was obeyed.
> If it were an order, it would be obeyed.

The first sentence is a simple statement of something that was true in the past; if signifies "when," and the subjunctive is not used. The second sentence, on the other hand, implies that "it" is not an order; the statement is a hypothesis about what would happen if it were, and the subjunctive is used. In the second sentence, time is understood to be present or future, in spite of the past-tense were.

Of course, with I, he, she, one, and it we can see the subjunctive in action with irregular verbs, because these pronouns take an unusual form of the verb. With we, you, and they the verb form doesn't change, but the context still alerts us to what's going on:

> If you had a horse, you were considered well-to-do. (Past tense)
> If you had a horse, you wouldn't have to walk. (Subjunctive)

The same distinction applies to other verb tenses as well:

> If you had had a horse, you wouldn't have had to walk. (Subjunctive)

The subjunctive is so well established in this contrary-to-fact context that "if I was you" sounds illiterate to a great many people, although oddly enough the locution was common a hundred years ago and is therefore an example of a trend in reverse.

2 *With wishes, recommendations, and exhortations followed by "that"* The subjunctive mood is used in the following sentences:

> It is important that you read the directions.
> I wish (that) he were here.
> It is essential that this be done quickly.
> I'll buy it on condition that it work.

It is also used with *lest* or *for fear that:*

> Be careful what you do, lest you be thought irresponsible.

The subjunctive is losing ground in these contexts; we often encounter sentences like "I wish he was here." Pity.

When to avoid the subjunctive As noted above, *if* does not always introduce a contrary-to-fact condition. Use the indicative verb form, not the subjunctive, in statements of concession, supposition, and doubt:

> If the treaty is (not *be*) signed, the troops will be withdrawn.
> If she plays trombone, she can join the band.

Whenever you can read *whether* for *if,* you can safely forget the subjunctive:

> She asked him if (whether) he was (not *were*) planning to attend.

that/which The choice between *that* and *which* in restrictive and nonrestrictive clauses depends on a few fairly simple rules.

In nonrestrictive clauses, use *which* preceded by a comma:

> Please return *Pride and Prejudice,* which is overdue.

In this sentence the clause *which is overdue* does not serve to specify the book; it merely provides additional information about it and can be removed without destroying the essential meaning of the sentence. It is a *nonrestrictive clause.*

In restrictive clauses, use either *that* or *which* without a comma:

> You'll have to pay for the library book that you lost.

In this sentence the clause *that you lost* specifies the book; in other words, it restricts the meaning to that book and no other and is essential to the sense of the sentence. It is therefore a *restrictive clause.*

Some writers prefer to use *that* exclusively in this construction, but *which* is so firmly established both in the vernacular and in literature that the distinction often seems arbitrary. However, even when *that* is the preferred word, there is a common exception: Many people prefer *which* in the expressions *that which, those which, this which,* and *these which:*

> These are the values *which* are being tested.

Please don't construe this discussion to mean that restrictive *thats* and *whiches* must always be supplied. Writing is often tighter and more euphonious without them:

> the book you lost
> the values being tested

Beware, too, the phantom *which* (or *that*):

> *Wrong:* The values we learned from our parents *and which* we live
> by . . . .

The *and which* requires the presence of a previous *which* to support it:

> *Right:* The values *which* we learned from our parents *and which* we live
> by . . . .

In nearby but unrelated restrictive clauses within a sentence, *that* or *which* may be changed to avoid repetition. Do not make this kind of change, however, if the two *that* or *which* clauses are related (attached to the same noun or parallel in some other way):

> Species *which* have become extinct as well as species *which* have survived . . . .

throughout the entire   The expression is redundant. *Throughout* implies entirety.

> *Wrong:* Philadelphia outplayed the Rangers throughout the entire series.

Throughout the series suffices; delete *entire*.

titles in text   A title is the name of a work and should not be used as part of the substance of a sentence:

> *Wrong:* Gesell's book on *The Child from Five to Ten*
> *Right:* Gesell's book *The Child from Five to Ten*
> *Right:* Gesell's book on the child from five to ten

An article at the beginning of a title may be dropped (1) after a possessive, (2) to avoid doubling of articles, and (3) in an abridged or familiar title:

> Sheridan's *Rivals*
> a *New Yorker* drawing
> a performance of *Merry Wives*

unattached modifiers   The best-known example of an unattached modifier is the *dangling participle,* but the problem takes other forms as well.

Whenever a descriptive or modifying element is placed in such a way as to modify the wrong term or to dangle in the sentence without relating to anything at all, it qualifies as an unattached modifier. The offending item can be a prepositional phrase, an adjective, an infinitive, a clause, an appositive—any element that should be closely connected to another element, but isn't.

> *Wrong:* While still a young man, the idea of personality as a dynamic process excited his interest.

The reader expects a man's name or a male pronoun to follow the words *while still a young man*, but neither is forthcoming. Reword:

> *Right:* While still a young man, *he* was excited by the idea of personality as a dynamic process.

Another example:

> *Wrong:* In poor health and out of work, the city seems a grim place indeed.

This sentence implies that the city is in poor health and out of work, when what is meant is:

> *Right:* To someone in poor health and out of work, the city seems a grim place indeed.

Sometimes the modifier is clumsily attached to a possessive:

> *Wrong:* Born in Chicago, her first visit to Easter Island convinced her that anthropology would be her life's work.

Because the subject of the sentence is *her first visit,* the modifier implies that the *visit* was born in Chicago. Don't even try to reword this in one sentence—you'll probably end up with a non sequitur.

Another source of error occurs when the modifier relates to only part of a compound subject:

> *Wrong:* Widowed now, Sarah and her children returned to Mandalay.

The children were not widowed (barring unusual circumstances). Reword:

> *Right:* Widowed now, Sarah returned to Mandalay with her children.

An unattached element can occur anywhere in a sentence:

> Alice Fletcher emerged as a proponent of change in federal Indian policies, culminating in the Dawes Act of 1887.

What, exactly, culminated?
The effect of a dangler is often ludicrous:

> Aging now in oaken casks, we look forward to sampling this year's vintage.
> Hastily summoning an ambulance, the corpse was taken to the mortuary.

Legitimate dangling participles   Note that some participles have lost the need to be identified with a noun:

> Judging by their appearance, the elms were infected.
> Considering that this was her first marathon, Sylvia did well to place fourteenth.

These indefinite participles and several others like them (including *assuming, concerning, given, owing to,* and *provided*) have become respectable by virtue of idiom and familiarity; no reader would expect them to modify a noun.

the universal present   If you think what's past is past, you might be tempted to change the verb *are* to the past tense *were* in the following sentence:

> Pasteur found that antibodies *are* produced by inoculation of rabies virus during the incubation of the disease.

The present tense is preferable, however. Even though the surrounding passage is expressed in the past tense, the present is properly used in stating something that is universally true or that was thought to be true at the time. Here's another example:

> The "control of nature" is a phrase conceived in arrogance, born of the Neanderthal age of biology and philosophy, when it *was supposed* that nature *exists* for the convenience of man. (Rachel Carson, italics added)

Do not confuse the universal present with the *historical present,* which is simply a literary device for recounting past events in a more immediate way. ("The slipper fits, and Cinderella and the Prince live happily ever after.")

unnecessary verbs in comparisons

> Dorothy is taller than I.
> Hilda is shorter than Dorothy.

These sentences are correct as they stand, with the second verb understood. For those who insist on expressing the second verb, the most natural place for it is at the end:

> Dorothy is taller than I am.
> Hilda is shorter than Dorothy is.

You would *not* say "taller than am I" or "shorter than is Dorothy." Why, then, do so many writers put the second verb in the wrong position? In the following examples, the verbs in parentheses are not only unnecessary but awkwardly placed:

> Second and third generations were likely to display more interest in the amenities of wealth than *(were?)* their hard-driving forebears.
> The length of an arc *AP* of a circle is greater than *(is?)* the length of the chord *AP*.

unparallel series   One of the most common and disconcerting errors in writing goes by several names: unparallel series, bastard enumeration, "A, B, 3."

> *Wrong:* Buffon's *Histoire naturelle* was brilliant, lucid, and was issued in forty-four volumes.

> *Wrong:* Such a regressive pattern (1) reflects enlargement of the land; (2) may be more or less destroyed at the top by erosion during regression; (3) shows a seaward shift of sedimentary facies; and (4) the deposits tend to coarsen upward stratigraphically.

In each sentence above we have been led to expect a part of speech that doesn't materialize. In the Buffon sentence we expect a third adjective to go with *brilliant* and *lucid* and get a verb form *(was issued)* instead. In the second sentence we expect a fourth verb and stumble instead on a new clause with a new subject *(the deposits)*.

To fix bastard enumeration, either eliminate the serial-comma construction:

> Buffon's *Histoire naturelle* was brilliant *and* lucid and was issued in forty-four volumes.

or change the faulty part of speech to correspond with the others in the list:

> Such a regressive pattern (1) *reflects* ... ; (2) *may be* ... ; (3) *shows* ... ; and (4) *is characterized* by the tendency of deposits to coarsen upward stratigraphically.

verbs: active or passive?   Strunk and White *(The Elements of Style)* and many other authorities encourage writers to avoid passive construc-tions. That is good advice for writers whose overuse of the passive voice leads to monotony of expression. But there are many situations in which the choice between active and passive depends entirely on the true subject of the sentence. Consider the following passive construction, and ask your-self where its emphasis lies:

> The plants should be watered once a week.

If the purpose of the sentence is to give instructions or directions to a person about an action to be performed, it could be recast with an active verb:

> You should water the plants once a week.

or the imperative:

> Water the plants once a week.

But if it is the plants and what happens to them that are important, not the agent that is going to act upon them, recasting the sentence into the active voice distorts the emphasis.

The moral here is that any rule of good writing should be applied thoughtfully and with discretion. If the passive voice suits your purpose, use it without guilt.

***whether or not*—or not**   Sometimes *or not* is required after *whether*, and sometimes it is redundant. You can easily tell by testing the sentence with-out *or not* to see whether (or not) it still makes sense. (Notice that in the last sentence the parenthetical *or not* is superfluous.)

When *whether* means "if," the existence of an alternative is already implied and you can safely forgo the *or not:*

Dorothy wondered whether she would like the snails.

But when "regardless" or "willy-nilly" is implied, *whether* or *not* (or *whether or no*) is correct:

Dorothy will eat the snails whether she likes them or not.

who/whom   In formal written English, *whom* is still considered the correct relative pronoun to use as the object of a preposition. In spoken English, however, the distinction seems to be fading. In many contexts it takes nerve to say: "Whom shall I give it to?"

It seems odd, then, that so many errors are made by introducing a faulty *whom.*

Wrong: Find an accountant *whom* you think is competent.

When a parenthetical expression of hope, supposition, or the like (in this case "you think") *comes between a relative pronoun and its verb, it does not change the case of the relative pronoun.*

Right: Find an accountant *who* you think is competent.

The relative pronoun *who* is the subject of *is* and remains in the nominative case.

Right: This is the accountant to *whom* I thought you spoke.

Here the relative pronoun *whom* is the object of *spoke to* and remains in the objective case.

words of more syllables than necessary   Mark Twain wrote:

. . . I would do away with those great long compounded words; or require the speaker to deliver them in sections, with intermissions for refreshments. To wholly do away with them would be best, for ideas are more easily received and digested when they come one at a time than when they come in bulk. Intellectual food is like any other; it is pleasanter and more beneficial to take it with a spoon than with a shovel.

Although Twain was talking about compounded German words, writers of English can find a moral here as well. When there is a choice between a complicated word and a simple one, lean toward the simple one. Say *use*, not *utilize*. Say *now*, not *presently*. One virtue of simplicity is that it gets ideas across effectively without undue strain on the reader's eyes. It also extends the life of typewriter ribbons.

wreak/wreck   Havoc and vengeance are *wreaked*, not wrecked. (They are also not racked.)

10

PUNCTUATION

In spoken language, natural pauses, combined with inflections of the voice, contribute important clues to the meaning of the message being conveyed from one person to another. In written language, however, we have to rely on punctuation to serve the same purpose; there is no other way to indicate these clues. A writer who ignores the conventions of punctuation can be likened to a composer who fails to give directions for the speed and expressive quality of the music, which are what enable the performer to interpret it correctly. Like the conventions for musical notation, the conventions for punctuation are fairly well defined (although not necessarily as strict).

To understand which mark of punctuation is best in any given construction, one has to try to understand the construction first. Writers do not, after all, start with a comma and look for a place to put it. They start with a group of words and have to find the mark that best clarifies its structure and meaning. This chapter begins, therefore, by identifying the various situations in which internal punctuation is needed and continues with a discussion of the marks that fulfill those needs.

10-1

TYPES OF SENTENCE

Only three sentence types need to be mastered: the simple sentence, the compound sentence, and the complex sentence. A fourth type is merely a combination of the second and third; it is called the compound-complex sentence.

Simple Sentence
A simple sentence consists of a *subject* (the person or thing that we're talking about) and a *predicate* (what the subject does or what is done to it). Generally a simple sentence expresses only one complete thought:

William S. Gilbert   wrote *The Bab Ballads.*

SUBJECT   PREDICATE

The subject can be compound (that is, consist of two or more nouns, or substantives):

Gilbert and Sullivan   wrote *The Mikado.*

COMPOUND SUBJECT   PREDICATE

And the predicate can be compound (that is, consist of two or more verbs, or actions):

Gilbert   wrote the libretto and supervised the production.

SUBJECT   COMPOUND PREDICATE

Any number of adjectives, adverbs, adverbial and prepositional phrases, and appositives may be added, but the sentence is still a simple sentence if it contains only one subject (compound or not) and only one predicate (compound or not). This, therefore, is a simple sentence:

> In 1885, William S. Gilbert, who wrote the libretto, and Sir Arthur Sullivan, the composer, collaborated on *The Mikado,* a comic opera which, although set in Japan, satirized English customs and pretensions.

This is also a simple sentence:

> Go!

(The subject *you* is understood.)

Compound Sentence

Enter the independent clause. An independent clause is a group of words which contains a subject and a predicate and which could stand alone as a simple sentence. A compound sentence consists of two or more such independent clauses. The clauses, which are sometimes called *coordinate clauses,* are often connected by a conjunction (a joining word, such as *and, but,* or *or*):

Gilbert wrote the libretto, and he supervised the production.

INDEPENDENT CLAUSE   INDEPENDENT CLAUSE

The pronoun *he* is a new subject. The appearance of a new subject is what removes the sentence from the "simple" category; each clause expresses a complete thought. (Compare the second independent clause with the compound predicate illustrated earlier.)

Sometimes no conjunction is used between the clauses:

Gilbert wrote the words;   Sullivan wrote the music.

    INDEPENDENT CLAUSE   INDEPENDENT CLAUSE

In both the foregoing sentences, we could place a period after the first independent clause and make a new sentence out of the remainder. The clauses are therefore independent, but they have been joined (in the one case by *and* and in the other by a semicolon) because they are closely related in thought.

Complex Sentence

The complex sentence consists of a main clause and one or more subordinate, or dependent, clauses. A subordinate clause is one that cannot stand alone because it does not express a complete thought:

They would have produced the opera earlier   if they hadn't quarreled.

    MAIN CLAUSE   SUBORDINATE CLAUSE

Notice that in this sentence the first clause is not a true statement until the condition under which it becomes true is expressed by the second clause. The second clause, by itself, is also an incomplete idea—if they hadn't quarreled, then what? The two clauses combine to make one complete thought.

In formal writing, a subordinate clause standing by itself is considered unacceptable:

The book is entertaining. Even though it is too long.

Such constructions tend to be acceptable, however, when one wants to convey the flavor of informal speech.

Compound-Complex Sentence

A sentence may have any number of main independent clauses with any number of subordinate clauses:

After a serious quarrel, Gilbert and Sullivan collaborated again on several other operas, but their friendship was never fully restored, even though their fame continued to grow.

Summary of Sentence Types

A *simple* sentence has a single subject and predicate:

Simple: _____A_____

A *compound* sentence consists of two or more independent clauses:

Compound: _____A_____ + _____B_____ + · · ·

A *complex* sentence contains one main clause and one or more dependent clauses:

Complex: _____A_____
                        _____a_____

A *compound-complex* sentence contains two or more independent clauses and one or more dependent clauses:

Compound-   _____A_____   + _____B_____
complex: _____a_____   _____b_____

10-2

PUNCTUATION IN SENTENCES

Punctuation between Subject and Predicate

Never use a comma that serves only to separate the subject from the predicate. In a short sentence it is easy to observe that such a comma is incorrect:

Wrong: Sullivan, wrote the music.

But in a longer sentence an unskilled writer will sometimes insert a similar comma without noticing that the subject and its verb have been separated:

Wrong: The unusually long period of drought experienced in the Northeast in 1980, resulted in severe restrictions on water consumption throughout the area.

Always delete the superfluous comma.

Interpolations

Do not confuse the superfluous comma just discussed with the pair of commas used to set off extraneous or parenthetical material:

> Sullivan, by the way, wrote the music.

This is not a question of separating subject from predicate, but of separating an interpolated expression from the rest of the sentence. Commas used for this purpose *always come in pairs*, as do parentheses and dashes if they are used instead of paired commas:

> Two-dimensional bodies do not, of course, exist in nature.
> The members own and (technically) control the cooperative.
> The mouth very rapidly—in fact by the second day after birth—acquires a large number and variety of both pathogenic and nonpathogenic microorganisms.

Notice that in these sentences the portions set off by commas, parentheses, and dashes may be removed from the sentence without destroying the completeness of the thought.

Be alert to supply the missing member of the pair:

> *Wrong:* Our several species of buntings for example, all belong to the order Passeriformes. (Set off *for example* with two commas.)
> *Wrong:* But now the clock—or rather the ticking of the clock, had obtruded into his consciousness. (Use two dashes or two commas—not one of each.)

Punctuation in a Compound Subject

Do not use a comma that serves only to separate two halves of a compound subject:

> *Wrong:* Gilbert, and Sullivan wrote . . . .
> *Wrong:* Interparty rivalries, and attempted coups have long characterized South American political life.

Delete the commas.

In a compound subject consisting of more than two items, use series punctuation (see Section 10-5):

> Red, blue, and yellow are primary colors.

If one of the items in a compound subject is subordinate or might be considered an afterthought, it may be set off by two commas:

> *Optional:* Several sets of stiffener angles(,) and a pair of bars used as stiffeners(,) support the cracking unit.

Punctuation in a Compound Predicate

In general, do not use a comma between parts of a compound predicate:

> *Wrong:* Gilbert wrote the libretto, and supervised the production.
> *Wrong:* Her work reflects her lack of commitment, and substitutes overstatement for creative energy.

There are four exceptions to this general rule, however.

1 If the predicate is composed of a series of three or more items, use series punctuation (see Section 10-5):

> Earle quit school, left home, and became a gunrunner for the Algerians.

2 If the verbs differ in tense or mode, a comma is optional:

> *Optional:* Earle quit school(,) and would have left home if his father had not been sick.

3 If a strong contrast is implied between the parts, a comma is optional:

> *Optional:* Leslie did not finish high school(,) but nevertheless became an eminent engineer.

4 If the parts of a compound predicate are very long, a comma may be used as a pause between them.

> A flat roof, although not as steeply pitched as other roofs, is slightly pitched to carry off the rain(,) and is generally covered with large sheets of roofing material which is supplied to the builder in rolls.

Punctuation in a Compound Sentence

with coordinating conjunction *And, but, or,* and *nor* are called *coordinating conjunctions* because they join coordinate (or equal) things. When they join coordinate clauses, they are usually preceded by a comma:

> Gilbert wrote the libretto, and Sullivan wrote the music.

Sometimes a semicolon is used before the coordinating conjunction, especially if one of the clauses already contains punctuation:

> *Optional:* Gilbert suggested a new plot; but Sullivan, we are told, did not like it.

The semicolon in this instance is not mandatory; a comma usually suffices. However, some sentences are too involved to be easily understood without the extra "stopping" force of a semicolon. Note how incomprehensible the following sentence would be without a semicolon after the term *heat exchangers:*

> The initial cost for the equipment includes expenses for foundations, supports, installation, pumps, blowers, and other auxiliaries such as instruments, controls, and heat exchangers; and operating costs include power for circulating the fluids, maintenance, labor, etc.

(That is an example of a *complicated* compound sentence, not of a *good* one. A better writer would undoubtedly have broken it in two.)

British writers tend to use no punctuation between the halves of a compound sentence—a practice that readers in the United States sometimes find disconcerting:

> The rainy season comes on with a series of downpours and tiny fishes magically appear in the swollen ponds.

Accustomed to seeing a comma in such sentences, an American reader might not realize right away that *fishes* is the subject of a new clause and wonder instead what "a series of downpours and tiny fishes" might be.

A compound sentence containing a series of three or more independent clauses is punctuated as follows:

> The reagent is allowed to react under mildly alkaline conditions, the excess reagent is then removed, and the protein is hydrolized with $6N$ HCl.

If any one of these clauses were complicated by further punctuation, semicolons would usually be used instead of the commas.

without coordinating conjunction When independent clauses are not joined by *and, but, or,* or *nor,* use a semicolon:

> Gilbert suggested a new plot; Sullivan did not like it.

Conjunctive adverbs are often used as transitional words between clauses. Among them are words like *consequently, hence, however, moreover, nevertheless, otherwise, therefore,* and *thus.* When used in this way, these adverbs are preceded by a semicolon, never a comma. *However* is always followed by a comma:

> Some complaints may be handled at the precinct station; however, General Order No. 14 requires that such complaints be passed on to Review Board headquarters.

But with the others the comma may be omitted at the writer's discretion, without regard to consistency:

> Alpha particles have zero spin; hence the total spin must also be zero.

In very short sentences, a comma after the conjunctive adverb seems especially superfluous:

> I think; therefore I am.

comma fault   Use of a comma rather than a semicolon between independent clauses not joined by *and, but, or,* or *nor* is a common error known as *comma fault* or *comma splice:*

> *Wrong:* Gilbert suggested a new plot, Sullivan liked it.
> *Wrong:* The feasibility study is an aspect of capital budgeting, therefore techniques used in capital budgeting are equally useful for feasibility studies.
> *Wrong:* Some transactional information requires longer processing time, in this event priorities must be assigned to incoming data.

In each of the three sentences above, the solution is to replace the comma with a period or a semicolon or to insert a coordinating conjunction after the comma.

the short compound sentence   If the clauses in a compound sentence are closely related and *very short,* they may, as an exception, be joined without punctuation:

> *Optional:* The fog lifted and the sun came out.

Punctuation in a Complex Sentence
Subordinate clauses that follow the main clause are generally not preceded by a comma:

The troops were sent home after the war was over.
The police are sometimes the focus of resentment because they represent
authority.

If the subordinate clause is introductory, however, it is followed by a comma:

After the war was over, the troops were sent home.
Because the police represent authority, they are sometimes the focus of
resentment.

(Remember that a clause contains a subject and a verb. "After the war was over" is a clause; "after the war," merely a phrase.)

10-3

MORE ABOUT CLAUSES

Restrictive and Nonrestrictive Clauses

restrictive   Clauses that limit or identify (that is, restrict) are not set off by commas:

The two Norwegians *who developed the process* were in their early twenties.

The clause *who developed the process* identifies the two Norwegians we mean.

The building *that had been proposed for the site* did not meet zoning requirements.

The clause in italic type identifies the building.

nonrestrictive   Clauses that do not restrict but merely provide additional information—in other words, that might be removed without altering the meaning of the sentence—are set off by commas:

Petersen and Sverdrup, *who were working in Cambridge,* developed the process.
Something should be said about critical attitudes, *which have not received the attention they deserve.*

In both examples, the italicized clause can be lifted out without altering the main point of the sentence.

Some further examples follow.

> The patients *who were given placebos* exhibited the same rate of improvement as those receiving the medication.

Not any old patients, but specifically those who got the placebos, as opposed to those who got the medication. The clause is restrictive.

> The patients, *who didn't know they had been given placebos,* showed marked improvement.

The clause *who didn't know* ... is incidental information here and is therefore nonrestrictive. For the clause to become restrictive, one would have to contrast those who didn't know with those who did know, making "the patients who didn't know" the subject of the sentence. That is clearly not the meaning here, however, and "The patients ... showed marked improvement" is a complete thought regardless of the *who* clause. Here are three more examples:

> *Restrictive:* The method *that they used* is limited to shallow depths.
> *Nonrestrictive:* The Sundburg method, *which they used successfully,* is limited to shallow depths.
> *Nonrestrictive:* See Chapter 3, *where complete references to the literature are given.*

clauses with *if, since, because, for*   *If, since, because,* and similar words expressing condition or cause are preceded by a comma or not depending on the degree to which they modify the sense of the preceding statement. Sometimes they are highly restrictive, and sometimes not. The choice requires a certain amount of judgment on the writer's part.

> The waves of immigrant nationalities that settled in the United States during the nineteenth and early twentieth centuries had to face the problems of poverty and discrimination, *since as foreigners they had not yet found their way in the community.*
> This method is impractical *because the vertical gradient may vary.*

In the first example above, the *since* clause seems mildly explanatory rather than restrictive. In the second example, the *because* clause seems to complete the meaning of the first clause: the method is impractical *for this reason.* There is no hard-and-fast rule here except that a sense for the completeness of the thought must govern. A comma should generally precede if the clause seems nonrestrictive and should be avoided if the clause seems restrictive.

Nonintroductory clauses beginning with *for*, however, are almost always preceded by a comma to prevent the possibility of misreading. See "Mistaken Junction" in Section 10-4.

Nonintroductory clauses beginning with *for, since,* or *because* should never follow a period or a semicolon. Those marks always precede a complete thought. Since these clauses can never express a complete thought but always modify another clause, use a comma or nothing, as appropriate, before them.

> *Wrong:* The outing was canceled; for it rained all day. (Use a comma instead.)

10-4

PUNCTUATION OF PHRASES

A phrase is a group of words, generally beginning with a preposition or a participle, that does not contain a subject and a verb.

Prepositional Phrases

Introductory prepositional phrases are correct with or without a comma:

> *Optional:* At the end of the war(,) the troops were sent home.

Consistency is unnecessary, except to achieve parallelism:

> *Wrong:* In 1920, average life expectancy at birth was 54.1 years; in 1976 it was 72.8 years. (Either delete the comma after *1920* or insert one after *1976*.)
> *Wrong:* On the one hand, the play is rich in witticisms. On the other it is lacking in plot. (Either delete the comma after *hand* or add one after *other*.)

Some introductory expressions look like phrases because they do not contain a verb but are really clauses with the subject and verb understood:

> *Right:* As before, she tripped over the extension cord. (*As before* is short for *as she had done before*.)
> *Right:* If so, please advise. (*If so* is short for *if that is so*.)

These expressions should always be followed by a comma.

Participial Phrases
Phrases beginning with a participle may be restrictive or nonrestrictive; they are preceded by a comma or not according to the same rules that apply to clauses (see Section 10-3):

> *Restrictive:* Another hypothesis *concerning the fermentation of acetic acid* is that . . . .
> *Nonrestrictive:* Mushrooms, *classified as Basidiomycetes,* are often grown commercially.

This phrase is nonrestrictive because all mushrooms are Basidiomycetes, not only those which are grown commercially.

Mistaken Junction
Be alert to supply a comma if the sentence could be misread without it, even in instances in which the use of a comma is normally optional:

> *Wrong:* After school children need fresh air and exercise. (Insert a comma after *school.*)
> *Wrong:* In general delivery of the mail has been prompt in spite of the strike. (Insert a comma after *general.*)

Mistaken junction is often unintentionally funny:

> *Wrong:* The audience cheered for the villain had been apprehended. (Insert a comma after *cheered.*)

10-5

OTHER RULES OF PUNCTUATION

Series Punctuation
A comma is needed for clarity before *and* or *or* in a series of three or more items:

> pressure, volume, and temperature
> lime, marl, gypsum, and other calcareous materials
> twenty, thirty, or forty children
> In this game one player has four "geese," the other player has the "fox," and the geese win if they can trap the fox before it reaches the last row.

Use semicolons between items in a series if any one of the items itself contains a series:

> The modules are 40 cm deep; 30, 45, or 60 cm long; and 35 cm high.

or as necessary where other internal punctuation exists:

> Among the agencies created during the New Deal were the CCC, Civilian Conservation Corps; the FHA, Federal Housing Administration; and the SEC, Securities and Exchange Commission.
> The McNary-Haugen Farm Relief Bill was vetoed by President Coolidge on the grounds that it sanctioned price fixing; was an improper use of taxing power; would antagonize overseas agricultural producers, thus inviting retaliation; and would lead to overproduction and profiteering.

Modifiers

Commas are used between adjectives that precede a noun when each adjective modifies the noun independently, that is, when the word *and* could be substituted for the comma:

> a small, dimly lit room

One could say that the room is small *and* dimly lit; thus the comma is correct. But:

> a frisky chestnut colt

One would never say that a colt is frisky *and* chestnut; thus a comma would be incorrect.

In technical material especially, commas are usually omitted from strings of adjectives when each adjective can be thought of as modifying the noun with all its other adjectives as a unit:

> present-day finned-tube coil design
> a 5-hp 230-V dc shunt motor

Elliptical Constructions

In an elliptical construction, one or more words have been left out, but their presence is understood, as in:

> One group represented the typographers; the other [group represented] the publishers.

This sentence may be correctly punctuated in two ways:

> *Right:* One group represented the typographers, the other the publishers.
> *Right:* One group represented the typographers; the other, the publishers.

Other examples:

> By 1890, 70 percent of Mexico's cultivated land was held by Spaniards, 15 percent by other foreigners, and the remainder by the original inhabitants.
> Of the 100,000 bales, South Carolina produced half; Georgia, a quarter.

Another form of elliptical sentence omits verbs altogether, taking the form of "the more the merrier." Sentences with this construction normally require a comma between the contrasted halves:

> The lower the measured value of the rating, the higher the approval by the average child in the test group.

If the sentence is very short, however, no comma is needed:

> The bigger the better.

Note that it is unnecessary to add a verb to either half of the sentence.

Appositives
Appositives can be either restrictive or nonrestrictive. Commas are used to separate only nonrestrictive appositives.

restrictive   In the following examples, the lack of a comma indicates that the appositive identifies (selects) a specific one from a field of more than one:

> my friend Steve (not my only friend, but this particular one)
> the river Alph
> Catherine the Great

The following mistake is common:

> *Wrong:* In his poem, "God's Grandeur," Gerard Manley Hopkins writes of . . . .

But Hopkins wrote other poems. Therefore:

> *Right:* In his poem "God's Grandeur" Gerard Manley Hopkins writes of . . . .

nonrestrictive In the following examples, each appositive is used only as a further description, not as a "selector" of what has already been identified:

> my best friend, Jeannine (my only best friend)
> his home town, Bridgeport
> Alph, the sacred river
> Beethoven's opera, *Fidelio* (his only opera)

Sometimes a nonrestrictive appositive and its noun are so close in concept that they are thought of as a compound, in which case the comma may be omitted:

> his wife Mary
> my uncle John

When preceded by *or*, appositives are sometimes confused with *alternatives*. An appositive is another name for something; an alternative is a different thing.

> *Appositive:* rickets, or Glisson's disease

Rickets and *Glisson's disease* are two names for the same ailment; a comma is required.

> *Alternative:* rickets or pernicious anemia

These are different ailments; a comma is not used.

Namely and Related Words
Set off terms like *namely* or *viz.*, *that is* or *i.e.*, *for example* or *e.g.*, and *etc.* with two commas unless they introduce an independent clause, in which case use a semicolon before the term and a comma after it:

> We seek an algorithm which reduces the number of computations, that is, an algorithm which permits elimination of some of the alternatives.
> The greatest disadvantage of the vacuum tube is that power is required to activate it; i.e., the vacuum tube depends on thermal emission of electrons in vacuum for its action.

A case can be made for not using a comma after *namely* and *for example* when phrasing is smoother without it (use judgment with these):

> . . . my favorite color, namely blue.
> He dislikes spectator sports, for example baseball.

Quotation Marks

punctuation with quotation marks   In the United States, periods and commas are conventionally placed inside a closing quotation mark:

> The prefix *inter-* signifies "between."

Semicolons and colons are always placed outside the closing quotation mark:

> The prefix *inter-* signifies "between"; *intra-* signifies "within."

Question marks and exclamation points go in or out according to sense:

> What is meant by "intramural"?
> "Why?" she asked.
> The band certainly knew how to ruin "Stars and Stripes Forever"!
> "Hurrah!" they cried.

In the United States, quotation marks are normally double; single quotation marks are used for quotations within quotations:

> "What is meant by 'intramural'?" she asked.

(In Great Britain, usage is just the opposite: 'What is meant by "intramural"?' she asked. And periods and commas are usually placed outside: ... signifies 'between'.) One conventional exception in the United States is found in linguistics and philosophy, where single quotation marks are sometimes used for definitions and to set off words under discussion. Periods and commas are then placed outside these special single quotes:

> Mexicans who live in the area say *el trocke*, 'truck'.

rhetorical questions   Quotation marks are not necessary with rhetorical questions:

> *Acceptable:* The question is "Can the species survive?"
> *Preferred:* The question is: Can the species survive?

Do not use quotation marks or a question mark when the question is phrased in declarative form:

> The question is whether the species can survive.

In general, do not use quotation marks for answers:

The answer is no.

The Colon
The colon is generally used in one of two ways.

1 The colon can "point" to the main idea to come, either following or taking the place of words like *as follows, to wit,* or *viz.:*

"Pointing" colon
This is the procedure: Dissolve the residue in 25 cc distilled water . . . .
. . . three components: nitrogen, phosphorus, and potash.

Note the use of a capital letter after the colon if a sentence or complete clause follows. Otherwise, lowercase is preferred.

2 The colon is used in place of a semicolon to balance two closely related ideas, one of which usually expands or illustrates the other:

"Balancing" colon
These situations are dynamic: they involve motion and change.

Note the use of lowercase after a balancing colon.

10-6

HYPHENS AND DASHES
To the trained eye, the hyphen and the various dashes differ noticeably in size:

Hyphen: -
En dash: –
Em dash: —
Two-em dash: ——
Three-em dash: ———

Figure 12-1 shows how hyphens and dashes are indicated in manuscript; Figure 12-4 shows how they are indicated in proof.

Hyphen

in compounds The hyphen is the familiar mark used for joining two words:

blue-green
Joliot-Curie
well-intentioned

in double numbers   The hyphen is also used in double numbering:

Section 24-9
Figure 4-18*a*

As a matter of design, a point (period or, sometimes, center dot) may be used instead of a hyphen in double numbers (Section 24.9), but an en dash should not be used because the numbers do not express a range.

En Dash

The uses of the en dash are not generally taught in high school or college. The mark is found only in printed materials. It does not exist on typewriter keyboards, and there is no graphic way to indicate it in typed copy except by doctoring a hyphen (see Figure 12-1). And yet the en dash has a distinct place in the written language, for it denotes relationships that the hyphen and the em dash cannot represent.

in ranges   The en dash is used in ranges:

the years 1949–1962
40–50 kg

This use of the en dash is recommended only for tables, footnotes, bibliographies, and other nontextual material. In text the word *to* is preferred:

the years 1949 to 1962

Use *to*, not the en dash, when the range is preceded by *from:*

from 40 to 50 kg

Use *to*, not the en dash, for ranges that contain a minus sign:

−5 to −10

in compounds   The en dash replaces the hyphen in certain compound expressions. See "En Dash in Compound Modifiers" in Section 1-2.

in headings The en dash often replaces the hyphen in all-capital-letter headings because, in most typefaces, the hyphen looks too small when surrounded by capital letters.

Em Dash

The em dash is now almost exclusively a mark of punctuation. (Formerly it was also a popular typographic device, usually placed after a run-in heading: *The Nervous System.*—The . . . .)

As a mark of punctuation, the em dash has been much maligned, perhaps because some writers rely on it too heavily. It has several legitimate uses:

interpolation A pair of em dashes may be used instead of commas or parentheses to set off words that are interpolated in a sentence and interrupt its flow:

> Derive a model for part of the respiratory system—the tracheal and bronchial tubes—as shown in Fig. 8.

summation A single em dash is used for summation after a list:

> Sapporo, Innsbruck, Lake Placid—these were the sites of recent winter Olympic games.

explanation A single em dash is often used to introduce an explanation or to expand on what has gone before:

> Basic plain weave produces the maximum number of *binding points*—areas in which a single weft is interlaced with a single warp.

interruption In dialogue, an em dash signifies that the speaker has been cut off abruptly:

> "If you ask me, there's a—"
> "Nobody asked you."

10-7

PUNCTUATION OF LISTS

In lists consisting entirely of sentence items, use a period after each item:

> 1. State the problem to be solved.

2. Formulate an algorithm for its solution.
3. Prepare general and detailed flow charts.

In lists consisting entirely of nonsentence items, do not use periods:

1. *Ma and Pa Kettle Go to Town,* 1950
2. *Ma and Pa Kettle at the Fair,* 1952
3. *Ma and Pa Kettle Back on the Farm,* 1954

If sentence and nonsentence items are mixed within a list, use a period after every item:

There were three main groups:

1. The *Hurrians:* An expansive people who settled northern Mesopotamia.
2. The *Hittites:* Possibly related to the Hurrians, these people became rulers of most of what is known today as Turkey.
3. The *Kassites:* Occupiers of Babylonia.

FROM MANUSCRIPT
TO BOOK

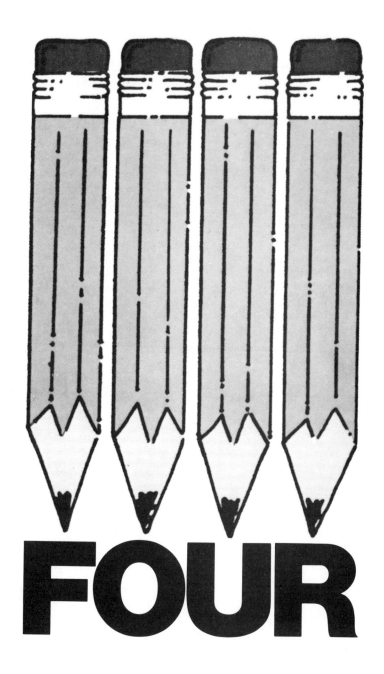

FOUR

PREPARING THE MANUSCRIPT

The word *manuscript*, which originally meant something written by hand, today usually means an author's typescript. By extension it also refers to any of the newer forms (disk or tape) in which an author can submit a work to the publisher. This chapter contains advice to authors and typists (or word-processor operators) on the preparation of a typescript for publication. If you are going to submit your manuscript on disks or tapes instead of in typewritten form, discuss your plans with your editor in advance to make sure that your system is compatible with the equipment to be used by the publisher or typesetter.

11-1

GENERAL INSTRUCTIONS FOR TYPING A MANUSCRIPT

If you are typing manuscript that is going to undergo a machine-readable process (optical character recognition, or OCR), your publisher can give you special instructions on what, if any, special typeface element to use and what typesetting codes, if any, to embed in the text.

Specific suggestions for typing technical material (mathematics and chemistry) are given in Section 11-5.

Paper

Use a good grade of standard-sized (not legal) bond paper. Avoid coated or so-called erasable papers, which cannot take editorial marking without danger of losing some of the type when an eraser or ink eradicator is applied. Also avoid thin or onionskin papers, which do not hold up well through the processes of production.

Clean, legible duplicates, such as those made on a good photocopier, are acceptable as manuscript.

Page Format

Type the manuscript on one side of the page only. Leave ample margins, at least 37.5 mm (1½ in) at the top and left and 25 mm (1 in) at the bottom and right. Some publishers supply their authors with special paper and ask them to type within preruled borders.

All copy, including lists, footnotes, bibliographies, and indexes, should be double-spaced.

Mounting Reprint Copy

Reprint copy (pages of previously printed material) should be mounted on standard-sized sheets of bond paper. If the copy was printed in a double-column format, mount only one column on each sheet. If you are using both sides of a previously printed page, obtain two copies of that page so that you can mount each side on a separate sheet. Paste the material down securely with rubber cement; do no use staples or transparent tape. (Some transparent tapes are difficult to write on, especially if you are using a fountain pen, which many copy editors prefer to ballpoint or felt-tip pens.)

Corrections

Make minor corrections in ink, not pencil. In typewritten material, make the correction directly *above* the affected word or words; if it won't fit there, write it in the margin. Never superimpose a correction on an existing character or word. If there are many corrections on a page, retype the page.

If material to be inserted does not fit, cut the page apart and paste it on a fresh sheet with the new material in place, so that the text reads consecutively. Also type insertions of more than five or six words.

In reprint copy, make corrections as you would in proof: Mark the location of the correction in the line of type, and show the desired change in the margin. When film or plates of a previous edition are to be corrected or tapes updated, reprint material to be deleted should never be completely obliterated—the typesetter must be able to see exactly what material is to be removed.

Always retain a complete copy of the final manuscript, containing the same corrections and showing the same page numbers as the final copy submitted to the publisher.

Numbering of Pages

Most manuscripts are numbered (folioed) consecutively from beginning to end, starting with the first page of the text, that is, with the first page of Part One or Chapter 1. Projects that have several authors, however, such as large technical handbooks, are frequently folioed by chapter (1-1, 1-2, 1-3, etc., signifying pages 1, 2, and 3 of Chapter 1). To avoid having to renumber a great many pages, inserted pages may be designated by letters (for example 18a, 18b). All page numbers should be written, typed, or machine-stamped in the upper right corner of the page.

Numbering of Other Items

Use arabic figures for chapter numbers, sections, figures, tables, and so forth. In technical books, numbered items are often double-numbered by chapter, with the chapter number first, followed by a hyphen and then the number of the section, figure, table, or equation. A double-numbering system is recommended whenever its use will simplify cross-referencing or facilitate renumbering in revisions. More complicated numbering systems, such as those employing triple or quadruple numbers, are cumbersome but sometimes unavoidable. (See Section 4-4.)

Just before the final draft is prepared, check the sequence of all numbered elements (sections, equations, tables, figures, examples, problems) to make sure that no numbers have been omitted or duplicated. This is one of the most neglected steps in manuscript preparation, along with failure to supply missing cross-references.

Chapter Titles

Begin each chapter or unit on a new page. Center the title, and type it in capital letters.

Headings

Headings are used to divide the text into topics and to serve as signposts for the convenience of the reader. As a general rule, the number of *values* (different ranks of headings) should be kept to a minimum, preferably no more than three. Try to follow a consistent method of positioning and capitalizing the headings in the manuscript to indicate their various levels. For example, the main headings used for major chapter breaks and for "Problems," "Bibliography," etc., can be typed on a separate line in capital letters, while second-value headings can also stand on a separate line but be typed in capital and lowercase letters. Third-value heads should be further distinguished, perhaps by being run in to the following text.

Submit an outline of headings with your manuscript to help the editor and the typographic designer to determine the best way of setting them in type. You can also help to ensure correct typesetting by identifying each heading in the left margin of the manuscript with a circled number—①, ②,③, etc.—marked lightly in pencil to represent the value (subordination) of each head.

Tables

Various types of tables, and their parts, are discussed in Chapter 6. Figure 11-1 shows a well-typed table.

Cross-References

General rules for referring to other parts of the same book are given in Chapter 4. Be sure to fill in any incomplete cross-references before you submit the manuscript. If any last-minute changes have been made in the numbering of chapters, figures, tables, or the like, double-check to make sure that all text references to these elements have also been changed.

Footnotes, References, Bibliographies

Double-space all notes and reference material, within items as well as between them. See Figure 11-2.

footnotes   For the numbering and styling of footnotes, see Chapter 5.

references and bibliographies   Instead of using footnotes at the bottom (foot) of the page, many authors place a list of *references* or *notes* at the end of each chapter or at the end of the book, particularly when there are

Table 5.   Equal annual rate which will amortize original investment over estimated life*

Life, yr	Annual rate of interest or return			
	6%	8%	10%	12%
10	0.13587	0.14903	0.16275	0.17698
15	0.10296	0.11683	0.13147	0.14682
20	0.08718	0.10185	0.11746	0.13388
25	0.07823	0.09368	0.11017	0.12750

*Amortization is by sinking fund earning interest at indicated rate.

FIGURE 11-1   Well-typed table.

many notes or it is necessary to refer repeatedly to the same source. Numbering is generally by chapter or, if notes are numerous, by page. *General bibliographies* or *readings* for which there are no references in the text may be placed either at the end of each chapter or at the end of the book. They are arranged alphabetically by author, and the items are unnumbered. For reference style, see Chapter 5. For methods of referring to bibliographies, see "General Rules for Credit Lines" in Section 11-2. (See also "Back Matter" in Section 4-7.)

Quoted Material (Extracts)
A quotation of more than five lines should be typed as a separate paragraph, not run into the text. Draw a vertical line in the left margin to show that the extract is a verbatim quotation from another source and should not be edited. Insert the footnote or bibliographic reference number at the end of the extract or in the introductory sentence preceding the extract. (See Section 4-1.)

Front Matter
Type the front matter (title page, contents, preface, and any other items that precede the text proper) in the same manner as the rest of the book, and submit it to the publisher with the manuscript. (See Section 4-6.)

FOR FURTHER READING

Allen, Elsa G.: The History of American Ornithology before
Audubon, Russell and Russell, New York, 1969.

Fisher, Allan C., Jr.: "Mysteries of Bird Migration,"
National Geographic Magazine, August 1979, pp. 154–193.

Pasquier, Roger: Watching Birds: An Introduction to Ornithology, Houghton Mifflin, New York, 1977.

Wallace, George J., and Harold D. Mahan: An Introduction
to Ornithology, 3d ed., Macmillan, New York, 1975.

FIGURE 11-2 Typed bibliography.

Index

The index is ordinarily not prepared until the book has been set in type and is in the page-proof stage. If you are going to create your own index rather than seek the services of a professional indexer, see Chapter 13, or follow your publisher's instructions.

11-2

OBTAINING PERMISSIONS

Whenever you plan to quote or reproduce material from another printed and copyrighted source, *you must obtain permission from the copyright holder.* This requirement applies not only to text passages, but to *tables, photographs,* and *line art* as well. Altering a drawing slightly does not relieve you of the obligation to obtain permission. Even if you provide a full credit line acknowledging the source of reproduced material, you will not be protected against a claim of copyright infringement unless you have received permission in writing for its use. A sample permission letter is shown in Figure 11-3.

Start writing for permissions long before submitting final manuscript to the publisher. Sometimes it take so long to get a reply that you may have to omit the material to avoid delaying publication of your book. Always write to the publisher, rather than the author, for permission. The publisher keeps extensive records and contract files and will check them carefully to determine who actually owns the rights. (Even if the author has already given permission, it's a good idea to consult the publisher.) And even if your own publisher has published the work from which you would like to quote, you must still obtain permission.

When an illustration or table bears a separate credit, permission to use it must be obtained from the person or publisher credited.

Unless otherwise specifically requested, permission to reproduce is assumed to be for domestic sale of one edition only. Discuss with your editor whether it is worth paying more than the single-edition fee to obtain the rights for subsequent editions, foreign sales, or other uses.

Copyright

All copyrightable works created after January 1, 1978, whether published or unpublished, are automatically protected by copyright under the Copyright Act of October 19, 1976. Duration of copyright under the new law is as follows:

1   Works created after January 1, 1978, are protected for the author's life plus 50 years.

[Date]

[Name of Publisher]

I am preparing a [book/textbook] tentatively entitled [Title] to be
published by [Publisher] in [probable date] and intended for use by
[junior high school students/graduate students/physicians, etc.]

I should like your permission to reproduce in my book, and in its
future editions and translations, the material indicated below.

Author(s):_____

Title and date of publication:_____

Selection or illustration: [first and last words if a quotation;
figure or page number if an illustration]

Page_____to page_____

Approximate number of words_____or pages_____

It is understood, of course, that full credit will be given to the
author and publisher, either as a footnote or as a reference within the text, or both.

If it will also be necessary to obtain permission of the author,
will you please provide me with [his/her] current address:

A release form is given below for your convenience. The duplicate
copy of this request is for your files.

Very truly yours,

[Requester's name and address]

....

Permission is granted for use of the material as stipulated.

Date:_____ Signature:_____

Title:_____

FIGURE 11-3 Permission letter.

2   Works that were in their first term of copyright when the new law went into effect (January 1, 1978) are renewable after 28 years, with the second term extended to 47 years for a new combined term of 75 years.

3   Works that were in their second term of copyright between December 31, 1976, and December 31, 1977, receive automatic extension to 75 years.

4   Works made for hire, as well as anonymous works or pseudonymous works of unknown authorship, are covered for 75 years from publication or 100 years from creation, whichever is shorter.

Fair Use

Although the safest course is to get permission before using any copyrighted material, under the doctrine of fair use a limited amount may be quoted without permission under certain circumstances. The Copyright Law states:

> 107. Limitations on exclusive rights: Fair use
> . . . the fair use of a copyrighted work . . . for purposes such as criticism, comment, news reporting, . . . scholarship, or research, is not an infringement of copyright. In determining whether the use made of a work in any particular case is a fair use the factors to be considered shall include—
> (1) the purpose and character of the use, including whether such use is of a commercial nature or is for nonprofit educational purposes;
> (2) the nature of the copyrighted work;
> (3) the amount and substantiality of the portion used in relation to the work as a whole; and
> (4) the effect of the use upon the potential market for or value of the copyrighted work.

Guidelines or rules of thumb for the number of words or lines that may safely be used have no legal significance, and therefore none are given here.

Public Domain

Works whose copyrights have expired or that have never been covered by copyright are in the public domain and may be quoted without permission. You can be certain that any work copyrighted before September 18, 1906, is in the public domain. Do not assume that lack of a copyright notice in a work (published or unpublished) created after January 1, 1978, implies that the work is in the public domain; copyright protection is automatic, and failure to include a notice no longer results in forfeiture of the copyright.

It is often incorrectly assumed that any work published by the U.S. government is in the public domain. That is true of works prepared *entirely* by a government agency. It is not necessarily true when the agency has commissioned a work or has quoted from another copyrighted source.

The safest course, therefore, is to write to any government agencies whose publications you wish to quote from. Ask them whether all the material may be freely used without permission. Also notify your editor about any substantial use you have made of government works; by law the copyright notice in your book may have to disclaim ownership of that material.

General Rules for Credit Lines

wording If a letter granting permission stipulates wording for the credit line, the wording may be edited to conform to a given book's reference style, as long as all the specified publishing information is included.

source footnotes In the text, a source footnote is dropped from the end of a quotation except in the following situations:

1 If the copyright holder requires that credit appear on the first page of the quotation, it may be necessary to drop the footnote from the line of text preceding the extract.

2 If an extract is so long that two or more pages are likely to intervene between the beginning of the quotation and the footnote, the footnote is dropped, for the reader's convenience, from the line of text preceding the footnote.

3 Credit to the source of complete poems, stories, articles, or chapters may be given either on the first page of the extract or in a list of acknowledgements in the front matter (usually on, or facing, the copyright page). This method of citing sources is especially common in anthologies and books of readings.

references to bibliography Bracketed [4] or superior[4] numbers keyed to the bibliography may be used instead of source footnotes. When a phrase such as "Used by permission" has to be incorporated, a footnote must be used; the footnote may contain either the full citation or a partial citation with reference to the bibliography for further publishing details:

*From Smith [4]. Used by permission.

Another method of giving credit is to cite, in parentheses, the author's last name and a date referring to an entry in the bibliography:

> ... as in the experimental models (Calderon, 1979).

In this system, letters (a, b, etc.) are used after the date to distinguish two or more works published in the same year by the same author, and initials are added to the name if two or more authors with the same surname are listed.

There is no need to give a full bibliographic reference for a quotation from a popular work that is in the public domain (for example, for well-known lines from Shakespeare, Lewis Carroll, or the King James version of the Bible).

See also "Source Notes" in Section 6-1 and "Legends" in Section 11-4.

11-3

ESTIMATING THE SIZE OF THE BOOK

Many contracts specify length in terms of published book pages. The publisher can estimate the final size accurately only after the design, an important variable, has been approved, the art has been sized, and an estimating process known as *castoff* has been performed.

The author can, however, make a rough estimate. Here are some sample calculations:

1 For a 6- by 9-inch book, 1.5 manuscript pages equal 1 book page, and 2 illustrations equal 1 book page:

900 manuscript pages	600 book pages
200 sketches (including parts)	100 book pages
Front matter and index	36 book pages
Total	736 book pages

2 For an 8½- by 11-inch double-column book, 3.5 manuscript pages equal 1 book page, and 3 illustrations equal 1 book page:

1300 manuscript pages	372 book pages
300 illustrations	100 book pages
Front matter and index	40 book pages
Total	512 book pages

11-4

ILLUSTRATIONS

Submit illustrations, whether sketches or finished art, as a separate package with a covering list that accounts for each piece of art by chapter. Manuscript for the accompanying legends, which are usually not typeset with the text, should be included with the art program as a separate item. (See "Legends" below.) It is best to compile the art program as you develop each chapter. The form for submission of final art is a matter to be decided on with your editor.

Some specific suggestions for the preparation of illustration copy follow.

Numbering

Illustrations are usually numbered and referred to in text by number. In technical books they are generally double-numbered by chapter (Fig. 12-1, 12-2, etc., meaning the first and second illustrations in Chapter 12). Call all illustrations *figures*—the use of separate sequences for "figures," "charts," "exhibits," etc., is confusing for the reader. Tables, however, are numbered in a separate sequence. If two or more drawings or photographs make up a single illustration, the separate parts should be labeled (a), (b), etc.

Line Drawings

1   The author should supply either finished drawings or carefully prepared and lettered pencil sketches for line illustrations. (See Figure 11-4.) The sketches must provide all the necessary detail. Curves must be plotted accurately on graph paper, and any essential variations in line weight noted. When coordinate paper is used in the preparation of graphs, be sure to indicate the density of grid lines wanted in the final drawing.

For biological drawings, provide aids in the form of photos, pages torn from books, and other instructions (attached to the back of the sketch) to enable the illustrator to understand precise detail, proportions, special ways of indicating surfaces, and so forth.

2   If you are rendering final illustrations yourself, prepare line figures for a common reduction (one-third, one-half, or same size). Lettering on the drawing should be large enough to be legible when reduced.

3   Make certain that labels, abbreviations, and symbols are consistent with those used in the text. Consult the most recent American National Standards Institute (ANSI) standards for current graphic symbols.

4 Take care that handwritten symbols on your sketches are clear; capitals and lowercase, "oh" and zero, Greek letters, and boldface symbols should be carefully distinguished. Pay particular attention to handwritten ι, υ, ω, κ, π, $\sqrt{\ }$, 2, z. Script and other special symbols should be clearly

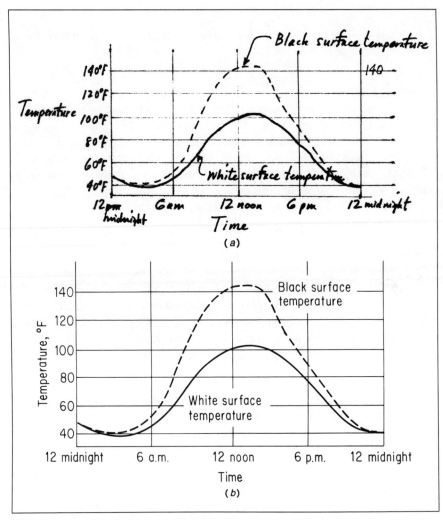

FIGURE 11-4 (*a*) Author's sketch; (*b*) finished drawing rendered by drafter.

identified. Boldface letters should be marked with a wavy underscore, not simply made heavy.

5   Wherever possible, plan illustrations to fit upright on the page so that they can be read without turning the book.

6   Descriptive material should be put in figure captions, not on the illustrations.

Photographs

1   Submit sharp black-and-white glossy prints. Do not submit photographs torn from other publications. For best results, have your photographic work done by a reliable custom firm.

2   Avoid submitting color slides or other color prints to be reproduced as black-and-white halftones.

3   Labels, arrows, and other markings that are to be added to a photograph should be indicated on a transparent overlay, not on the print itself. Tape the overlay to the back of the print, and fold it down over the front. Do not staple or clip the overlay in place. Write lightly with a soft pencil to avoid making an imprint on the glossy surface of the photograph. (Do not use hard lead pencil or ballpoint pen.)

4   The figure number for a photograph should be marked lightly in a lower corner on the back of the illustration.

5   The publisher cannot return original prints until the book is published, and there is always some risk of loss. The author should therefore keep duplicates of all irreplaceable photographs.

Computer Printouts
Computer printouts of more than a few lines seldom look right when set in type. The author should provide clean copies of printouts ready for reproduction ("camera copy"). If printouts are long or numerous, they can be numbered in the regular sequence of figures.

Legends
Legends, or captions, for illustrations should be typed double-spaced in the form of a separate list and submitted along with the illustrations. Do not type them on the manuscript or on the illustrations themselves. Type legends just like text, that is, with a capital letter at the beginning and a period at the end. Include credit to all persons, organizations, or publishers who gave permission for the use of the material. See "Legends" in Section

4-3. If the legend list is long, start the legends for each chapter on a new page.

Shipping the Illustrations

Illustrations are usually sent with the manuscript, but always separated from the text. Submit small drawings on separate sheets; large drawings should be rolled, not folded. Ship photographs flat, and avoid the use of paper clips.

When submitting copy for revision, send the original drawings and photographs, whenever possible, for illustrations that are to be reused in the new edition. This is particularly important when an old illustration is to be corrected.

Original art (reproduction copy) is often sent separately by registered mail to ensure special handling. Wrap the illustrations in plastic to prevent water damage.

Keep a photocopy of all sketches sent so that they can be discussed over the telephone or reconstructed if lost.

11-5

SUGGESTIONS FOR TYPING TECHNICAL MATERIAL

If mathematical and chemical notation is inaccurate or ambiguous in the manuscript, it is bound to cause costly errors when set in type. Some practical suggestions are given here for ensuring the clarity and accuracy of a technical manuscript.

Many typewriters today are available with complete sets of Greek letters and mathematical or other symbols, either in the form of spherical elements or as individual characters that can be attached to, or substituted for, little-used keys on the ordinary typewriter. *Symbols should be typed whenever possible,* but where specially equipped machines are not available, a reasonable approximation of a symbol can sometimes be improvised on an ordinary typewriter. The remaining symbols should be carefully drawn in by hand, in ink.

Signs of Operation

Use one space before and after all signs of operation (for example, $+$, $-$, $\div$, $=$, $\leq$).

For an equals sign, use two hyphens, backspacing and turning the roller slightly to type the second hyphen. For a minus sign, use one hyphen with space at both sides.

Unless it is available on the typewriter, do not attempt to type a plus sign. Write it by hand instead.

Do not type a letter X for a times sign where it might be mistaken for the mathematical symbol X or χ; instead insert the sign in ink.

Center Dots

For a center multiplication dot $(x \cdot 2y)$, turn the roller a half turn and type a period. Allow a single space on each side. A center dot in a chemical formula $(Na_2CO_3 \cdot H_2O)$ or a compound unit of measure $(3N \cdot m)$ has no space around it.

Spacing of Symbols

In general, symbols indicating a simple product should be typed without space $(2\pi r)$. Use space, however, before and after trigonometric functions, ln, and similar abbreviations.

Show space before and after differentials like $dx\ dy$ and $d\omega t$ and similar combinations like δt and Δt. If you have forgotten to omit or add space, mark $d\overset{\frown}{\ }x$ to indicate closing up and mark $\sin x$ to indicate space.

Special Symbols

Two Greek letters can be satisfactorily reproduced on the ordinary typewriter: lowercase phi (ϕ) can be shown as an "oh" with a slant bar through it, and lowercase theta (θ) as a zero with a hyphen through its center. Lowercase mu (μ) can be approximated by typing lowercase u and adding the first upstroke in ink. All other Greek letters should be written by hand in ink unless available on the typewriter.

If Greek letters are typewritten or drawn unmistakably, further identification is rarely necessary. Distinctive letters like Δ or Σ need never be identified. Symbols that may be ambiguous, such as δ or ∂, Θ or θ, ω or w, should be identified at the beginning of a chapter or section of the manuscript. Never clutter up the manuscript by marking Greek letters every time they appear.

The Greek capitals A, B, E, Z, H, I, K, M, N, O, P, T, X are identical with roman letters and should therefore not be used as symbols. If they must be used, they should be identified by marginal note so that they will not be improperly set in italic.

Script and German symbols may be indicated by circling the corresponding English letter in a distinct color or by marking over it with a pastel felt-tip highlighter pen. Use different colors for script and German symbols if both are called for.

Ambiguous Symbols

Differentiate symbols that may be ambiguous as follows: underline the letters l and o; leave the numerals 1 and 0 unmarked. If an isolated symbol must be handwritten, be sure to distinguish between capital and lowercase letters that resemble one another, such as C and c, K and k, S and s, U and u, W and w. Mark c̲ to indicate a capital letter and ¢ for lowercase if not perfectly clear. It is particularly important to identify capital and lowercase "oh" (O, o) in subscripts.

Vectors or other symbols that are to be set in boldface should be identified with a wavy underscore F̰. Use a similar wavy underscore to identify a vector cross or dot:

$$\text{A } \underset{\sim}{\times} \text{ B} = \mathbf{\epsilon}\text{AB sin } \theta$$

Dash
For a dash, type two hyphens with no space before, after, or between.

Prime
For a prime, use an apostrophe.

Superscripts and Subscripts (Superiors and Inferiors)
Superscripts and subscripts should be typed clearly above and below the line by moving the typewriter roller a half turn up or down. If the typing is not exact, use the mark ˅ , as in n$\overset{x}{˅}$, to show a superscript and the mark ˄ , as in p$\overset{}{˄}$o, to show a subscript. Mark various levels of subscripts and superscripts that are not typed clearly like this:

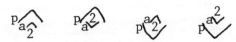

Unless very clearly typed, subscript letters that carry primes should be marked as follows:

since otherwise it is assumed that the prime belongs with the symbol on the line.

In typing fractions containing subscripts or superscripts, allow a separate line for the fraction bar, spacing one full line below before typing the denominator:

$$\frac{x_1}{p^2}$$

Equations

In equations, make sure that plus signs, minus signs, equals, etc., line up with the horizontal bar of a built-up fraction:

$$x = -\frac{mA}{R} e^{-Rt/m} + B$$

Center an isolated (displayed) equation on the width of the page. Whenever possible, run in successive short parts of a displayed equation containing two or more equals signs:

$$x = a^2 + b^2 = c$$

not
$$x = a^2 + b^2$$
$$= c$$

Two or three very short displayed equations may be typed horizontally on the same line to save space when the book is set in type. (Do not show two equations with different equation numbers on the same line, however.) Leave at least five spaces between the equations:

$$e_c = E_{cc} + E_{gm} \qquad e_b = E_{bb} - E_{plm}$$

In a vertical sequence of related equations, the equals signs should be aligned:

$$\alpha + \beta = (a_1, \ldots, a_n) + (b_1, \ldots, b_n)$$
$$= (a_1 + b_1, \ldots, a_n + b_n)$$
$$c\alpha = c(a_1, \ldots, a_n) = (ca_1, \ldots, ca_n)$$

Figure 11-5 shows what a well-prepared page of technical manuscript looks like.

Chemistry

Draw and type chemical structural formulas with the greatest care, since the compositor must follow the manuscript exactly. Be sure that bonds are

14-4. <u>The parallel-T null network.</u> A network of consider-
able importance is the parallel-T combination shown in Fig.
14-13a. It has the unique property that V_b is zero at one
frequency. See Sec. 11-11. The solution is easily obtained
by the node analysis. The source is replaced by two current-
source equivalents, as in Fig. 14-13b.

The determinant of the network is

$$\Delta = \begin{vmatrix} 2(G + j\omega C) & -G & 0 \\ -G & G + j\omega C & -j\omega C \\ 0 & -j\omega C & 2(G + j\omega C) \end{vmatrix}$$

$$= G^3 \left(1 + j\frac{\omega}{\omega_0}\right) \left[2 - \left(2\frac{\omega}{\omega_0}\right)^2 + j8\frac{\omega}{\omega_0}\right]$$

where $G = 1/R$ and $\omega_0 = 1/RC$. The cofactors Δ_{12} and Δ_{32}
are needed.[1] They are

$$\Delta_{12} = 2G(G + j\omega C) \qquad \Delta_{32} = j2\omega C(G + j\omega C)$$

The potential V_b is

$$V_b = \frac{\Delta_{12}(V_a/R) + \Delta_{32}(j\omega C V_a)}{\Delta}$$

The steps following the substitution of formulas for the
determinants are omitted. Expressed as the ratio of V_b/V_a,
the response is

$$\frac{V_b}{V_a} = \frac{1 - (\omega/\omega_0)^2}{1 - (\omega/\omega_0)^2 + j4(\omega/\omega_0)} \qquad (14\text{-}16)$$

[1] A cofactor of row m and column n of a determinant
is $(-1)^{m+n}$ times the minor of that row and column.

FIGURE 11-5   Well-typed page of technical material.

shown in the exact position in which they are to appear and that labels under parts of a chemical equation are placed in the proper position:

$$2RCHOHCOOH \underset{H_2SO_4}{\rightleftarrows}$$

a lactide

11-6

SHIPPING THE MANUSCRIPT

Stack the manuscript carefully so that the edges will not become ripped or dog-eared. Place heavy cardboard under it and above it, and secure the bundle with rubber bands or twine. An empty typewriter-paper box makes a convenient shipping carton.

Wrap the bundle in strong paper. Address the package *to your editor* or another specific person at the publisher's address, showing that person's floor or room number if you know it. Ship the package manuscript rate, insured for the minimum so that it can be traced if lost in the mail.

Be sure to retain a copy of the entire manuscript.

12

COPY EDITING
AND PROOFREADING

Although this chapter is addressed primarily to professional copy editors and proofreaders, authors too will find it useful for revising their work, preparing their own copy for composition, and proofreading their galleys and pages.

12-1

DEFINITIONS

Copywriter, Copy Editor, Proofreader
For those who are unsure of the distinction between these three terms, note that in each case *the name of the job defines the job*.

A *copywriter* writes advertising copy—blurbs and other promotional material—for an advertising agency or for the advertising or marketing department of a firm. Since the job of copywriter is not related solely to publishing, it will not be considered further here.

A *copy editor*, on the other hand, is a member of the publishing community. The copy editor's work takes place *before* type has been set. *Copy*, in publishing, is the term applied to any material that the keyboarder will read from during the composition (typesetting) process. Copy may take many forms; it is thought of most often as the author's typescript, but it may also be handwritten material, pasted-up pages from an earlier edition or another printed source, the printout from the disk of a word processor, or the text as it appears on the screen of a video display terminal. The copy editor is the person who edits the copy, in whatever form it takes, to prepare it for composition. (The instruction "Follow copy" is an exhortation to make no changes in the original material.)

The *proofreader's* job is performed *after* type has been set, as implied by the name. *Proof* is the term applied to a preliminary printing of typeset material to verify ("prove") the accuracy of the typesetting and to show what the material looks like in type. A proofreader reads the proofs to make sure that they are free of typographical errors and certain other faults.

Style

In the context of editing and proofreading, the word *style* does not refer to literary merit. Instead it encompasses the conventions of capitalization, spelling, abbreviation, and so forth, that require consistency throughout a work. Many publishers have their own *house style*—a preferred style often issued to authors, editors, and proofreaders in the form of a published or unpublished *style manual.*

In addition, some technical fields and academic disciplines have their own distinct styling requirements; what may seem, for example, to be a minor difference in spacing, spelling, or capitalization, may signal a major difference in meaning in a particular context. Clearly, then, the job of copy editing, and that of proofreading as well, requires not only an eye for detail but the ability to recognize and apply appropriate rules according to circumstance.

12-2

ELECTRONIC TEXT PROCESSING

With the growing use of electronic text processing (including word processors and various types of computerized typesetting systems), some of the methods used in editing and proofreading are in a state of transition. In many applications, the steps described below can be performed at a video display terminal (VDT) using a television screen or cathode-ray tube (CRT) to display the text. By positioning a bar of light (called a *cursor*) under the point on the screen at which a change is to be made, the operator can easily add, delete, or change material or move it to another location. The text on the screen spreads out to accommodate additions and closes up when characters are deleted. This gives the operator a chance to review the corrected text before entering it onto the disk or tape. Many text processors are also equipped to search for and correct specific errors on command.

Most text-processing systems have an attached printer so that material can be edited on paper rather than on the VDT. The corrections are then keyboarded into the text as a subsequent step.

12-3

MARKING MANUSCRIPT AND PROOF

Typed or printed-out manuscript is marked interlinearly, with corrections being made above, not below, the affected line (see Figure 12-2). Corrections in proof, on the other hand, are shown in the margin, with a mark being made within the line to indicate where the correction is to be located (see Figures 12-4 and 12-5). The reason for the two different procedures is inherent in the compositor's (or keyboarder's) role: In keyboarding from copy, the compositor has to look at every word, just as a typist does, and thus saves time if corrections are indicated at the point at which they occur. In correcting type that has already been set, however, the compositor merely glances down the margin to find the lines that require attention—looking through the text to find corrections would be a waste of time. Thus the copy editor's interlinear corrections and the proofreader's marginal marks are placed where they serve their purpose best.

Color of Ink or Pencil

Use colored ink or pencil as preferred by the publisher. Choose a color that has not been used before in the manuscript. Traditionally, authors use blue or black ink; designers brown; and copy editors and proofreaders red, green, or violet. Fountain pens and fine felt-tip pens containing *washable ink* are preferred by many editors to pencils or ballpoint pens because ink eradication is less time-consuming, and often neater, than erasure.

Eradication

Liquid chlorine bleach is an inexpensive ink eradicator. Keep it in a small dropper bottle, apply it sparingly, and blot it carefully. Since you won't be able to write over the damp area for a while, try superimposing a correction in ordinary lead pencil *before* applying the eradicator. The pencil mark will remain as the ink disappears, and it can be inked over after the bleach has dried.

Never eradicate or erase any marks except your own. Cross out what you wish to overrule, but do not obliterate it.

12-4

COPY EDITING

The chief purposes of copy editing are to achieve consistency in details of style and to correct linguistic errors and infelicities. Sometimes a copy editor is also expected to check facts, verify mathematical answers, remove biased language, or rewrite and reorganize the entire work. When a book has been well edited, its reader is likely to credit the author with being a good writer. But if editing is inadequate, the reader (and often the reviewer) is likely to blame the publisher. Thus editing comes to the average reader's attention more in its absence than by its presence. The better the copy editor's work, the less noticeable it will be in the finished product.

One widely held misconception is that a copy editor must be an expert on the subject of the work at hand. Most editors will agree, however, that a copy editor contributes best by bringing experience in *editing* to the job—an understanding of book production, facility with language, and familiarity with editorial usage and nomenclature in the given field. Most of all, a copy editor needs good judgment. It's not enough to know the rules; the editor must also know when it is permissible to break them.

Publishers often turn to full-time professional freelancers for copy editing, sometimes paying an agreed-on fee for the job but more often paying an hourly rate. When freelancers are employed, someone in-house (editor, production editor, or editing supervisor) is usually responsible for determining the overall style of the project, answering the freelancer's questions, resolving editorial problems, and checking the acceptability of the completed job.

Step-by-Step Working Procedure

Since copy editors are responsible for correcting many types of errors, from faults in the overall organization of the manuscript to the minutest inconsistency in hyphenation, they usually break the work into steps, reading the manuscript through quickly several times, but concentrating each time on only a few aspects of the work.

The most efficient procedure will depend on the requirements of a given assignment and the personal working preferences of the copy editor; the steps recommended below, therefore, need not be performed in the order in which they are described.

1   check numerical sequences   The sooner missing material is identified, the better. The first step, therefore, should be a review of all numerical sequences in the manuscript, starting with the page numbers. Manuscripts are usually numbered (folioed) in the upper right corner; you need only use a rubber fingertip and turn the corners—a tedious but essential preamble to editing.

In checking chapter numbers, mark the first page of each chapter with a paper clip for ease in locating cross-references or other material later on. Make sure that there are no gaps in list, footnote, table, and equation number sequences. Numbering errors that have obvious solutions should be either fixed on the spot or clipped for attention during a later reading. If, however, you suspect that an item is misnumbered because something is missing, query the author or the editor. (See "Querying" below.) Remember that an uncaught error in a number sequence can throw all the subsequent numbers off and result in costly proof corrections later on.

2   style the headings   A second major step, sometimes performed at this stage and sometimes later, during the sense reading, is to check all the headings and subheadings in the manuscript. There are several things to watch for and mark.

Subordination   Before they are set in type, headings should be assigned their proper value, or rank; that is, the relation of one heading to another should be plotted in a systematic way. Each heading should then be numbered or lettered to indicate its place in the hierarchy of headings. For example, suppose you are editing a chapter on small-boat construction. The chapter number and title itself ("Chapter 8. Small-Boat Building") is not part of the internal heading sequence but will be coded separately. The main headings in Chapter 8 turn out to be:

> Wood Construction
>
> Aluminum Construction
>
> Plastics

Since they represent the main divisions of this chapter, these three headings can all be considered number 1 heads and identified by a circled ① in the left margin.

You discover that each main heading is followed by a subordinate heading. For instance, "Wood Construction" is followed by "Properties of Wood"; this becomes a number 2 head, identified by a circled ② in the left margin. Under the number 2 heading are further subdivisions: You find paragraphs headed "Mahogany," "Teak," and "Plywood," which you identify as number 3 heads. Your heading scheme, if formalized in an outline, would now look like this:

①   Wood Construction

② ☐ Properties of Wood

③   Mahogany

③   Teak

③ ▱ Plywood
① Aluminum Construction

and so forth. The circled numbers will eventually refer to the design specifications for the book; each value of heading will be set in a different size
of type or have other features that will make its relationship to other headings clear to the reader. (The copy editor may or may not know the design
specifications at the time the heads are marked.)

Wording   Whenever possible, related headings should be worded in a
consistent or parallel way. If one heading is "Aluminum Construction" and
another is "Construction Using Steel," change the second to "Steel Construction" for parallelism.

Capitalization in headings   If the final, approved design specifications are
known, indicate upper- and lowercase letters whenever the typing is not
accurate.

Adequacy of headings   Headings can be thought of as signposts. If there
are too few, or if they point in the wrong direction, the reader can easily
get lost in a forest of text. If the structure of the heading scheme is not
obvious at this point, wait for the sense reading before making any drastic
changes or suggestions.

3   style the text   This step is sometimes called the *mechanical reading.*
It is a separate reading for the purpose of establishing consistency in spelling, capitalization, abbreviation, numbers, hyphenation, use of italics and
quotation marks, etc. The skill of spotting details of style without reading
for sense is difficult to master but is a necessary technique for efficient copy
editing.
    Sometimes styling is divided into several separate steps. For exam-
ple, in a book with many equations, it is wise to style all the mathematical
material in a separate reading: underscoring symbols for italic, aligning
equals signs, converting fractions, and so forth. In a history book, you may
decide to capitalize historical terms as a separate step to ensure consistency.
    Figure 12-1 shows how hyphens and dashes are marked in manu-
script.

4   style recurring features   Tables, problems, end-of-chapter bibliographies and glossaries, and other features of the book that recur are best
handled in separate readings—again for the purpose of achieving consistency.

Citations Bibliographies and footnotes require special care. It is best to style an extensive or comprehensive bibliography first, according to the style established for the book. Then you can start on the footnotes, checking to make certain that the spelling of authors' names and other details of the citations are identical with those in the bibliography. If discrepan-

---

a. They couldn't see the road--the fog was thicker now.

b. An 80-km speed limit was in effect.

c. A handheld voice synthesizer can produce up to four words at a time, using three-digit codes.

d. See pages 318-325.

e. A model of part of the respiratory system-the trachea and bronchial tubes - is shown in Fig. 8.

f. Lady B- was seen at Claridge's with Col. W-.

g. Huxley, Francis: <u>Affable Savages</u>, Rupert Hart-Davis, London, 1956; Viking, New York, 1957.

Huxley, Francis: <u>The Invisibles</u>, Rupert Hart-Davis, London, 1966; McGraw-Hill, New York, 1968.

FIGURE 12-1 Indicating hyphens and dashes in manuscript. (*a*) The em dash need not be marked if it is clearly typed as two hyphens. (*b*) The hyphen, too, is clearly recognizable and need not be marked if it is typed without space on either side. (*c–g*) Otherwise, hyphens and dashes generally have to be identified as shown here. For clarity, it is recommended that en and em dashes be represented by capital N and M rather than lowercase n and m.

cies are found, the copy editor is not normally expected to resolve the problem, which would require library research; instead, the discrepancies should be brought to the author's attention. (See "Querying" below.)

5   read for sense   This is the step in which the copy editor assumes the identity of the prospective reader and reviews the logic and coherence of the author's presentation. Writing style, organization of ideas, and continuity are approached as a separate step because they need undivided attention. (If you have to worry about capitalizing titles or italicizing symbols at this time, you can easily overlook a non sequitur or a contradictory statement.) This is also the step in which grammar, usage, and punctuation are corrected.

Punctuation as part of the sense reading   Some punctuation has merely a design function—for example, the period used after some headings or between table number and table title. That kind of punctuation should be taken care of when the heads or the tables are styled. Similarly, commas in four- or five-place numbers are styled during the mechanical reading. But structural punctuation—the internal punctuation in a sentence—is too dependent on syntax and meaning to be styled mechanically. It is unwise to make any changes in the internal punctuation of a sentence until the structure of the sentence is fully understood. (See Chapter 10.)

Factual accuracy   The author of an advanced or technical work usually bears sole responsibility for the accuracy of the material. Unless paid to do research, the copy editor should not be faulted for failing to correct obscure historical facts, mathematical errors, or the misspelling of unfamiliar names. Still, erudition is an important attribute for copy editors; the opportunity to point out fallacies and absurdities is one of the pleasures of a sometimes tedious and often unappreciated profession.

Watching for libel and plagiarism   A copy editor should be alert to passages with legal implications. Any statement that seems to libel or ridicule an individual, whether a public figure or not, should be brought to the attention of the publisher, as should remarks that appear to question the motives or competence of organized or professional groups (such as particular religious or medical organizations).

   Plagiarism is the passing off of another's work as one's own. Plagiarism can be difficult to spot and often more difficult to prove. If you have reason to suspect that a passage purporting to be original is not, notify the publisher at once. (Writers who forget to jot down sources when they add material to their idea file run the risk of later assuming that the material was their own and incorporating it in their work—an innocent lapse, perhaps, but a possible infringement of someone else's copyright.)

Rewriting Some degree of rewriting may be necessary at the sense-reading stage of the editing job. The amount of rewriting that is wanted can vary from publisher to publisher and from project to project. Beyond the correction of grammatical and syntactical faults, the copy editor should not rewrite without a clear mandate to do so.

If extensive rewriting is called for, it is wise to submit a few pages of the edited manuscript to the editor or author, showing the kind of rewriting you plan to do. In that way you can obtain approval in advance and not have to worry about overstepping the author's or the publisher's expectations.

Always remember that *the best rewrite is the least rewrite.* A beginner often tries to recast an entire sentence, when a more experienced editor would look for the least drastic correction—perhaps a simple word transposition or the substitution of one preposition for another. The urge to make unwarranted changes should be suppressed.

Any rewrite undertaken should sound as though the words were coming from the author's pen, not the copy editor's. If the author writes in a breezy or colloquial style, you should try to match it. If the author tends toward formal cadences, you should not introduce verb contractions and informal or slangy expressions. Also, needless to say, any rewrite should clearly be an improvement on the original.

The sense reading may include the adjustment of vocabulary and sentence length for a predetermined grade or reading level (see "Reading Levels" below).

Editing for bias A copy editor may be asked to rewrite to eliminate various types of discriminatory language. See Section 12-6.

Querying It is sometimes necessary to write a note to the author or editor questioning the accuracy of a statement, asking for clarification of a confusing passage, or recommending an improvement in wording or organization. Write short queries in the margin close to the affected line. Circle queries so that the compositor will not mistake them for copy to be set. If a query will not fit in the margin, write it on a flier (paper with a gummed edge, available in small pads). Attach the gummed edge to the back of the manuscript page, and fold the flier over to form a writing surface on the face of the page. (All fliers should be placed on the same side of the page—right or left—so that the person reviewing the queries can find them all easily.) Put the author's name and the manuscript page number on each flier so that if the flier falls off, it can be restored to the right place in the right manuscript. Address all queries to either the author *(Au:)* or the editor *(Ed:)*.

Keep queries as concise and to the point as possible. A vague question mark *(Au:?)* may be clear to you at the time, but the author probably won't know what it refers to. A precise query *(Au: Peterson here, but Petersen on p. 260—which?)* is more helpful and more likely to get results.

Don't clutter a manuscript with queries. If a problem recurs frequently, describe it the first time it appears, and then mark each subsequent occurrence with a light check mark in the margin. Note the page numbers of subsequent occurrences in the original query.

Don't query the obvious. If a correction is clearly called for, you needn't add *Au: OK?* Do query, however, when you are in doubt about a change. You can suggest a new wording or ask for clarification, but don't actually make a correction unless you are convinced of its soundness.

6   mark type   Some publishers expect their copy editors to mark up the manuscript with typographic specifications for the compositor—type size, typeface, leading, width of measure, and so forth—or, with the new technologies, to use a set of codes that identify the various elements in the book's format. Many of these codes are mnemonic and easy to use: *CN* for chapter number, *TT* for table title, and so forth. These simple codes are then translated into computer commands. In other publishing houses, the designer performs this step. Figure 12-2 shows an edited manuscript page with typographic codes inserted by the copy editor.

To communicate typographic information correctly, you have to understand the terminology of the printing industry, the meanings of typographic codes, and various other details of composition and production. This is not an area for amateurs.

7   prepare a style sheet   *Preliminary and working style sheets*   The publisher usually provides the copy editor with a *preliminary style sheet* indicating points of style that have already been determined for a particular project. During the editing, however, the copy editor will have to make decisions about many other details of style. Which of two spellings will be used? When is a certain word capitalized? Don't rely on memory; keep a record of your decisions by compiling a *working style sheet* as you go along. (See the "Style-Sheet Checklist" below for the kind of items to be included.)

Final style sheet   When the editing has been completed, the copy editor should prepare a *final style sheet* combining the preliminary and working style sheets. The final sheet is typed and returned to the publisher with the manuscript. Figure 12-3 shows a short, well-presented style sheet.

136

(CN)   Chapter 4

(CT)   THE PLANT KINGDOM

① THE STUDY OF BOTANY

Botany is a science that deals with plants: what kinds of
of plants are there how they live and grow, how they respond
to their surroundings, what diseases they are susceptible to,
and how they influence man's daily life. lives.

② Branches of botany. For convenience of study, the subject
of botany has been divided into several important branches.
Taxonomy, or systematic botany, deals with the classification of
plants. Morphology considers the form and structure of plants,

Au: not clear / together with plants to each other physiology is concerned with
the life processes of plants, and with the functions of the
different organs and tissues. Pathology deals with the diseases
of plants; ecology, with the relations of plants to their surroundings; paleobotany, or fossil botany, with the plants of
past geologic periods; and plant genetics, with the study of
heredity in plants. ¶ Other branches of the subject are concerned with separate groups of plants. Thus bacteriology is confined to the study of bacteria, mycology to the study of fungi,
algology to the study of algae, and bryology to the study of
mosses and liverworts.

② KINDS OF PLANTS. An excursion into the woods or fields
during the summer or fall reveals a wide diversity of form and
structure in the plants encountered. Some are tall trees;
others are lowgrowing herbs and shrubs. Some have beautiful

FIGURE 12-2 Edited page of manuscript.

Notice that there are no extraneous words; problems are generally *illustrated* rather than described.

The final style sheet will be referred to by both the author and the proofreader in checking proofs. It may also be used in future if the work is revised, when it will form the basis for styling the new edition.

STYLE-SHEET CHECKLIST

General
Italics or quotes for words as words, terms defined, unusual usage, coinages
Use of italics for emphasis
Punctuation (commas in series, any variation from usual style)
Grammar (5 lb is, mathematics is)
Style for genus and species
Spelling (any general rule or authority other than *Webster's* that is to be followed)
Formality (use of contractions, etc.)
References (representative footnotes and bibliographic entries; source notes for tables, i.e., whether handled as complete citation or by reference to end-of-chapter references or bibliography)
Legends [representative legend showing handling of (*a*), (*b*) parts and credit line]

Numbers, Measurements, Abbreviations, and Symbols
Give examples of each:
Numbers in general (spell below 10 or 100; 1000 or 1,000; 0.10 or .10; approximations; fractions; ordinal numbers)
Measurements (group all simple abbreviated measurements, all simple spelled-out measurements, all compound measurements—show with numbers)
Numbers as adjectives (35-mm camera)
Ranges (text and tables)
Vectors
Ratios
Percentages (text and tables)
Temperature (text and tables)
Angles
Money
Ages
Time [A.M., A.D., century, decade (e.g., 1920s), month and year]
"times" (10 times)
e.g., i.e., et al., op. cit., vs., etc.
Symbols [symbols combined with words (B-H curve, β ray); mathematical

variables; abbreviations in subscripts and superscripts; chemical notation]

Computer terminology

Abbreviations and acronyms (capital initial-letter abbreviations, lowercase initial-letter abbreviations, capital-and-lowercase combinations, abbreviations formed by shortening words, letter-and-number combinations, letter-and-symbol combinations, use of periods and plurals with abbreviations)

Cross-references [part, chapter, section, figure (include *a* and *b* style), problem, equation, example, page ranges in text and footnotes]

Capitalization
List items alphabetically, and include trade names. Include terms that should be lowercased, when appropriate.

Italics
List foreign-language terms and Latin binomials alphabetically. Include anglicized terms to be set in roman type. Do not list italic symbols here.

Spelling and Hyphenation
List items alphabetically. Include proper names on which there is a question of spelling rather than of capitalization. Show hyphenation in typical compound modifiers.

Reading Levels
Textbooks and other educational materials are usually written for specific grade levels; the reading level of the text must be suitable for the intended readers of the book. Many different measurements are used for determining reading level, among them the Dale-Chall formula, the Spache formula, and the Fry reading scale. The formulas are similar in that passages of roughly the same length are chosen at random for the purpose of counting such things as sentence length, number of syllables, and the number of words in the passage that are considered unfamiliar for students at the intended grade level. To edit for this kind of readability, a copy editor must be familiar with the required formula and applicable word list and with the educational concepts behind their use.

In another, nonformula type of test, the difficulty of the material and the comprehension of an individual student can both be measured by the student's success in supplying missing words in selected passages. Such tests include the cloze procedure and the Degrees of Reading Power test.

Even when writing (or editing) to a given grade level is not at issue, expository text should be as clear and comprehensible as possible. See the Bibliography for books on developing or improving one's writing style.

FINAL STYLE SHEET

Anderson: Marketing Research, 1/e

GENERAL

is called a <u>micromodel</u> (ital for definition, emphasis, word
    as word)
"optipessimist" (quotes for coinages, irony, inexact use)
to classify as "small" those which... (quotes for classifi-
    cations in discussions of surveys)
don't (contractions OK--follow copy); ad (advertisement, OK)

Footnotes:

    Jane A. Author and John B. Coauthor: <u>Book Title</u>, Harper &
    Row, New York, 1980.

    Jane A. Author, "Chapter Title," in John B. Compiler (ed.),
    <u>Book Title</u>, 3d ed., Prentice-Hall, Englewood Cliffs, N.J.,
    1978.

    F. J. Author, "Title of Article," <u>Journal Title</u>, 3(8):46-52
    (1976). (Follow copy on spelled first name or initials)

Bibliography:

    Alphabetical, unnumbered; same as footnotes, but first
        author's name inverted; colon after author's name:

    Author, Jane A., and John B. Coauthor: <u>Book Title</u>, etc.

NUMBERS, MEASUREMENTS, ABBREVIATIONS, AND SYMBOLS

Generally spell below 10, including time; figures with units
    of measurement

1000; 10,000; 2 billion
nine respondents; 13 cities
a value of 1; a score of 9; a factor of 10
coded 0 and 1 (not zero and one)
.05 confidence level; correlation of .971 (otherwise zero
    before decimals)
a 35-mile (56-km) radius
2-L bottles
three-point scale
two to four responses
a 10 to 1 chance
a/b ratio; male-female ratio
5 percent (% in tables)
10 cents; 6 francs; $7 million
a 2-year-old
nine minutes; 60 days; three months' duration
11 <u>A.M.</u>
mid 1960s; mid-seventeenth century
December 1981; December 12, 1981

FIGURE 12-3 Final style sheet.

NUMBERS, MEASUREMENTS, cont'd.

e.g.; i.e. (OK)
brand A; cake B; sample A
J scale
Q-sort technique
U-shaped curve
CBS; NBC
M.S.I.; M.I.T.
TV (or television--follow copy)
Chap. 3; Fig. 4; Table 14; Appendix B

CAPITALIZATION

Brand Rating Index
Bureau of Business Research; the bureau
Federal Advisory Council; the council
federal statutes
law of costs; Reilly's law of retail gravitation
marketing research director
Midwest
Omaha, Nebraska (text); Neb. (footnotes)

SPELLING AND HYPHENATION

analog
behavioral-science techniques
break even (v.); break-even
   point
closed-circuit television
culturally defined
data-based methods
direct mail brand purchasing
   test (au. pref.)
financial-management function
first repeat purchase curve
fixed-ratio method
four-state model
go no-go decision
intermedia evaluation
key-word scrutiny
land-use planning
last in first out (lifo)
long-range action
lower-level manager
marketing information system
market-share goals
market test experiment
mini-market
model building
n-dimensional
new-product information
newsmagazine

nonbusiness
paired-comparison method
postdecision
product line; product-line
   price
product preference studies
product testing technique
product-user test
quality-control program
random-access capability
rank-order (v.)
real-world applications
reevaluation
sales-level predictions
second-order criteria
small-group theory
test-market sales
three-dimensional
time-series analysis
trade-area boundaries
trademark
trade name
user-oriented system
user-system interface
vice president
word-association test

PROOFREADING

A professional proofreader performs a wide variety of tasks, depending on the type of proof (galleys, page proofs, final film proofs, or computer printouts), the needs of the assignment, and the instructions received. A proofreader may be asked only to compare the typeset material with the original copy. Other responsibilities require more judgment: correcting grammar and punctuation or checking type specifications and page makeup. To do this, a publisher's or compositor's proofreader must be familiar with the practices and terminology of the printing industry.

General Considerations

Proofreaders' corrections fall into the following categories.

compositor's ("printer's") errors The proofreader looks for (1) typographical errors (typos); (2) incorrect typefaces, type sizes, spacing, indentions, and so forth; and (3) failure to follow page makeup instructions (such as page length and placement of tables and illustrations). Sometimes an innocuous compositor's error is allowed to stand if extensive work would be required to correct it. For example, if a heading appears with incorrect but consistent spacing above and below or has been set one size too large or too small throughout, the proofreader should bring it to the attention of the editor to find out whether the error will be allowed to stand.

errors in style A proofreader is expected to have a thorough knowledge of the publisher's house style. If the same stylistic error occurs frequently in an assignment, the proofreader should check with the editor before marking it; the editor may let it stand if it is an acceptable variation. Occasional oversights are corrected without querying.

errors in grammar, usage, punctuation A proofreader is responsible for correcting clear-cut errors in grammar, such as disagreement of subject and verb or the use of faulty antecedents. Cases in which the grammatical issues are debatable may be queried—for example, the number of the verb used with a collective noun. The proofreader should correct, without querying, errors in word usage, such as *affect* for *effect* and *militate* for *mitigate*, and clear-cut errors in punctuation. Comma corrections should be handled judiciously; rigid application of the rules of comma usage can result in heavy proof corrections. The following principle is a good general guide: Where the meaning of a sentence is unclear and the addition or deletion of a comma will clarify it, make the correction.

See Section 12-6 for methods of eliminating bias.

Marking the Proofs

color of ink or pencil   See Section 12-3.

proofreader's marks   A proofreader's correction has two parts. First, the point in the text at which the correction is to be made is indicated, and then the correction itself is shown in the margin. If it is not shown in the margin, the correction will not be made, because compositors do not reread typeset copy—they simply run their eyes down the margin to see what lines need their attention.

Marks should be clearly made and be unambiguous in meaning. Figure 12-4 illustrates the proofreader's marks in common use, and Figure 12-5 shows a marked galley proof.

what not to mark   A proofreader's skill is not judged by the number of marks on the proof. It is the number of meaningful marks that counts. If, after reading a batch of proof, you have found little or nothing to mark, resist the impulse to put something down just to prove that you've been on the job. Publishers know that it is possible for a proofreader to do a thorough job and yet find little to correct. Most of the minor physical imperfections seen on proofs today are the result of poor xerographic copying and have nothing to do with the quality of the typesetting. Nevertheless, some proofreaders insist on cluttering the proofs with marks such as X and *Clean*—largely a waste of time. Call attention only to conspicuous instances of battered or dirty letters, type out of line, etc.

queries   Short queries to the editor may be written directly on the proof. Address them to *Ed.* and circle them. Longer queries should be written on gummed fliers, attached to the underside of the proof and folded over.

Queries should always be concise and specifically worded. A vague *Ed: OK?* may be clear to you but not to the editor. In addition to the query, indicate exactly where in the line the editor should look to find the problem: a small check above the word in question or a light circling of the passage in lead pencil will direct the editor's eye to it.

Excessive queries take up your time and delay the editor's work later. Try not to query unnecessarily. If the same problem recurs, do not repeat the same query at each occurrence; a single query will suffice, with later instances lightly circled in pencil and checked in the margin.

rewriting   The proofreader should not attempt to rewrite or polish at the proof stage. If the quality of the writing is so consistently poor as to cause concern, bring the problem to the editor's attention before attempting to solve it on your own.

word division   It is, at present, impossible to reconcile all the traditional rules of word division with the practices of modern computer composition. Rigid application of the rules is therefore unrealistic. A word break that is actually misleading to the reader should, of course, be corrected; e.g., "pro/gress" as a noun should be changed to "prog/ress." Be consistent: if you change a particular break once, change it throughout.

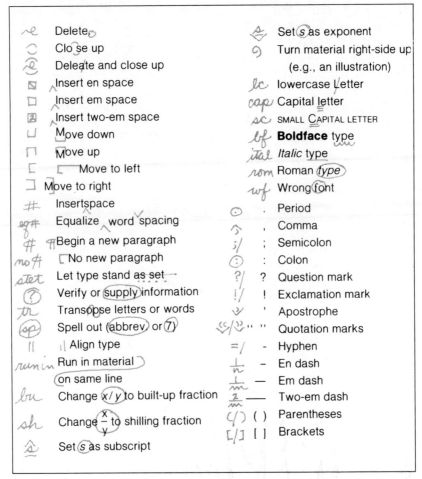

FIGURE 12-4   Proofreader's marks.

7020A$4　　UG　　McG-H　　Thompson: Introduction to Natural History 99

Chapter 4

THE PLANT KINGDOM

THE STUDY OF BOTANY

Botany is a science that deals with plants: what kinds of plants there are, how they live and grow, how they respond to their surroundings, what diseases they are susceptible to, and how they influence our daily lives.

Branches of botany. For convenience of study, the subject of botany has been divided into several important branches. *Taxonomy,* or systematic botany, deals with the classification of plants. *Morphology* considers the form and structure of plants, together with plants to each other. *Physiology* is concerned with the life processes of plants and the functions of the different organs and tissues. *Pathology* deals with the diseases of plants; ecology, with the relations of plants to there surroundings; *paleobotany,* or fossil botany, with the plants of past geologic periods; and *plant genetics,* with the study of heredity inplants.

Other branches of the subject are concerned with separate groups of plants. Thus, *bacteriology* is confined to the study of bacteria, *mycology* to the study of fungi, *Algology* to the study of algea, and *bryology* to the study of moses and liverworts.

Kinds of plants. An excursion into the woods or fields during the summer or fall reveals a wide diversity of form and structure in the plants encountered. Some are tall trees; others are low-growing herbs and shrubs. Some have beautiful flowers and produce seed, while others, like the ferns, produce no flowers at all but reproduce by means of tiny structures called spores. Some live on land, others in water, some are giants, while others are so small as to be seen only with a microscope. These wide differences led botanists years ago to attempt to arrange plants into different groups for the convenience of study and discussion. Many different systems of classification have been used, but the ones most generally accepted are based upon fundamental similarities or relationships and are called natural systems. According to these systems, the entire plant kingdom is usually subdivided into several large main divisions. Each of these is then subdivided into appropriate groups.

Among the plants lowest in development, with the least structural differentiation, are the bacteria, the fungi, and the algae. These plants have no roots, stems, or leaves. A plant body of this type is called a **thallus.**[1] The simplest of these plants are the bacteria, most of which

[1]From the Greek *thallos,* from *thallein,* "to sprout."

are unicellular, *i.e.,* the entire plant consists of but a single cell. Hence, the individual plants are visible only under the high magnification of a microscope. They are commonly called microbes. These organisms

FIGURE 12-5 Marked galley proof.

Step-by-Step Working Procedure

The procedure given here is for page reading. (In galley proofs, of course, omit checking for running heads and folios, widows, page length, and other elements applying only to page makeup.)

1   check the schedule   With the first batch of proof, you should receive a schedule for the return of first and final pages to the compositor. Missed deadlines can ruin production schedules and cause a costly delay in the publication of the book.

2   examine the working material   You will normally receive a style sheet and a composition order (type specifications) with the first batch of proof. There will often be other specific instructions as well. Familiarize yourself with all this material and resolve any major discrepancies before starting to work on the proofs.

3   check the sequence of pages (or galleys)   Make certain that no proofs are missing by checking the folios. If any pages (or galleys) are missing and not accounted for, call the editor as soon as possible. In the page-proof stage, all blanks (pages with nothing on them) should be indicated, preferably on the preceding page.

4   read running heads and folios   Check the composition order for specifications, and then read the running heads and folios for typographical errors, position, and wording. Check the spacing between running heads and text. Note that the specified space between running head and text is always maintained—do not alter this space for purposes of makeup adjustment or any other reason.

5   check the sequence of numbered elements   Any numbered sequence, such as artwork, footnotes, equations, tables, and numbered paragraphs, involves the possibility of error. Check every sequence as a separate step. Be especially alert to any author addition or deletion that affects numbering.

6   check the galley corrections   If you have received the previously corrected galleys, it is important to check the corrections against the page proofs. Check the line above and below each correction, as well as the line itself.

7   check the artwork   If artwork is shown on the proofs, you should verify each piece of art by comparing it with the illustration proof supplied. Check the illustration proof for any art corrections, and make certain that they have been made. Carefully read any labels (words, symbols, numbers) on the art for errors.

In some offset books it is impractical to show the artwork in the pages. In these books, space (called a *window*) is left for the insertion of the artwork later. Measure this space against the illustration proof to make sure that the illustration, with specified space around it, will fit.

8   read legends   Legends must be read against the manuscript, since normally they will not have been read before. Check the sequence, and be alert for any change that might affect the numbering.

9   check cross-references   References to pages, sections, chapters, and other elements of the work, whether already set in type or merely indicated in handwriting on the proof, should be verified whenever possible.

10   check makeup   Read the makeup instructions carefully, and then check to see that the compositor has followed them. Do this with particular care in the first batch of proof so that the compositor can be alerted early to prevent the recurrence of the same makeup errors.

In dummied books, you are responsible for making sure that the compositor has followed the dummy exactly. (Do not write corrections on the dummy or alter it in any way.)

In books that are to be printed in more than one color of ink, you may receive either a separated set, that is, a set of proof for each color, or a master set on which colors are merely noted. In either case, verify that all elements, color and black, are correctly designated. Sample pages are your guide to the "color breaks."

Correct widows and "blocks"—three or more lines of text beginning (or ending) with the same word or ending with hyphens.

Never make changes in makeup on the basis of subjective preferences. For example, if you think artwork would look better in another place, make the suggestion to the editor, but do not move the art unless its position violates the makeup instructions for the book. If an author has requested repositioning of artwork or tables, you are not responsible for making the decision, but can help the editor by setting forth what is involved: how many pages would have to be remade. how many lines reset, and so forth.

In page proofs, if any addition or deletion (whether made by you or by the author) involves resetting more than two or three lines, try to add or delete a corresponding number of characters to keep resetting to a minimum. This is especially important when changes will affect more than one page. If you cannot work out a practical solution, explain the problem on a flier.

Check the specifications for page size, and, taking facing pages (a verso and its facing recto) as a unit, measure page depth. Unless instructed otherwise, follow these rules: (*a*) facing pages are to be the same depth with an allowable variation of 6 points; and (*b*) facing pages may run one line long or one line short, as necessary. Problems of page depth must be handled by the proofreader, except for major compositor's errors, which the compositor will have to handle. Exercise judgment in making these corrections. The devices used for making page adjustments are, in order of preference: (*a*) manipulation of spacing; (*b*) editorial cutting or creation of lines; (*c*) as a last resort, line transpositions from one page to another.

If you are uncertain of the best way to handle a makeup problem, explain the alternatives on a flier.

11 read the text This is often the heart of the proofreader's work. It requires the reading of every word and character on the proofs. In the past, proof used to be read aloud with another person (the "copy holder"), but that is an expensive luxury today. Proofs are rarely compared word for word with the manuscript nowadays—publishers have found that the process yields too few errors to justify the time and effort involved. Instead, the manuscript or previous proofs are supplied for reference in case the proofreader suspects that words have been left out, transposed, or otherwise set incorrectly. Material set by a computerized process is subject to electronic error as well as manual (input) error and should be read as carefully as proofs set by other methods.

12 initial the proofs As a final step, initial each galley or page of proof in the upper right corner.

Returning the Proof
Be sure to return all corresponding material (manuscript, galleys) with each batch of proof, and all instructional materials (style sheet, composition order, and so forth) with the last batch.

12-6

BIAS-FREE PUBLISHING

Publishers recognize that textbooks carry a social as well as an educational message. The publishing industry supports the belief that the acceptance of human diversity is a fundamental American value and maintains that through exposure to such diversity children develop a sense of respect for themselves and for people of different backgrounds.[1]

In the 1960s and 1970s, momentous changes in social awareness, such as civil-rights legislation and the women's movement, prompted educators, parents, and publishers to reexamine educational materials to make sure that women and minority groups were represented without prejudice and in fair proportion. The concern has since widened to include disabled and elderly people as well.

Most educational materials today emphasize the inherent dignity and worth of every human being and encourage all students—whatever their cultural group, sex, or physical handicap—to pursue their own academic and vocational interests to the best of their ability.

Bias against Minority Groups

A minority group is one that differs in some respects from a larger or more dominant population. Minority groups include ethnic, cultural, national, religious, and what are sometimes loosely referred to as racial groups. Discrimination against these groups can manifest itself in many ways in both language and illustration. Some guidelines follow for avoiding bias against minority groups.

1   Educational materials should reflect the diversity of American society. Do not imply that any group is more or less worthy than any other, but emphasize the achievements of minority groups and the value of diversity in a multicultural society.

2   Members of minority groups are physicians as well as patients, homeowners as well as tenants, golfers as well as caddies. They should be portrayed, in fair proportion to population ratios, as integrated participants in every aspect of contemporary life. The aim is not to present an unrealistic or utopian view, but to make sure that educational materials reflect the ideal society toward which the United States is striving. At the same time, do not avoid frank discussion of the difficulty and hostility that some groups have encountered in trying to achieve full acceptance in the United States.

3   In choosing illustrations, avoid those which stereotype any group by economic status, life-style, or mode of dress. Reject drawings that over-

---

[1]"Textbook Publishers and the Censorship Controversy," School Division of the Association of American Publishers, New York, 1981.

emphasize (caricature) the physical characteristics sometimes associated with particular groups.

4   In choosing fictional names for characters in stories, examples, problems, case studies, and the like, select names from a variety of language groups.

5   In using terms to designate minority groups, try to be sensitive to the preferences of the groups themselves. This suggestion is sometimes difficult to follow, because the acceptability of a term can vary with time and place. The following list indicates terms that are currently acceptable, as well as some that are deprecated or questionable.

COMMONLY ENCOUNTERED
MINORITY-GROUP DESIGNATIONS

aborigine/aboriginal. Widely used to refer to the aboriginal peoples of Australia, although some prefer the term *Australian blacks.* Capitalization depends on whether the term is regarded as a proper name or a descriptive designation.

alien, resident alien. Acceptable when it refers to a non-U.S. citizen.

American. The use of the term *American* to refer to a citizen of the United States is acceptable. *United States citizen* is generally used when it is necessary to emphasize the distinction between a U.S. citizen and a citizen of, say, a South American country or Canada. Immigrant groups that have settled in the United States are described as *American* (as in *Irish-American*).

American of Hispanic background. See *Latin American.*

American policy, American economy. The terms *United States policy* and *United States economy* are preferable. (See also *we/our.*)

Amerind, Amerindian. Not recommended. The term *American Indian* or *Native American* is preferable.

Anglo-American. Not recommended. Use *English-speaking* or *white,* depending on what is meant.

Asian. Widely used to refer to various peoples from the near and far east. Acceptable, but be specific if possible (e.g., *Chinese, Japanese*). (See also *oriental.*)

black. Widely accepted. Like *white, black* is considered a generic or descriptive term and is therefore usually not capitalized.

Boricua. Carib word for natives of Puerto Rico. Not recommended as an English-language substitute for *Puerto Rican.*

Chicano, Chicana. Often used by Mexican-American activists instead of *Mexican-American.*

coloured. Has application in South Africa for people of mixed African and other ancestry.

Cosa Nostra. Use *organized crime.*

English. Should be distinguished from *British* and *Briton.* Not everyone in Great Britain is English.

Eskimo. Widely used. However, the term *Innuit* (singular, *Innuk*) is preferred by Arctic and Canadian peoples and is often an acceptable alternative. These terms are sometimes spelled with one *n: Inuit, Inuk.*

ethnic, ethnics. Colloquialism. Usually refers to "new immigrant" nationalities from southern and eastern Europe, but may be applied to any group.

gringo. Colloquialism. Not recommended.

Hebrew. A language. Not acceptable for reference to a person or a religion, except in the context of ancient Israel.

Hispanic (adj.) See *Latin American.*

Hispanic-American. See *Latin American.*

Ibero-American. See *Latin American.*

Indian. The preferred term is *American Indian* or *Native American.* Acceptable when used to refer to an individual from India.

Irish-American, Italian-American, Polish-American, etc. Used in political and sociological writing to refer to people of foreign heritage who have settled in the United States.

Israeli. Citizen of Israel; not all Israelis are Jews.

Jew. Person whose religion or religious background is Jewish.

Latin American. There is wide confusion over what term to use when referring to Spanish- and Portuguese-speaking people in the western hemisphere. *Hispanic* is often used instead of *Latin American* in referring to residents of the United States who speak Spanish or are one or two generations removed from Spanish-speaking people from one of the Central American, South American, or Caribbean countries. However, some groups object to the term *Hispanic* on the grounds that it emphasizes a shared European cultural heritage rather than a shared new world cultural heritage. And certainly not all Spanish-speaking people from Central America, South America, or Caribbean countries are of Spanish descent. When possible, be specific.

Some resent *Latin American*, saying it is insensitive to national differences; some find it inaccurate, since not all people referred to as Latin American speak a Latin-based language. Further, it usually does not include French speakers.

Again, when possible, be specific. *Central American* or *South American* can also be used. *Latin American* is preferable to *Hispanic-American* (often used for Spanish speakers who have settled in the United States). *Ibero-American* is acceptable, but clumsy; use *Brazilian* instead of *Luso-American*.

Latino. Preferred by some groups to *Hispanic.*

Mafia. Use *organized crime.*

Mexican-American. Acceptable.

Mongoloid, Negroid, Caucasoid. Not recommended. The names from which these terms were derived—*Mongolian, Negro, Caucasian*—are no longer considered valid as terms for designating races. Further, *-oid* has a pejorative connotation.

mulatto. Not recommended. The term is from the Spanish *mulo,* "mule," and is used to refer to a person of mixed ancestry. Use *person of mixed ancestry.*

Muslim, Moslem, Muhammadan. These terms refer to persons whose religion is Islam. *Muslim* is preferred in the United States. *Muhammadan* is not recommended. (Note that the term *Muslim* is not interchangeable with *Arab.*)

Native American. Preferred by some groups to *American Indian.* When this term is used with a lowercase *n,* it can refer to a person born in the United States (sometimes called a *native-born American*).

native peoples. Acceptable.

Negro. Acceptable in the appropriate historical context. Preferred by some groups to *black.*

North American. Acceptable.

oriental. Not recommended. Use *Asian,* or be specific.

Québecois, Quebecker, Quebecer. French speakers in Quebec prefer *Québecois;* English speakers in Quebec prefer *Quebeckers.* (*Quebecer,* occasionally used in the United States, can lead to mispronunciation.)

Scottish, Scots, Scotch. Scottish is the preferred adjective; use *Scots* for the people, *Scotch* for certain products or objects (such as whisky).

Spanish-speaking people. See *Latin American.*

third world. Often used to refer to developing countries, especially those not aligned with either the Soviet Union or the United States. In the United States, also used to refer to minority groups taken as a whole. Not recommended. If the term is used, care should be taken to make sure that the intended meaning is clear from the context in which it appears.

WASP. Colloquialism of limited application. Stands for "white, Anglo-Saxon Protestant."

we/our (when referring to the United States). Not recommended.

Gender-Related Bias
Sometimes called *sexism,* gender-related bias can occur in the form of attitudes and assumptions or as an outgrowth of our language itself, which has long used male terms to represent humankind in general. This discussion covers many of the problems associated with editing to eliminate sexism, whether in one's own writing or another's.

sexist assumptions Some authors ascribe maleness to general, non-gender-related terms such as *farmer* or *pioneer.* Consider this example:

> Wave after wave of immigrants arrived from Europe, bringing with them their wives and children.

This sentence implies that "immigrants" must be men (since immigrants have wives)—but what were the women and children if not immigrants themselves?

As recently as 1976, a book on the subject of good writing asked:

> Who is this elusive creature, the reader? . . . He is assailed on every side by forces competing for his time; by newspapers and magazines, by television and radio and stereo, by his wife and children and pets. . . .

The author of this passage might be able to defend the use of *he* as a generic pronoun, but the reference to *his wife* is the giveaway—readers, to this writer, were male.

stereotypes   Stereotyping ascribes certain characteristics to a group of people as a whole, often inaccurately and emotionally. The sexes are frequently stereotyped, girls being characterized as weak, frivolous, or timid; boys as strong, rational, or brave. Avoid the clichés that further such notions:

> the weaker sex   all brawn and no brains
> feminine intuition   she thinks like a man

Also avoid gender epithets:

> *male* nurse
> *lady* doctor
> *woman* anthropologist

except in the unlikely context that would also require you to say "*female* nurse, "*gentleman* doctor," or "*man* anthropologist."

courtesy titles   Use a courtesy title with both male and female names or with neither:

> *Avoid:* Schmidt and Mrs. Thatcher
> *Prefer:* Helmut Schmidt and Margaret Thatcher
>   *or:* Mrs. Thatcher and Mr. Schmidt
>   *or:* Prime Minister Thatcher and Chancellor Schmidt
>   *or:* Schmidt and Thatcher

Ms. is an acceptable and useful designation in place of Miss or Mrs.

anthropomorphic sexism   There is a tendency to ascribe dominant characteristics to the male of the species, whether biologically warranted or not:

> a bull seal watches over his harem. [Photo caption]

One might just as well say that the females had hired the bull as their bodyguard.

sentimental feminine abstractions Personifications of nature (e.g., "Mother Earth") generally do not belong in expository writing.

> *Avoid:* The changing face of nature can never be understood unless her metabolism is also studied.
> *Prefer:* The changing face of nature can never be understood unless its metabolism is also studied.

In nautical jargon, ships—even those with masculine names—are referred to as *she*, but the feminine pronoun should be avoided in other contexts:

> *Avoid:* When the *Speedwell* proved unseaworthy, she was abandoned at Plymouth and the entire company crowded aboard the *Mayflower*.
> *Prefer:* When the *Speedwell* proved unseaworthy, *it* was abandoned at Plymouth . . . .

Do not refer to countries as *she:*

> *Avoid:* Romania had claimed the whole of the Banat as the price of her adherence to the Allied cause in 1916.
> *Prefer:* Romania had claimed the whole of the Banat as the price of *its* adherence to the Allied cause in 1916.

sexist language Many people believe that the English language itself does much to shape attitudes and have suggested that the word *man* and the male pronouns *he, him,* and *his* be replaced in all generic senses. Whether such a radical change in the vernacular can ever be accomplished by willing it so is open to question. But wherever you stand on this issue, you should be aware that the people responsible for purchasing textbooks (adoption committees, administrators, and teachers) will generally reject a text that inadvertently uses sexist language.

occupational titles Except in a few firmly entrenched terms like *actress* and *waitress*, words or suffixes indicating gender are best avoided. Some representative occupational titles follow. A complete directory of job titles can be found in *Dictionary of Occupational Titles*, U.S. Department of Labor, Employment and Training Administration.

Avoid	*Prefer*
aviatrix	aviator
chairman	chairperson; chair

Avoid	*Prefer*
coed	student
delivery boy or man	deliverer
draftsman	drafter
fireman	fire fighter
foreman	supervisor
houseboy	house cleaner; housekeeper
housewife	homemaker
maid	house cleaner; housekeeper
poetess	poet
policeman; policewoman	police officer
postman	letter carrier; mail carrier
repairman	repairer
salesman	sales representative
sculptress	sculptor
usherette	usher

avoiding generic male pronouns   Traditionally, male pronouns *(he, him, his)* have been used in English to represent the generic third person singular: "Everyone will turn in his assignment by Thursday." Avoiding such locutions can be time-consuming, but is not as difficult as some people think. The simplest but least graceful way to eliminate a generic male pronoun is to change *he* to *he or she* (or *she or he*), which often leads to a clumsy retinue of *her or him, his or hers,* and *himself or herself.* Consider this sentence:

> When an adolescent starts to define himself as a person, he does so by separating his likes and dislikes from those of his parents.

Recast in a *he or she* mold, the sentence becomes ludicrous:

> *Poor:* When an adolescent starts to define himself or herself as a person, he or she does so by separating his or her likes and dislikes from those of his or her parents.

Clearly, that won't do. With practice and a little care, however, one can apply some simple corrective methods to create an expository prose style that is neither sexist nor ungainly.

Before applying any of the following suggestions, think a passage through to the end. Otherwise you may find that your solution, which solved the problem so aptly at the start, no longer works at the end of the passage, causing you to go back and start over. And be sure to carry through. If you have changed *he* to *they*, don't overlook the verb that needs correcting as well. The following paragraphs suggest several ways of recasting the same original sentence:

> *Original:* When an investor buys common stock, he receives a certificate of ownership indicating the number of shares he purchased and their par value.

1 *Pluralize.* Pluralizing is often the best and easiest choice:

> When investors buy common stock, they receive a certificate of ownership indicating the number of shares they purchased and the par value of the shares.

The "adolescent" example lends itself admirably to this solution:

> When adolescents start to define themselves as persons, they do so by separating their likes and dislikes from those of their parents.

2 *Recast in the passive voice.* Don't be afraid of the passive voice. It need not produce tedious prose.

> When an investor buys common stock, a certificate of ownership is received . . . .

3 *Use "you."* Being informal and immediate, this works well in self-help and how-to books, problem sections of textbooks, and so forth:

> When you invest in common stock, you receive a certificate of ownership indicating the number of shares you purchased and their par value.

4 *Use "we."* This device also has an informal tone:

> When we invest in common stock, we receive a certificate of ownership indicating the number of shares we purchased . . . .

5 *Use "one."* Although *one* may sound stiff and formal in some contexts, it is often extremely useful:

> When one buys common stock, one receives a certificate of ownership indicating the number of shares purchased . . . .

(Note "one . . . *one*," not "one . . . *he*.")

6   *Use a relative pronoun.* Often overlooked, this construction can solve many wording problems:

> An investor who buys common stock receives a certificate of owner-
> ship . . . .

7   *Use a participle.* A participle can serve the same function as the *who* construction:

> An investor buying common stock receives a certificate of ownership . . . .

8   *Use "she or he" (or "he or she").* As noted above, this is the most obvious solution, but it can also be the most inelegant and soporific:

> *Poor:* When an investor buys common stock, he or she receives a certif-
> icate of ownership indicating the number of shares he or she pur-
> chased and their par value.

Reserve *he or she* for isolated occurrences.

9   *Recast without pronouns.* It's astonishing how expendable pronouns can be:

> An investor in common stock receives a certificate of ownership indicating
> the number of shares purchased (or *that were* purchased) and their par
> value.

10   *Repeat the noun.* Many writers are reluctant to resort to repetition, but the result is not always inelegant:

> When an investor buys common stock, the investor receives a certificate
> of ownership . . . .

Overreliance on repetition, of course, can create leaden prose.

11   *Rephrase.* If all other attempts fail, rewrite the sentence. For example:

> A certificate of ownership indicating the number of shares purchased and
> their par value accompanies every purchase of common stock.

12   *Supply a qualifying statement.* Some writers object to changing generic male pronouns. There are also subject areas in which the task proves very difficult. For example, in a discussion of pediatric nursing, it may be expedient to call the nurse *she* and the infant *he* throughout for clarity. In such instances, publishers often recommend that a statement be given, in the preface or in a footnote, calling attention to the fact that the pronouns were chosen for the sake of convenience and are intended to be universal.

Several of the foregoing methods can often be combined in what might be called a mixed solution:

> *Original:* By his fourth year, the child's phonological system approximates the model, and he usually corrects the remaining deviations by the time he enters school.
>
> *Mixed solutions:* (1) By the fourth year *(elimination of pronoun),* the child's phonological system approximates the model, and the remaining deviations are usually corrected *(passive voice)* by the time the child *(repetition of noun)* enters school.
>
> (2) Between the ages of three and four *(rephrasing),* the child's phonological system approximates the model, and the child *(repetition of noun)* usually corrects the remaining deviations before entering *(participle)* school.

Other solutions are possible as well. Needless to say, if you are editing someone else's work, the less drastic your revision the better.

Bias against Disabled People

In fiction, disabilities often form the basis of cliché: writers have long used them to represent frightening or sinister characters (Captain Hook, The Boot) or to play upon the reader's sympathies (Clara, Tiny Tim).

In educational materials, disabilities are often not represented at all, except to provide object lessons in perseverance and nobility. And yet it is estimated that more than 35 million citizens of the United States have some form of disability. They, and their needs, should not be ignored in textbooks and reference books.

Some of the curriculum areas that provide good opportunities for including disabled people are career and vocational education, language arts, mathematics, science, social studies, health studies, and physical education. Writers should try not to limit the portrayal of handicapped people to those who are visually impaired or use wheelchairs or crutches—other, less obvious disabilities should also be represented if possible: for example, learning disabilities and mental retardation.

Most physically impaired people lead full and useful lives—as teachers, artists, workers, business executives, parents. They should be fairly represented as integrated members of a larger community.

Discrimination against disabled people is sometimes called *handicapism.* The terms *handicapped person, disabled person,* and *exceptional person* are used interchangeably.

Age Bias

In children's books especially, old people are often stereotyped as infirm and ill-tempered or, at the other extreme, as totally good-natured and child-nurturing. Like any other group, however, elderly people should be represented realistically, with recognition of their diverse human qualities and of their value as vital members of their communities.

Discrimination against old people is sometimes referred to as *ageism*.

MAKING
THE INDEX

This chapter provides instruction for preparing an index in the traditional manner from page proofs—how to select the entries; record them on separate index cards; arrange, alphabetize, and mark the cards; and prepare the final manuscript. The revision of an old index for a new edition is also discussed. Although certain simple indexes can be compiled and alphabetized by computer, a subject index with complex subentries still requires the judgment of a qualified indexer—someone skilled in selecting the most appropriate wording for an entry and in arranging the entries for maximum usefulness to the reader.

Some authors enjoy the challenge of compiling their own index, but unless they have the time and skill to attempt it, the job is best left to a professional indexer. Most publishers can arrange to have an index compiled by a freelance indexing service; the cost of this service is usually deducted from the author's royalties.

13-1

TIMING

Preparation of the index is usually the last editorial step to be completed before the book is manufactured, and if it is not performed on schedule, publication may have to be delayed. Although it is possible to compile an index from the manuscript or galleys, most indexers prefer to work from page proofs because these proofs generally include all corrections, as well as final page numbers. In the absence of final page numbers, more steps are required and the possibility of error is greater.

Start indexing immediately upon receipt of the first installment of page proof. Do the indexing for each subsequent installment of proof as it arrives, and complete the alphabetizing and typing within a few days after receiving the last of the page proofs, so as not to delay publication.

13-2

SELECTING THE ENTRIES

Keep in mind the people who are going to read the book. Include all the items that they will be likely to look for when they consult the index, and put the items in the form in which readers will expect to find them. For every entry, ask yourself the following questions:

1   Is the reader likely to look for this information in an index?

2   What is the most significant word in this discussion? (If more than one word might be looked up, make an entry for each of them.)

3   What other, related information is the reader likely to want to know? (Perhaps a cross-reference to a related entry should be provided for the reader's convenience.)

Main Entries and Subentries

An index heading (main entry) should be a noun or a substantive phrase. If an adjective constitutes the first part of a well-known term and would naturally be sought by the user of the index, it retains its leading position and determines the alphabetical placement of the term:

Alimentary canal	Domestic economy
Carbolic acid	Real estate

An adjective alone does not constitute a complete entry.

A long string of page numbers after a single heading is objectionable. For example, in a book on petroleum, reference to every page on which the word *petroleum* appears would obviously be worthless. The solution lies in concise qualifications of the main entries to reduce to a minimum the actual number of page references following each heading.

Chapter titles and section headings may suggest important subjects that belong in the index, but the exact wording of such headings may not be suitable for index entries. An index is an alphabetical arrangement, which means that in every entry the important word should come first. For example, "What is a transistor?" may be acceptable as a section heading in a book, but the important word is *transistor;* a proper index entry for the page on which that heading appears might be:

Transistor, definition of, 36

The same principle applies to subentries; the important word should be considered first for purposes of alphabetizing. Thus, although prepositions may be used for clarity, they are disregarded in alphabetizing: "of France" precedes "in Great Britain" as a subentry.

Nontext Sources of Entries

Certain items that appear as regular features in a book, such as problems or bibliographies, need not be indexed. Illustrations (including maps and diagrams) and tables are often worth indexing, especially if they do not appear on the same pages as the text referring to them. An identification such as *(illus.)*, *(map)* or *(table)* may be given before the page number.

Bibliographic references and citations within the text are sometimes indexed. The author should decide whether they are necessary. Separate items within bibliographies, tables, or glossaries are not usually indexed.

Footnotes are indexed if they give information that is not in the text on the same page. Insert the italic letter *n.* after a page number to indicate a footnote. If the text reference to a subject is on the same page as the footnote, list the page number only once:

> Rayonism, 182
> *not* Rayonism, 182, 182*n.*

If the names of more than about a hundred persons are indexed, a separate author index or name index may be needed.

13-3

PREPARING INDEX CARDS

In the procedure described here, each index item is recorded on a separate 3- by 5-inch index card, after which the final index manuscript is prepared on a typewriter. If you are using a computer or word processor to create an index, change or adapt this procedure as necessary to reflect the capability and sophistication of your particular system.

Underscoring Entries

In the page proof, underscore or circle items that should be included in the index. If the exact word or phrase that is wanted for the index does not appear in the text, it can be written in the margin of the proof. This marking is meant for your convenience as an indexer—do as much or as little of it as you find necessary.

Transferring Entries to Cards

Copy the index items on 3- by 5-inch cards. Use a separate card for each main entry and subentry, repeating the main entry at the top of each card. This is done for convenience and accuracy in the final arrangement of the index. The cards should look like this:

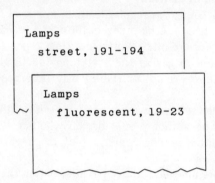

```
Lamps
     street, 191-194
```

```
Lamps
     fluorescent, 19-23
```

Arranging the Cards

Some indexers wait until all the cards are written before arranging them in alphabetical order. Then they combine all duplicate entries, eliminate synonymous terms, and list all page numbers for an entry in correct order on one card.

Other indexers prefer to put cards in alphabetical order as soon as they are written. This avoids duplication of cards and helps in the planning of a consistent arrangement. It also saves time in the final revision of the cards, which may be important in meeting deadlines.

In revising the cards, you may find that you have listed the same subject in different forms. For example, both "Atomic energy" and "Nuclear energy" may have been used. Watch for singular and plural forms of the same word, such as "Mouse" and "Mice," and for phrases which may be in more than one form, such as "Inheritance of acquired characteristics" and "Acquired characteristics, inheritance of." If you decide to keep both forms, make sure that the same page numbers are given in both places.

Cross-references (*see* and *See also*) should be carefully checked to ensure that the items to which they refer have not been changed or eliminated.

Marking the Cards for Typing

After the cards have been arranged, they should be marked for typing. In a group of subentries under one heading, all main entries except the one on the first card should be crossed out but not obliterated. If a subentry is followed by a secondary item, both main entry and subentry should be crossed out. For example:

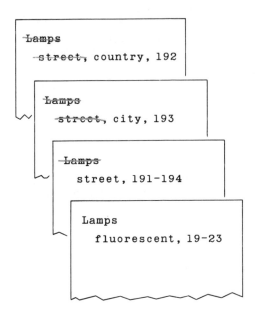

In terms that include an adjective, however, the adjective must be repeated before each noun that it modifies (see "Repeated Adjectives" in Section 13-4).

In a printed index, subentries are indented 1 em, and secondary items (sub-subentries) 2 ems. This is shown on the index cards by the marks ▢ and ▣ . (Complicated arrangements using more than two steps of indention should be avoided. They are confusing to readers and awkward in appearance.) The items on the cards above would be combined and marked for indention as follows:

Lamps:
▢ fluorescent, 19–23
▢ street, 191–194
▣ city, 193
▣ country, 192

chronological style for subentries In some types of books, especially biographies and histories, index subentries are arranged in chronological order rather than alphabetical order. They are often printed in run-on form:

> Jefferson, Thomas: Declaration of Inde-
> pendence, 105–110; minister to
> France, 125–128; secretary of state,
> 130–135; President, 140–150

If it is necessary to save space, the run-on arrangement may be used for subentries in any index that does not contain more than one level of subentry.

13-4

FORM OF ENTRIES

Page Numbers

When a main entry is not followed by page numbers of its own, it stands on a separate line, followed by a colon. The first subentry appears on the next line:

> Drawing:
> architectural, 621–630
> mechanical, 642–651

If a subentry has no page numbers but is followed by secondary subentries, this form is used:

> Electric power, 531–552
> home use: rural, 541–545
> urban, 537–540

Give page numbers in full:

> 172–178 (*not* 172-8)

Arrange page references in numerical sequence:

> Converters, 3, 26–28, 44, 119

Use inclusive page numbers for three or more consecutive page references, regardless of whether the discussion is continuous or interrupted:

> 236–238 (*not* 236, 237, 238)

If only two consecutive pages are listed, use an en dash between them if the discussion is continuous from one page to the next; use a comma for two separate mentions.

Prepositions

Prepositions are used in subentries to show how the subitem is related to the main entry:

Stars:
    masses of, 623–624
    in spiral nebulae, 642

These subentries are to be read "masses of stars" and "stars in spiral nebulae."

Repeat appropriate prepositions with each entry:

Surveys:
    of community resources, 88
    of handicapped children, 40

Use prepositions instead of the possessive case:

Health of workers, 144   *rather than*   Health, workers', 144

except where a change to the prepositional form would change the meaning:

Engineer's level, 44
Engineer's scale, 46

not Engineer:
    level of, 44
    scale of, 46

Abbreviations

If possible, avoid the use of abbreviations; spelled-out forms are preferred (see "Abbreviations" in Section 13-5). When abbreviations are used, the abbreviated form may be given in parentheses after the spelled-out form in cross-references:

ac (*see* Alternating current)
Alternating current, 27–35
Alternating-current (ac) circuits,
        104–115

Names

Give names of persons in full. Supply first names or initials if possible, even if they do not appear in the text. Repeat identical surnames:

Davis, Evelyn G., 152
Davis, Michael, 138

These rules hold for names as entries in a subject index as well as for name indexes.

Punctuation
A comma is used after the last word of an entry, and page numbers are separated by commas.

If a noun is followed by a single modifying phrase, use a comma only when it is needed for sense:

Coagulation of colloids, 436
or Colloids, coagulation of, 436
not Coagulation, of colloids, 436

Repeated Adjectives
Because adjectives cannot be used alone as entries, they must be repeated in each entry to which they apply:

Weak acids, 350–351   Weather forecasting, 464
Weak bases, 352   Weather maps, 465

Repetition
If an item is likely to be looked for under either of two key words, enter it twice—once in natural order and once in inverted form. Be sure the same page numbers are given with both forms:

Absolute temperature, 64
Temperature, absolute, 64

Cross-References
Cross-references are of two kinds: *see* and *See also*. A *see* reference directs the reader from an entry that is not used to one that is used. It is run in after an entry, and no page numbers are given:

Labor unions (*see* Unions)

This means that all information on the subject will be found under "Unions." If only a few page numbers appear under "Unions," it is better to repeat them under "Labor unions," but if the item is several lines long a *see* reference should be given.

A *See also* reference shows where related information can be found. It appears on a separate line after the entry or subentry to which it refers:

Erosion, 29–37
   annual rate of, 46
   (*See also* Soil conservation)

Insurance, 402–426
   group, 410–415
     (*See also* Hospitalization plans)

Note that a *See also* reference applying to a main entry appears after the last subentry and aligned with it. One applying to a subentry appears after that subentry, indented 1 em more.

The *S* in *See also* is capitalized; in *see*, it is not. Both forms are italicized.

13-5

ALPHABETIZING

First Solid Word
Alphabetize by the first solid word:

Hybrid vigor, 21
Hybridization, 38

Hyphened Words
Words in which a hyphen is used after a prefix are alphabetized as one word:

Panama Canal, 172–183
Pan-American Exposition, 194
Panel discussions, 78–80

Hyphened adjectives preceding a noun (sometimes called *unit modifiers*) are treated as two words:

Voltage-regulator tubes, 48
Voltage saturation, 96

In chemical terms a prefixed symbol or number is disregarded:

Benzophene, preparation of, 737
o-Benzoquinone, 435
Benzotrichloride, 199
2-Benzoylbenzoic acid, 739
4-Benzoyl catechol, 757

Note that the last two entries illustrate an alternative form of alphabetical arrangement: letter by letter, ignoring word divisions, as in dictionaries. This style is often used for indexes of chemical or medical terms that may or may not be printed as separate words, as in the example above. The style may be difficult to follow in indexes containing phrases and proper names. The difference between the two styles is illustrated by the following lists:

Word by word	Letter by letter
New Jersey	Newark
New towns	New Jersey
New York	Newspapers
Newark	Newtown
Newspapers	New towns
Newtown	New York

The disadvantage of letter-by-letter alphabetizing in a subject index is that it tends to separate related items:

pump efficiency, 51
pumpernickel, 146
pumpkins, 185
pump operation, 50

Abbreviations

Alphabetize according to the sequence of letters. An abbreviation beginning with a single letter precedes words beginning with that letter: "B & O" stands before all words beginning with B.

There is one exception to this rule: Certain abbreviations, especially Mt. (mount) and St. (saint), are always alphabetized as if they were spelled out. Thus, "Mt. Wilson Observatory" appears before "Mountains," and "St. Paul, Minn." appears before "San Diego, Calif." The abbreviation "U.S." is alphabetized as "United States," and "U.S.S.R." as "Union of Soviet Socialist Republics."

Letters used as symbols are alphabetized according to their alphabetical sequence:

k, 163
K lines or series, 468, 479
Kaufman, J. B., 495

Nuclear reactions:
  energy relations of, 575, 606–609
  with radioactive products, 625–647
    Ag^{106}, 627
    As^{74}, 628
    Co^{58}, 645

Words Spelled Alike
A proper name precedes a common noun with the same spelling:

Joule, J. P., 111   Wells, M. H., 232
Joule (unit), 102   Wells, artesian, 123, 156

Words which are spelled alike but which have different meanings should be given as separate entries:

Bonds (adhesives), 273–276
Bonds, chemical, 14, 18

Numbers
Alphabetize incidental numbers, years, and so forth, as if they were spelled out:

Cleveland Children's Bureau, 181
  reports of: on death rate, 187
    1960 survey, 250
    on playgrounds, 182

A series of dates or other numbers in subentries is more conveniently arranged in chronological or numerical sequence. Where serial numbers are listed, either as main entries or as subentries, place them in numerical order:

Census: Scattering matrix, 517
  1790, 21–24   707B cavity oscillator, 250
  1860, 263–269   723A/B klystrons, 31
  1960, 456–461   Shot noise, 270

Subentries

Alphabetize subentries by the first significant words, ignoring prepositions and articles:

> Agencies:
>   charity, 112, 126
>   health, 135–141
>   in large cities, 136
>   for scientific research, 235

Articles

Eliminate the articles *the* and *a* in ordinary index entries. As part of a proper name or a title, they may have to be retained. In a main entry, to preserve the appearance of alphabetizing by the significant word, transpose the initial article to follow the key word. In a subentry, keep the natural sequence, but disregard the article in alphabetizing:

> *New York Times, The,* 500
>
> Industrial statistics:
>   sources of, 66, 77, 83
>   Bureau of Manufactures, 77
>   *The Economic Almanac,* 67
>   Industrial Commission, 85

Names

Alphabetize names beginning with *Mc* or *Mac* as if all were spelled *Mac:*

> Macartney, C. A., 127
> McClellan, G. S., 505
> McDonald, J. D., 455
> MacDonald, Ramsay, 347
> Macedonia, 43
> McGovern, W. M., 732

Foreign names containing prepositions are generally alphabetized according to the style used in the country of their origin. For example, in French the preposition *de* is placed in inverted form, and the article *La* is alphabetized:

> Lafayette, Marquis de, 97
> La Fontaine, Jean de, 72–73
> Lamb, Charles, 251

Anglicized names and those which are more familiar under prefixes are entered with the prefixes first and alphabetized as solid words:

Debt, foreign, 35–40   Vanderbilt, B. M., 59
de Gaulle, Charles, 139–142   Van Doren, Carl, 64
Delancey, R. C., 215   van't Hoff, J. H., 331

Names beginning with contractions like *L'* and *O'* are alphabetized as solid words:

Lasher, John, 32   Olney, Richard, 16
L'Asseur, Gabriel, 46   O'Malley, F. W., 63
Latham, Beverly, 62   Omar, K., 31

Names of popes, saints, and sovereigns precede family names of the same spelling:

George III, king of Great Britain,
    29–33
George, Henry, 109
George School, 256

Personal names precede geographic names:

Washington, George, 54–60
Washington, D.C., 89–92

13-6

PREPARING THE INDEX MANUSCRIPT

Typing
After the cards have been edited, arranged alphabetically, and marked for indentions, have the index typed in a single double-spaced column on standard-size sheets of bond paper, or use a word processor.

Indention
Show subordination of subitems by indention, using two spaces on the keyboard for each step (em) of indention. Avoid using more than three indention steps, if possible.

Figure 13-1 shows a section of a typed index manuscript.

13-7

REVISION OF THE INDEX FOR A NEW EDITION

The preparation of a completely new index for a new edition is generally less time-consuming than attempting to check page numbers, delete old entries, and add new entries to an old index. Take full advantage of the experience gained in constructing and using the old index, and make revisions where necessary.

If you have decided, however, not to start from scratch but to update the old index, be sure to perform the following steps:

1 Delete entries referring to material deleted from the current edition.

2 Add entries for new material.

3 Check the form of all entries.

4 Check page numbers.

5 Prepare a new index manuscript (see Section 13-6).

```
AFL-CIO, 36-48, 192
    arbitration, 114-120
    in automobile industry, 230-232
    history, 37-39
Agricultural marketing, 608-628
    agricultural production and, 608
    channels of distribution for, 610-
        617
    cooperatives, 621-626
    market structure:   changes in,
        613-616
    traditional, 610-613
```

FIGURE 13-1 Typed index manuscript.

If the revision is very slight, reprint copy of the old index can be cut and pasted, and index items covering new material can be handled as typed insertions. If you have ever tried doing this, however, you will appreciate the advantage of retaining the old index on tape or disk and updating it on a computer or word processor.

BIBLIOGRAPHY

GENERAL REFERENCE MATERIALS

Certain reference books are updated frequently. Where the date of publication is not provided in the entries that follow, the reader should consult the most recent edition.

Atlases
International Atlas, Rand McNally, Chicago.
National Geographic Atlas of the World, National Geographic Society, Washington, D.C.

Biographies
Current Biography, H. W. Wilson, New York. (Published monthly and cumulated annually. Names in the news.)
Who's Who in America, Marquis, Chicago. (Published biennially.)

Books Currently in Print
Books in Print, Bowker, New York. (Published annually in several volumes. Entries arranged by authors, titles, and subjects.)
Cumulative Book Index, H. W. Wilson, New York. (Published monthly and cumulated annually.)
Publisher's Trade List Annual, Bowker, New York.

Business Directories
Conover Mast Purchasing Directory, Conover Mast, Denver. (Published annually in three volumes. Lists manufacturers alphabetically and by products. Also lists trademarks.)
Encyclopedia of Associations, Gale Research, Detroit. (Updated quarterly.)
Poor's Register of Corporations, Directors, and Executives, Standard & Poor's, McGraw-Hill, New York. (Published annually.)

Copy Editing and Proofreading

Butcher, Judith: *Copy Editing: The Cambridge Handbook,* Cambridge University Press, London, 1975.

O'Neill, Carol L., and Avima Ruder: *The Complete Guide to Editorial Freelancing,* Dodd, Mead, New York, 1974.

Proof Corrections, ANSI Z39.22-1981, American National Standards Institute, New York, 1981. (A comprehensive illustrated guide to proofreaders' marks.)

Dictionaries (General)

American Heritage Dictionary of the English Language, Houghton Mifflin, Boston. (Indicates the preferences of a "usage panel" composed of writers and editors.)

Random House College Dictionary, Random House, New York. (Indicates italicizing of foreign words and phrases.)

Webster's New World Dictionary, Collins + World, Cleveland, Ohio.

Webster's Third New International Dictionary of the English Language, Unabridged, Merriam, Springfield, Mass. (The most comprehensive dictionary published in the United States. For recent words not found in *Webster's Third,* consult *Webster's New Collegiate Dictionary,* Merriam, Springfield, Mass., and *6,000 Words: A Supplement to Webster's Third New International Dictionary,* Merriam, Springfield, Mass.)

Dictionaries (Special Subjects)

Blakiston's Gould Medical Dictionary, McGraw-Hill, New York.

De Sola, Ralph: *Abbreviations Dictionary,* Elsevier, New York, 1978.

Dictionary of Occupational Titles, U.S. Department of Labor, Employment and Training Administration, Washington.

McGraw-Hill Dictionary of Scientific and Technical Terms, McGraw-Hill, New York. (Lists many technical terms not found in *Webster's.*)

Webster's New Biographical Dictionary, Merriam, Springfield, Mass.

Webster's New Geographical Dictionary, Merriam, Springfield, Mass.

Wentworth, Harold, and Stuart Berg Flexner: *Dictionary of American Slang,* Crowell, New York.

Encyclopedias

Encyclopaedia Britannica, Encyclopaedia Britannica Educational Corporation, Chicago. (Thirty volumes.)

The New Columbia Encyclopedia, Columbia University Press, New York. (A single-volume work.)

Facts and Current Events

Information Please Almanac, Atlas and Yearbook, Simon and Schuster, New York. (Published annually.)

New York Times Index, Microfilming Corporation of America, Glen Rock, N.J. (Generally used in connection with microfilm of past issues.)

Statesman's Year-Book, St. Martin's, New York. (Current information on all nations. British spellings.)

U.S. Government Manual, U.S. Government Printing Office, Washington, D.C. (Published biennially. Contains names of government departments, agencies, and officials.)

World Almanac and Book of Facts, Newspaper Enterprise Association, New York. (Published annually.)

Periodical Literature
Reader's Guide to Periodical Literature, H. W. Wilson, New York. (Published monthly and cumulated annually.)

Publishers' Names
Literary Market Place, Bowker, New York. Published annually. (Contains names and addresses of many publishing houses, as well as names and addresses of nontechnical journals and newspapers, literary agents, translators, and other publishing services.)

Quotations
Bartlett's Familiar Quotations, Little, Brown, Boston.
The Oxford Dictionary of Quotations, Oxford University Press, New York.

Synonyms
Roget's International Thesaurus, Crowell, New York.

Trademarks
The Merck Index: An Encyclopedia of Chemicals and Drugs, Merck & Co., Rahway, N.J. (Lists generic and trade names of thousands of drugs.)

United States Trademark Association. (The USTA prints lists of trademarks in various fields. The lists are available free from USTA, 6 East 45th Street, New York, NY 10017.)

PUBLISHING AND PRINTING

General
Bailey, Herbert S.: *The Art and Science of Book Publishing,* Harper & Row, New York, 1970.

Balkin, Richard: *A Writer's Guide to Book Publishing,* 2d ed., Hawthorn, New York, 1981.

Dessauer, John P.: *Book Publishing: What It Is, What It Does,* 2d ed., Bowker, New York, 1981.

Lee, Marshall: *Bookmaking: The Illustrated Guide to Design/Production/Editing,* 2d ed., Bowker, New York, 1979.
Melcher, Daniel, and Nancy Larrick: *Printing and Promotion Handbook,* McGraw-Hill, New York, 1966.
Pocket Pal, International Paper Company, New York. (A small but useful handbook for graphic arts production.)

Copyright Law
Johnston, Donald F.: *Copyright Handbook,* Bowker, New York, 1978. (General copyright standards, user rights, copyrightable material, copyright notices, deposit, registration, transfers and licenses, infringement, etc.)

Elimination of Bias
Bias-Free Publishing, McGraw-Hill, New York, 1982. (Guidelines for equal treatment of the sexes and fair representation of minority groups and disabled people in McGraw-Hill Book Company publications. *Pamphlet.*)
Guidelines for Creating Positive Sexual and Racial Images in Educational Materials, Macmillan, New York, 1975.
Guidelines for Selecting Bias-Free Textbooks and Storybooks, The Council on Interracial Books for Children, New York, 1980.
Miller, Casey, and Kate Swift: *The Handbook of Nonsexist Writing for Writers, Editors, and Speakers,* Lippincott & Crowell, New York, 1980.
Ward, Jean: "Check Out Your Sexism," *Columbia Journalism Review,* May-June 1980, pp. 38–39.
Without Bias: A Guidebook for Nondiscriminatory Communication, International Association of Business Communications, San Francisco.

Reading Ability
Chall, Jeanne: *Learning to Read: The Great Debate,* McGraw-Hill, New York, 1967. Updated 1982.
———: *Stages of Reading Development,* McGraw-Hill, New York, 1982.
Kibby, Michael W.: "The Degrees of Reading Power," *Journal of Reading,* February 1981.
Spache, George D.: *Good Reading for Poor Readers,* 9th ed., Garrard, Champaign, Ill., 1974.

Textbook Selection Policies
Censorship: The Challenge to Freedom in the School, Association for Supervision and Curriculum Development, Washington, D.C.
Policies and Procedures for Selection of Instructional Materials, American Association of School Librarians, Chicago.
Selection Guidelines: School Library Resources, Textbooks, and Instructional Materials, New York State Education Department, Bureau of School Libraries, Albany, N.Y.

STYLE

General Style

A Manual of Style, University of Chicago Press, Chicago. (Consult latest edition.)

Sabin, William A.: *The Gregg Reference Manual,* 4th ed., McGraw-Hill, New York, 1977. (Primarily an office and business reference.)

U.S. Government Printing Office Style Manual, rev. ed., Washington, D.C., 1973. (Primarily a guide for government publications, but contains much valuable information not easily found elsewhere—e.g., rules for word division in various languages.)

Words into Type, 3d ed., Prentice-Hall, Englewood Cliffs, N.J., 1974. (Based on studies by Marjorie E. Skillin, Robert M. Gay, and others.)

Newspaper Style

The Associated Press Stylebook, Lorenz Press, Dayton, Ohio, 1977.

Jordan, Lewis: *The New York Times Manual of Style and Usage,* Times Books, New York, 1976.

Webb, Robert A. (ed.): *The Washington Post Deskbook on Style,* McGraw-Hill Book Company, New York, 1978.

Style for Dissertations and Papers

Gibaldi, Joseph, and Walter S. Achtert: *MLA Handbook: For Writers of Research Papers, Theses, and Dissertations,* Modern Language Association, New York, 1977.

Style for Some Special Fields

The American National Standards Institute (ANSI) publishes standards for many fields. For a complete list of all American National Standards, write to American National Standards Institute, Inc., 1430 Broadway, New York, NY 10018.

biochemistry

Nomenclature Committee of the International Union of Biochemistry (ed.): *Enzyme Nomenclature 1978,* Academic, New York, 1979.

biology

Style Manual for Biological Journals, 4th ed., American Institute of Biological Sciences, Conference of Biological Editors, Arlington, Va., 1978.

chemistry

Directions for Abstractors, American Chemical Society, Columbus, Ohio, 1975.

Handbook for Authors, American Chemical Society, Columbus, Ohio, 1978.

law

A Uniform System of Citation, Harvard Law Review Association, Cambridge, Mass.

mathematics

Swanson, Ellen: *Mathematics into Type: Copy Editing and Proofreading of Mathematics for Editorial Assistants and Authors,* rev. ed., American Mathematical Society, Providence, R.I., 1979.

medicine

List of Journals Indexed in Index Medicus, National Library of Medicine, National Institute of Health Publication, Rockville, Md. (Published annually.)

mental measurement

Buros, Oscar K.: *Tests in Print II,* Gryphon Press, Highland Park, N.J., 1974. Available from University of Nebraska Press, Lincoln. At this writing, *Tests in Print III* is in preparation.

metric usage

ASTM/IEEE Standard Metric Practice, ANSI Z210.1-1976, American National Standards Institute, New York, 1976.

The International System of Units (SI), U.S. Department of Commerce, NBS Special Publication 330, Washington, D.C., 1981.

Metric Editorial Guide, American National Metric Council, Washington, D.C., 1978.

"Metric Style Guide for the News Media," U.S. Department of Commerce, National Bureau of Standards, Washington D.C., 1976. (Three pages of essentials in foldout form.)

physics

Symbols, Units, and Nomenclature in Physics, International Union of Pure and Applied Physics, Document U.I.P. 20, 1978.

psychology

Publication Manual of the American Psychological Association, 2d ed., APA, Washington, D.C., 1974.

science and technology

Encyclopedia of Science and Technology, McGraw-Hill, New York. (Consult latest edition.)

Mathematical Signs and Symbols for Use in Physical Sciences and Technology, ANSI Y10.20-1975, American National Standards Institute, New York, 1975.

Writing Style

composition and rhetoric

Elsbree, Langdon, et al.: *College Handbook of Composition,* 9th ed., Heath, Boston, 1977. (Two versions, one covering usage only and the other rhetoric and usage.)

Flesch, Rudolf: *The Art of Plain Talk,* Macmillan, New York, 1962. (Paperback.)

Hodges, John C., and Mary E. Whitten: *Harbrace College Handbook,* 8th ed., Harcourt, Brace, Jovanovich, New York, 1977.

Strunk, William, Jr., and E. B. White: *The Elements of Style,* 2d ed., Macmillan, New York, 1972.

Zinsser, William: *On Writing Well: An Informal Guide to Writing Nonfiction,* 2d rev. ed., Harper & Row, New York, 1980.

grammar and usage

Bernstein, Theodore M.: *The Careful Writer: A Modern Guide to English Usage,* Atheneum, New York, 1965.

————: *Dos, Don'ts & Maybes of English Usage,* Times Books, New York, 1977.

————: *Miss Thistlebottom's Hobgoblins: The Careful Writer's Guide to the Taboos, Bugbears, and Outmoded Rules of English Usage,* Farrar, Straus and Giroux, New York, 1971.

Bryant, Margaret M. (ed.): *Current American Usage: How Americans Say It and Write It,* Funk & Wagnalls, New York, 1962. (Nonprescriptive; presents statistical evidence.)

Cottle, Basil: *The Plight of English,* Arlington House, New Rochelle, N.Y., 1975.

Curme, George O.: *English Grammar,* Barnes & Noble, New York, 1953. (A scholarly, not prescriptive, guide to grammar.)

————: *A Grammar of the English Language,* Verbatim, Essex, Conn., 1978.

Follett, Wilson: *Modern American Usage,* Warner Books, New York, 1974. (Paperback.)

Fowler, H. W.: *A Dictionary of Modern English Usage,* 2d ed., revised by Sir Ernest Gowers, Oxford University Press, London, 1965.

Lamberts, J. J.: *A Short Introduction to English Usage,* McGraw-Hill, New York, 1972. (A refreshing approach.)

Morris, William, and Mary Morris: *Harper Dictionary of Contemporary Usage,* Harper & Row, New York, 1975.

Newman, Edwin: *A Civil Tongue,* Bobbs-Merrill, Indianapolis, 1976.

Nicolson, Margaret: *Practical Style Guide for Authors and Editors,* Holt, Rhinehart, and Winston, New York, 1970.

Partridge, Eric: *Usage and Abusage: A Guide to Good English,* British Book Centre, Elmsford, N.Y., 1965.

Perrin, Porter G.: *Reference Handbook of Grammar and Usage,* Morrow, New York, 1972.

INDEX

ABOUT THE EDITOR

MARIE M. LONGYEAR is the former director of publishing services at the McGraw-Hill Publishing Company. In that capacity she directed a division that is responsible for editorial training, copy editing, proofreading, indexing, copyrights, and permissions. She served on the committee that developed American National Standard Z39.22-1974 (rev. 1981), "Proof Corrections," and on Subcommittee 14.1 of The Institute of Electrical and Electronics Engineers, which developed "IEEE Standard Metric Practice" (ANSI Z210.1-1976). She has lectured on editing at the Radcliffe Publishing Procedures Course and elsewhere and serves as a career counselor for college graduates who want to enter the field of book publishing.